DRUM CHART SUPPLEMENT
by Alan Hall

THE REAL EASY BOOK
TUNES FOR BEGINNING IMPROVISERS

3-HORN EDITION - LEVEL 1

A Sher Music Co. Publication
Produced in conjunction with
the Stanford Jazz Workshop
stanfordjazz.org

Publisher - Chuck Sher
Graphic Design - Attila Nagy, Santa Rosa, CA
©2021 Sher Music Co. • P.O. Box 445, Petaluma, CA 94952 • www.shermusic.com
All Rights Reserved. International Copyright Secured. Made in the U.S.A.
No part of this book may be reproduced in any form without written permission from the publisher.
ISBN 978-0-9910773-9-7

Table of Contents

Section 1

- A note to the jazz the ensemble teacher ... i
- A note to the jazz the ensemble drummer ... i
- Simplified parts and grooves ... 1
- Jazz Time in this book ... 1
- Notation variations ... 2
- Simple setups and hits ... 3
- The "4-feel" and the "2-feel" ... 4
- Mix and Match: 2-bar jazz comping ideas in 4/4 ... 5
- The difference between "1/2 time" and "1/2 time feel" ... 6
- The Map of the Tune ... 7–9

Section 2

- Bag's Groove ... 10
- Big Bertha ... 12
- Blue Seven ... 14
- Blues by Five ... 16
- Blues in the Closet ... 18
- Cold Duck Time ... 20
- Contemplation ... 22
- Doxy ... 24
- Edward Lee ... 26
- Equinox ... 28
- Freedon Jazz Dance ... 30
- Gingerbread Boy ... 32
- Groove Merchant ... 34
- Jive Samba ... 36
- Jo Jo Calypso ... 38
- The Jody Grind ... 40
- Killer Joe ... 42
- Listen Here ... 44
- Little Sunflower ... 46
- Mercy, Mercy, Mercy ... 48

Table of Contents

SECTION 2 *continued*

Midnight Waltz	50
Mr. P.C.	52
One for Daddy-O	54
Red's Good Groove	56
Revelation	58
Road Song	60
Short Stuff	62
Shoshana	64
Sir John	66
Sister Sadie	68
So Dańco Samba	70
Song for My Father	72
Sonny Moon for Two	74
St. James Infirmary	76
St. Thomas	78
Straight Life	80
Tenor Madness	82
Trail Dust	84
When the Saints go Marching In	86
Work Song	88
Yardbird Suite	90
Z's Blues	92

SECTION 3

Stop-Time "Work Song" analysis	94
"Elvin" Style	95
The Jazz Shuffle	96
Mix and Match: Two bar jazz comping ideas in 3/4	97
12/8 feel	98
Advanced Latin Jazz Drumset Grooves	99–101
References	102

A NOTE TO THE JAZZ ENSEMBLE TEACHER

These drum parts and grooves are written with the beginning to intermediate level drummer in mind. The accompanying videos (jazzdrumming.info/charts) are designed as a practice aid for drummers working on the tunes. There are also supplemental pages and videos (jazzdrumming.info/more) to help with the numerous drumming concepts encountered in these tunes: 4-feel and 2-feel, stop-time, simple set-ups and hits, Latin jazz grooves, the map of the tune, 1/2 x feel, Elvin Feel, Jazz Shuffle and more.

Each drum chart covers the basic groove and important melody, background, shout chorus and harmony figures in the 3-horn arrangements. You may choose to have your drummer catch all or some of the written figures. Set-ups are written minimally, with the beginning drummer in mind.

The variety of drum notation used in this book is intended to familiarize the student with the varieties he/she may encounter. Most charts are detailed; some are vaguer. I utilized rhythm slashes, section notation, and rhythmic notation as well as full scoring. If your drummer is new to chart reading, these charts will introduce them to the skills required while also giving them a clear path towards supporting the band musically. If your drummer is more advanced, he/she will find the charts to be a useful guide to the musical events in the arrangements.

A NOTE TO THE JAZZ ENSEMBLE DRUMMER

As a jazz ensemble drummer, you have SEVERAL roles to play. First and foremost, keep a solid pulse in the style of the arrangement. In addition, you serve as a conductor of sorts, telegraphing important musical events. That is done with *fills, set-ups* and *hits* which align with important rhythmic events in the tune. Your musical use of dynamics can also greatly affect the volume and intensity of the band. The band and audience need you to step up to these roles.

If you're new to chart reading, there are playthrough / play-along videos available (jazzdrumming.info/charts) designed to help you prepare to play these charts. Be sure to also check out the "simplified set-ups and hits" pages and video (jazzdrumming.info/more).

If you're new to jazz comping, I encourage you to work through the 4/4 and 3/4 "Mix and Match" pages. Also check out the "4-feel, 2-feel" page and video (jazzdrumming.info/more). The tools provided in this book and accompanying videos are designed to help you get comfortable in your role as the jazz ensemble drummer.

SIMPLIFIED PARTS AND GROOVES
The parts and grooves written here are simplified.

The grooves are generally based on an early recording of the tunes. I encourage you to search on YouTube or Spotify for the earliest recording of each tune so you can get a solid idea of the way the original drummer, who often worked under the direction of the composer, approached the tune. This is NOT to say you must play it THAT WAY. But that knowledge will provide a starting point from which you can musically build and modify the groove, under the guiding hand of your band director.

"JAZZ TIME" IN THIS BOOK
In this book jazz time is indicated like this...

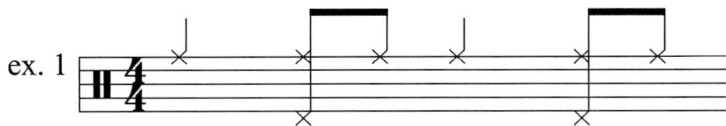

...but this a short-cut, to writing this, which is more of the story, but not all:

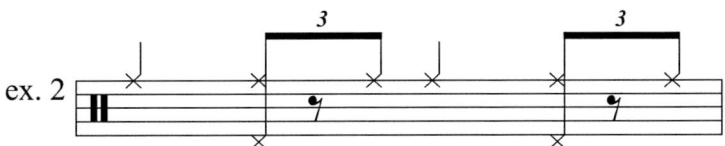

You'll also see jazz time written out like this:

swing 8ths

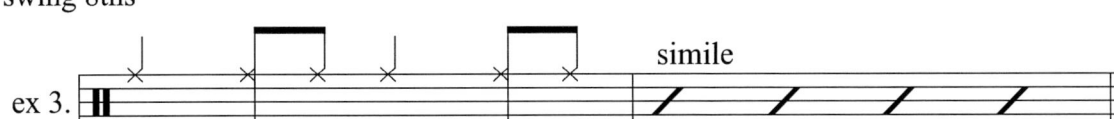

Neither version is complete because Jazz, and consequently jazz drumming, has **improvisation at the heart of it!** So generally, you determine how to play jazz time.

The word *simile* here means continue playing jazz time generally as indicated but use your own triplet-based variations at will. Jazz comping variations occur in the ride pattern, but mainly in the snare and bass drum "jabs" (light hits) played against it.

TIP:
If you're interested in developing a jazz comping vocabulary, check out the "Mix and Match" 2-bar jazz comping ideas in this book. You can also look at the video entitled *4-feel and 2-feel*, found at jazzdrumming.info/more. There are additional resources in the reference list at the back of this book

SECTION 1 — DRUM CHART SUPPLEMENT

NOTATION VARIATIONS

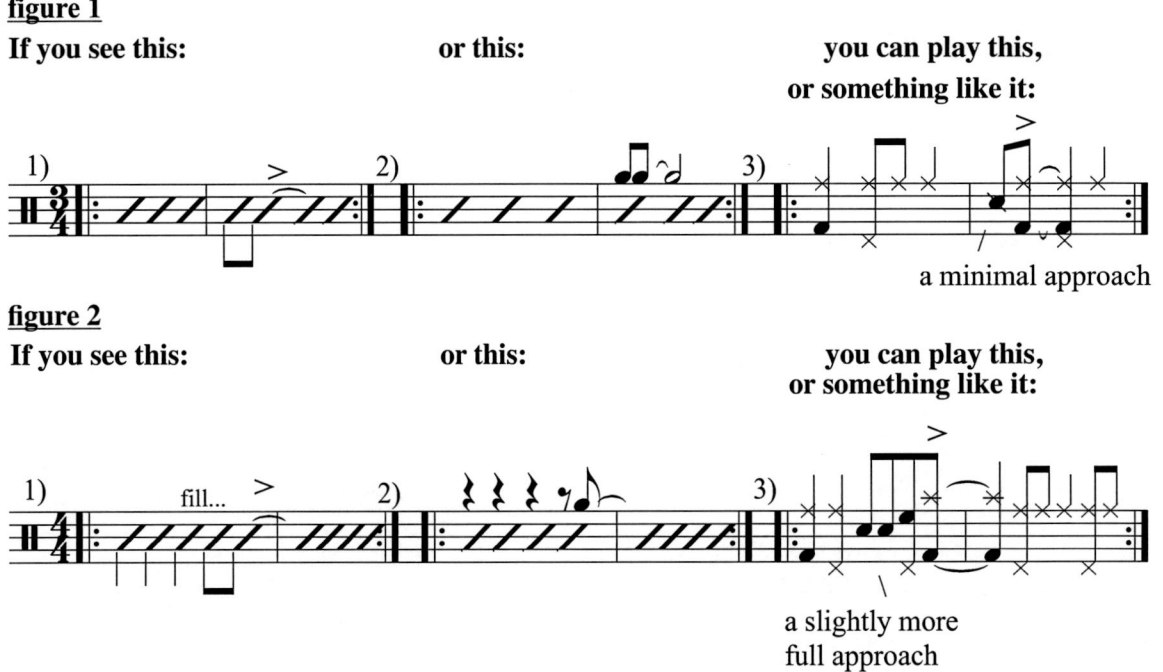

Figures 1 and 2 above each illustrate three different ways an arranger might notate the same rhythm on a drum chart. Example #1 on each line above utilizes *time slashes* with *rhythmic notation*. Example #2 on each utilizes *time slashes* with *section figure notation*.

Example #3 on each line is *fully scored* and includes a **fill, set-up**, and **hit**. This is the approach I've used in most of these charts. You will also see some *rhythmic notation, time slashes* and *section figure* notation as well. In those cases, you will need to come up with your own approach to fills, set-ups, and hits. If your new to chart-reading I'd suggest using the fully transcribed examples to guide your decisions.

Drumset Legend

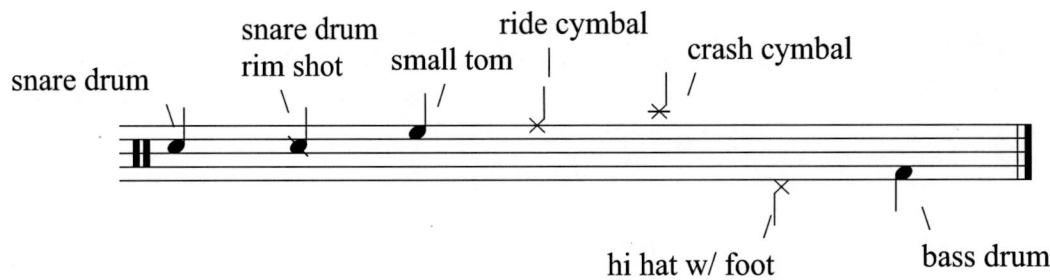

Simple set-ups and hits

video at: jazzdrumming.info/more

KEY TERMS:
hit (or **figures**): the rhythm or rhythms the arranger has explicitly indicated we are meant to catch.
set-up: the final <u>down beat</u> we play immediately before the hit (or figures),
fill: a group of notes we play to add excitement prior to a set-up note.

Example 1 through 3 represent three different ways an arranger might notate a particular rhythm he'd like the drummer to emphasize. What is not indicated above is EXACTLY how the drummer should do that. That is left up to the drummer. Most charts in this book indicate *exactly* what a drummer might play to **set-up** and catch the various **hits**. However, in some charts I've provided a more general guide to the arrangement, more like the examples above. In those charts the fill and set-up are literally in your hands.

Examples 4 and 4a below are complete drum parts written for the figures above. Because this book is geared toward the beginner or intermediate drumset player I've primarily notated a minimal approach to **fills, set-ups,** and **hits,** as in example 4 below. An advanced student might choose to play a fill leading up to the set-up, more like example 4a.

In the charts in this book, I've predominantly notated each set-up as a simple *stick shot* and the hits as either a bass drum/crash, bass drum/ride or bass drum/choked hi hat. Click on the above link and view the Simple *Set-ups and Hits* video to see specific examples of the concepts and techniques introduced here.

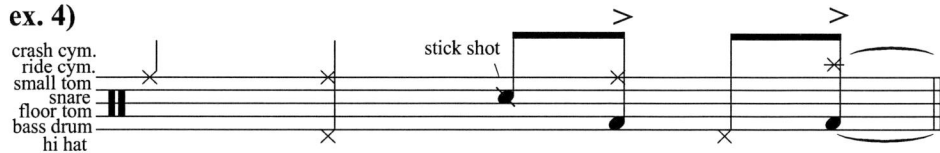

Here is a busier version, with some suggested stickings included:

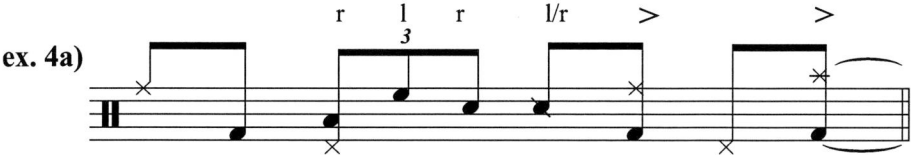

Advanced drummers: I'd suggest trying the minimal approach indicated here before trying out a more elaborate one for setting-up and catching the figures in this book. Bear in mind the size of the band and nature of the room while making those creative decisions.

The "4-Feel" and "2-Feel"

video at: jazzdrumming.info/more

Ex. 1) with no jabs — basic "walking bass"," 4-feel" drumset jazz ostinato

"Walking bass" and "4-feel" are terms that refer to the bass line being played primarily in steady quarter notes, 4 notes per measure, while outlining the harmony. Most of the tunes in this book utilize this 4-feel. It's also referred to as "Jazz Feel," "Swing Feel" "Bebop Feel" or "Straight Ahead."

Ex. 2) with no jabs — basic "2-feel" drumset jazz ostinato

"2-feel" refers to the bass line being played primarily in half-notes, 2 notes per measure, while outlining the harmony. This feel allows for a more spacious groove.

The little O above the ride pattern refers to the opening of the hi hat which will occur if you play the 2-feel cymbal pattern *on the hi hat cymbal* (it's a function of the hi hat closing on beats 2 and 4). The parenthesis around the bass drum notes indicate that they should be played softly (ghosted).

Improvisation
Remember jazz music is based on improvisation. Occasionally we will be asked to trade 4's or take a solo, but that is relatively rare. We are mainly support players, but within that role we can improvise our snare jabs, bass jabs and ride pattern somewhat, as long as the "groove-feel-flow" of the tune isn't disturbed too much.

Comping Lingo
The next page has some 2-measure jazz comping "jab" patterns you can work on to get familiar with drumset comping lingo.

MIX AND MATCH: TWO BAR JAZZ COMPING IDEAS IN 4/4

basic jazz ostinoto*
(with no "jabs")

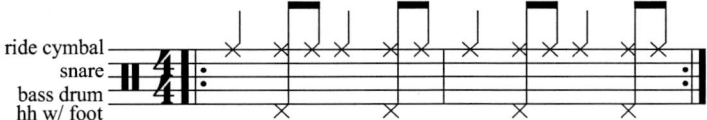

ex.1) <u>**with snare "jabs" added:**</u>

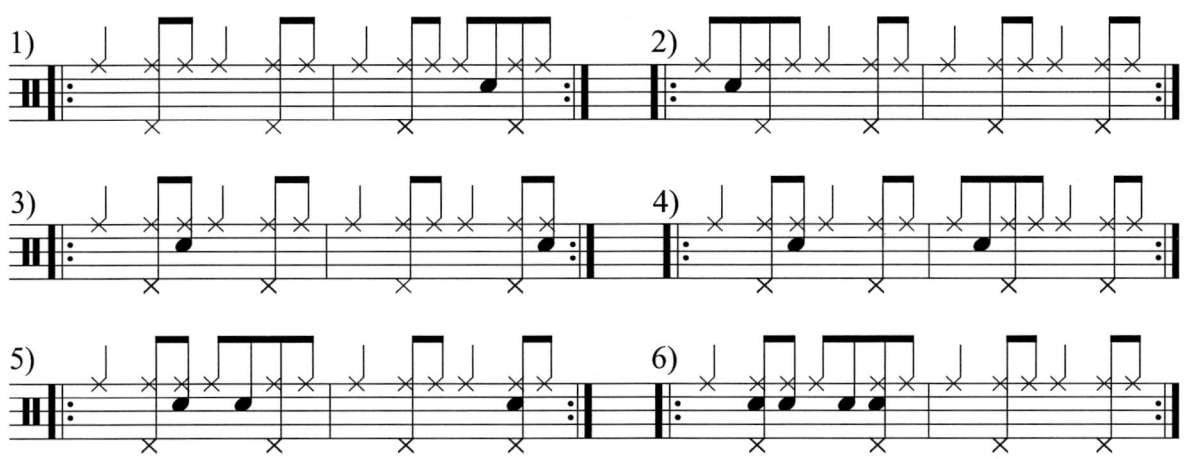

* Throughout these examples, the ride cymbal and hi hat patterns remain unchanged.

ex 2) <u>**with snare and bass drum "jabs" added:**</u>

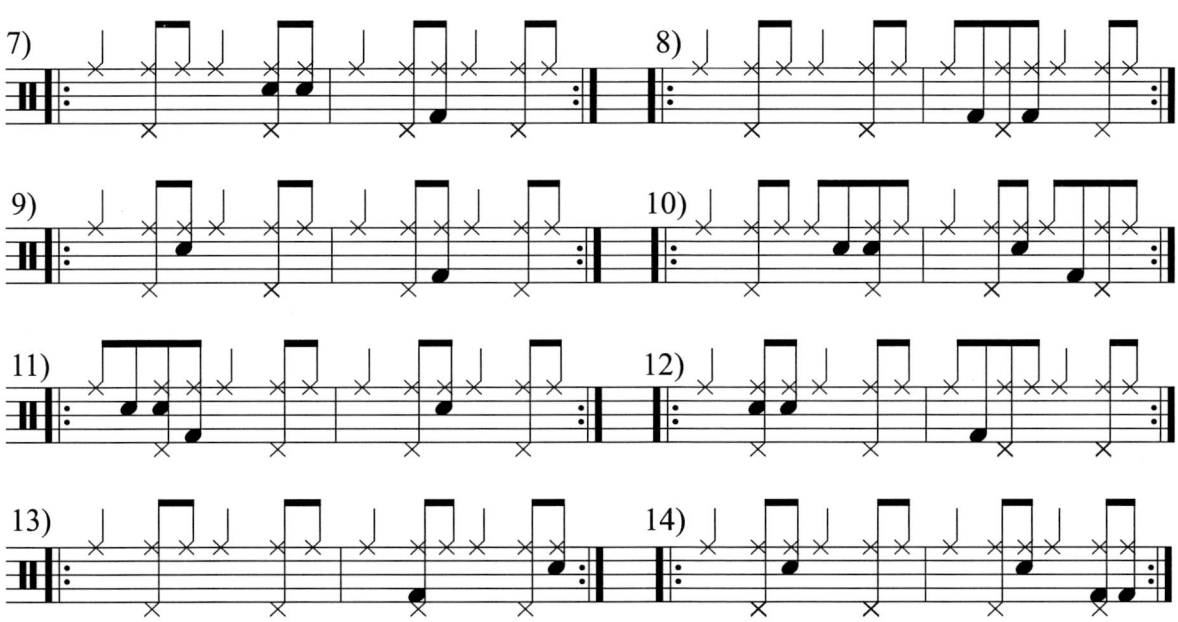

The ability to move freely between comping phrases like those above should be one of the main goals of any aspiring jazz drummer. At first, I'd encourage you to work out these patterns, with this fixed cymbal ostinato, to start developing your limb independence. Of course, there are many more possibilities than these, and you'll want to find your own over time.

The Difference Between "1/2 Time" and "1/2 Time Feel"

1/2 time

video at: jazzdrumming.info/more

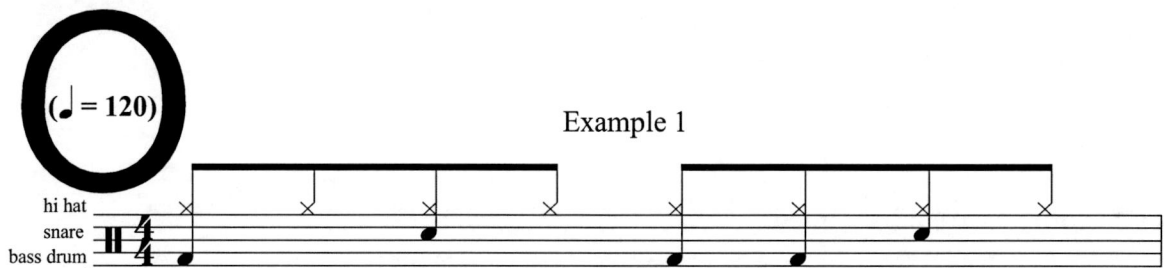

This is a standard rock beat, notated at 120 beats per measure (bpm). This is the standard way it would be notated in 4/4 time. Notice the snare "back beats" on counts 2 and 4.

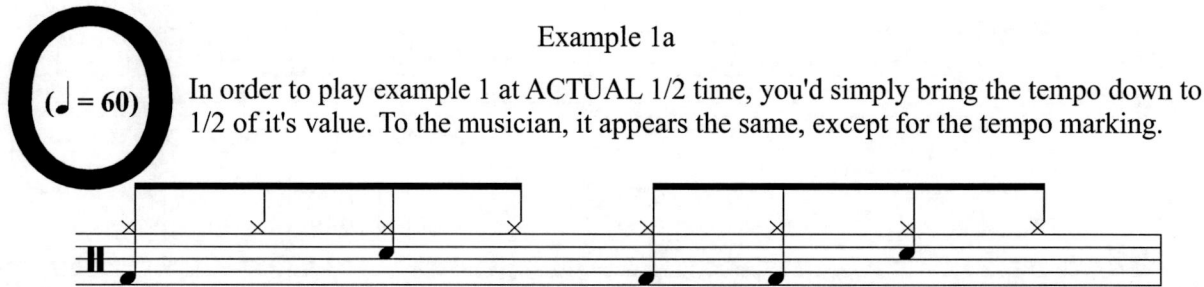

In order to play example 1 at ACTUAL 1/2 time, you'd simply bring the tempo down to 1/2 of it's value. To the musician, it appears the same, except for the tempo marking.

The audience, who would not be looking at any music, would perceive the slow down immediately, and the musician would be reading the music at half the original tempo.

Now compare example 1, to the beat in example 2:

1/2 time feel

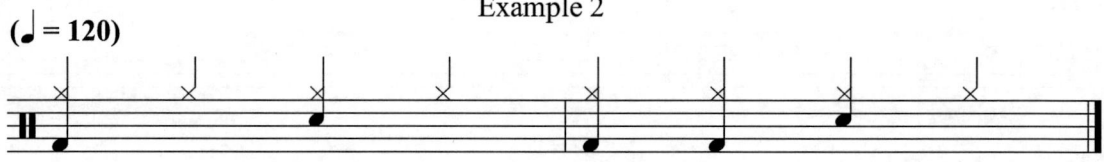

This beat in example 2, *also played at 120 bpm,* is the same *structurally* as example 1, but will sound half as fast. This is what 1/2-time FEEL is: it feels 1/2 as fast as the actual tempo indicates.

IMPORTANTLY, it doesn't LOOK like it normally would on the page TO THE MUSICIAN.

The "back-beats" of the beat structure are now played on count "3" in each measure of a two-measure pattern as opposed to being on counts "2 and 4" of a one measure pattern.

The "Map" of the Tune

Where do you go and when do you go there?

Repeat Marks

These repeat marks tell you: **"Play these 4 bars, two times."** (also notated as : 2x)

A repeated section can be 2 bars long, 4 bars long, 32 bars long, or anything in between or beyond. Repeat marks can be placed anywhere in a tune.

1st and 2nd Endings

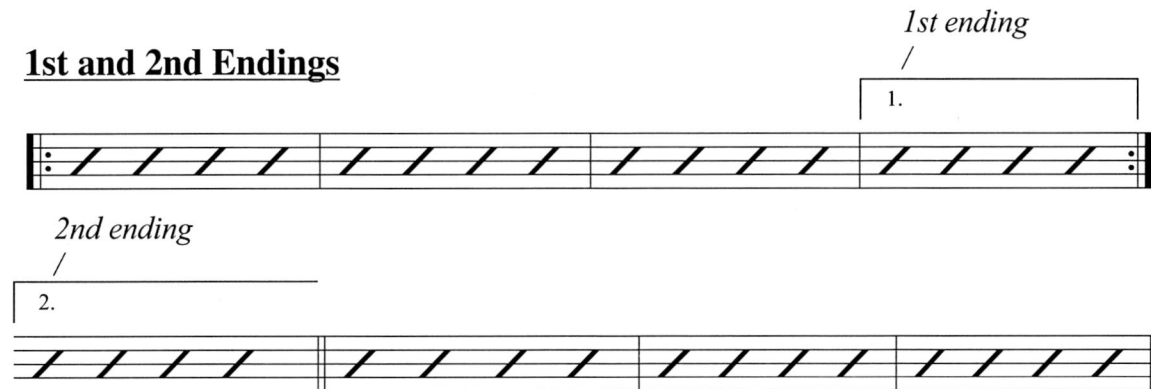

This is a variation on repeat mark mapping which tells you to: **"Go the 1st ending the first time through the phrase, but on the repeat, SKIP THE 1ST ENDING, AND TAKE THE 2ND ENDING INSTEAD."** Then you can proceed on to the rest of the chart.

Go Back

These terms and symbols direct you to GO BACK to some place in the chart: **D.S.** and **D.C.**

- **D.S.** is an abbreviation for an Italian term, "Del Signo", which means: to the sign.

The symbol for the sign is this: 𝄋

- **D.C.** is an abbreviation for an Italian term, "Da Capo", which means: to the very beginning. There is no symbol for the beginning

Go Forward

These terms and symbols direct you to go FORWARD to some place in the chart: Coda and Fine

- **al Coda** means "go to the Coda", the symbol for the Coda is: ⊕

- **al Fine means** "to the Fine" (pronounced FEE-nay) it looks like this: Fine

Map example #1

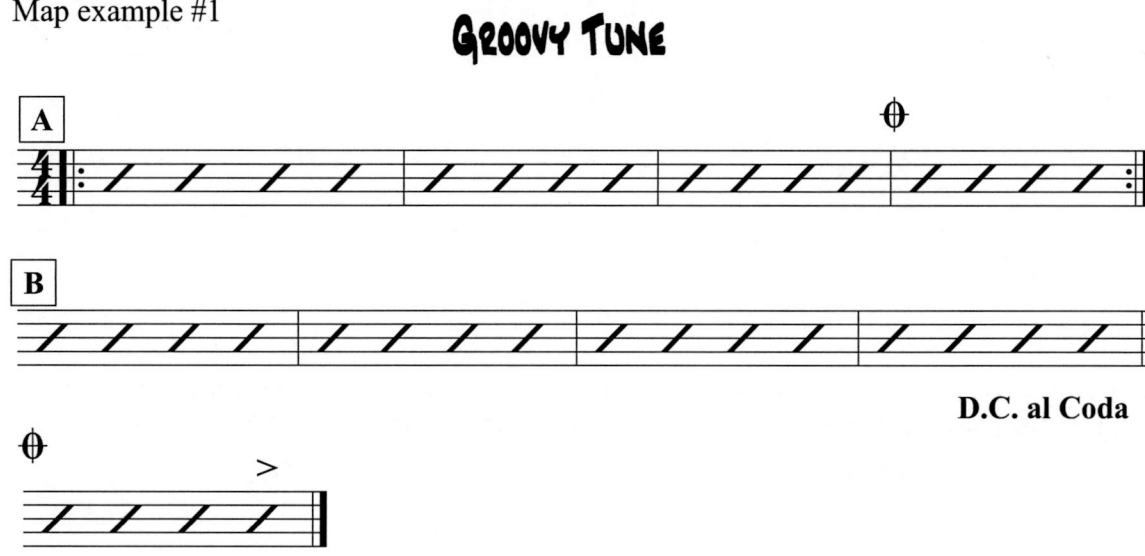

In "Groovy Tune" you'd play the A section 2 x (noticing the repeat marks and the coda sign) then go to the B section. After playing the B section, you would **D.C.** (go to the beginning), play 3 bars, then, at that Coda sign (⊕) you'd jump down to the CODA (⊕), and end the tune on beat 4

Map example #2

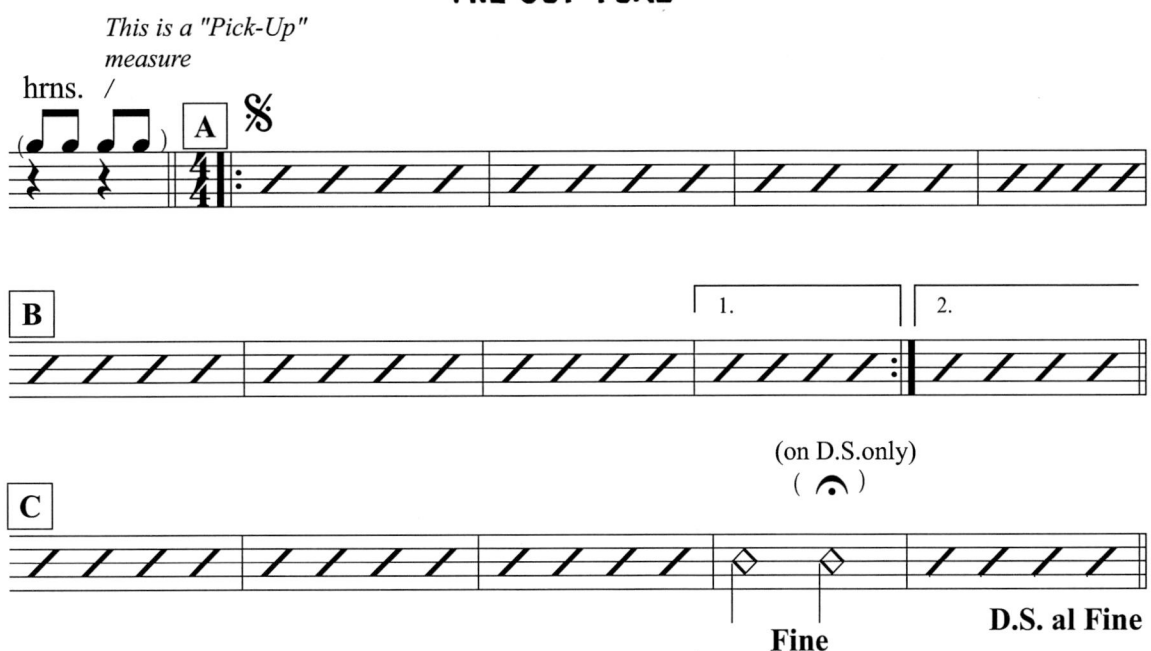

In "Far Out Tune" you first come in at A (after the pick-up measure), play through B, take the first ending, and repeat back to A. Then again play through B, but this time, take the 2nd ending INSTEAD of the 1st ending, going on to C. Note the location of the *fine, fermata*. At the end of C, you'd go back to the SIGN (𝄋), which is at A in this case, and play through A 2 x, taking the 2nd ending the 2nd time, then go on to C, where you would end at the FINE, which is on beat "3" of the 4th bar of C, and you'd hold that note, because of the fermata sign. Cut off when directed.

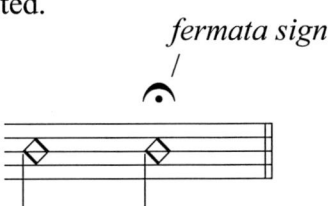

In the chart, the fermata is in parenthesis with a note above which says "on D.S. only". This is telling you that when you first come to this measure, you should ignore the fermata. You only play the fermata after you arrive here from the D.S.

Suggested basic drum set part

Bags' Groove

comp. by Milt Jackson
drum arr. by A. Hall

"2-feel"

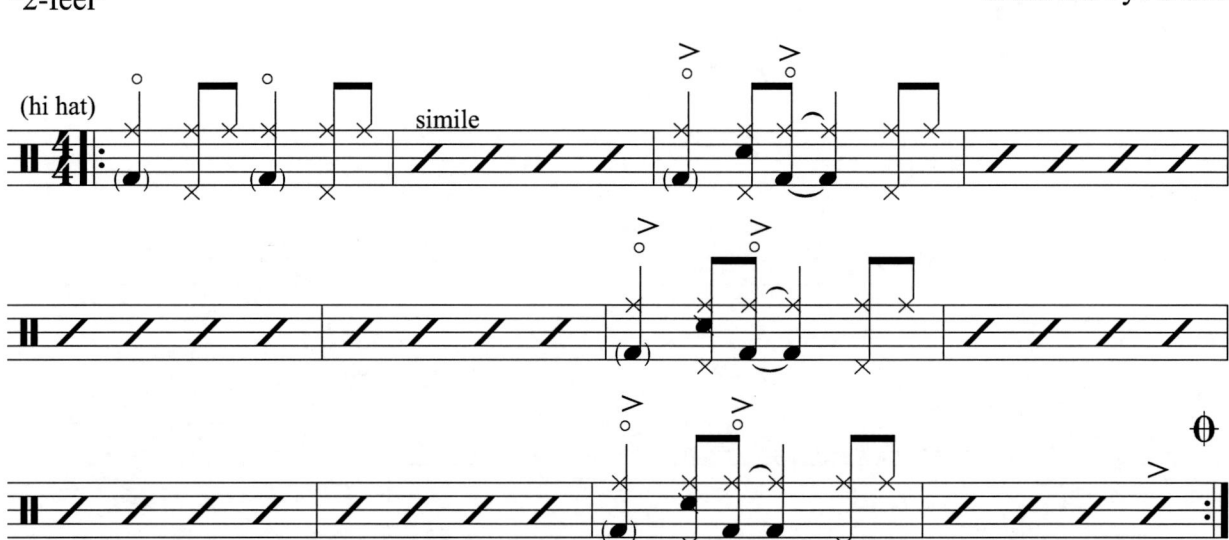

For solos:
Play time with "4-feel", freely in 12 bar phrases, listen, interact, hold the pulse.
Watch for the cue to "background for solos" and "shout chorus".

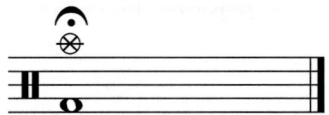

On Cue: Background for solos

"4-feel"

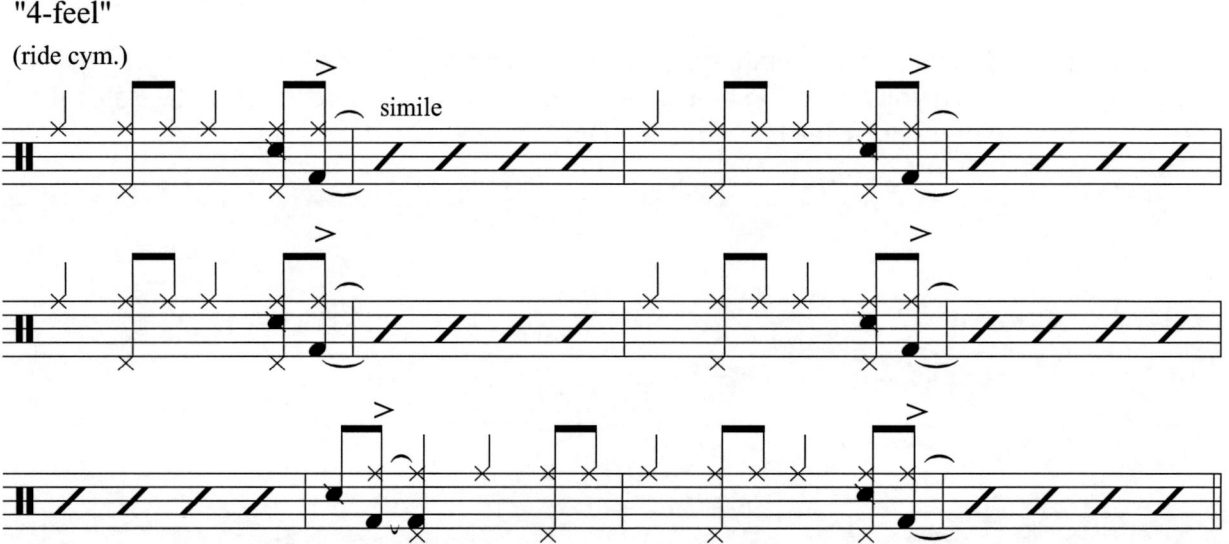

DRUM CHART SUPPLEMENT — SECTION 2

playthrough video - jazzdrumming.info/charts

SHOUT CHORUS. PLAY AFTER SOLOS (OPTIONAL)

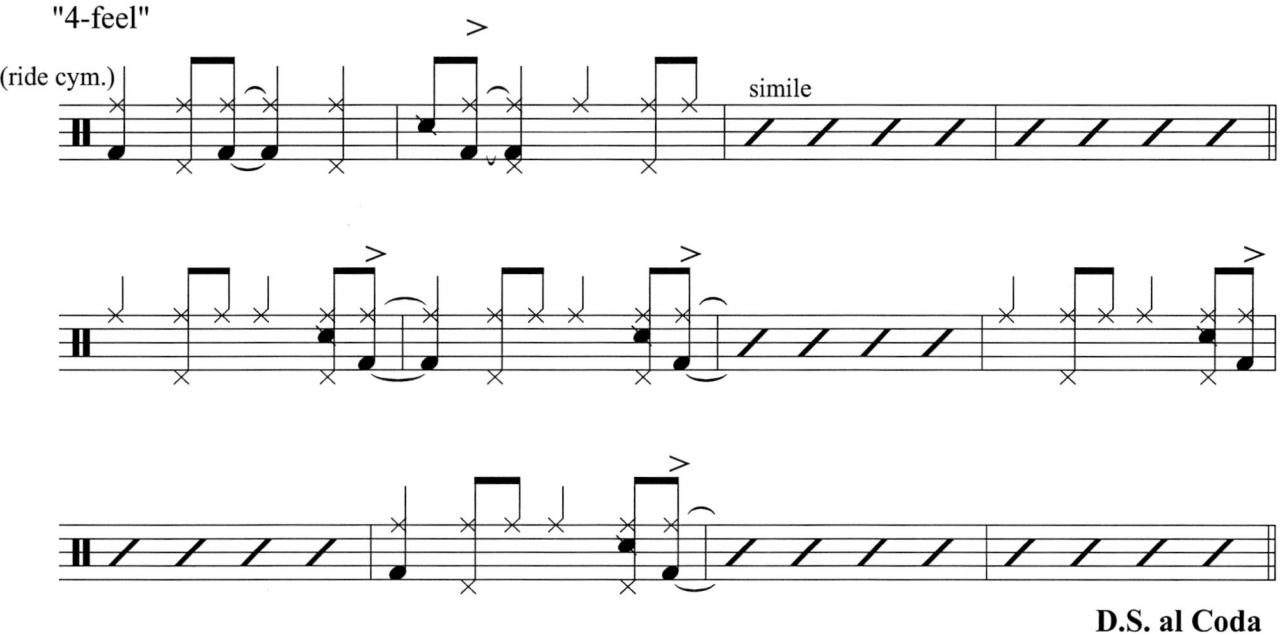

D.S. al Coda

Drum Set Legend:

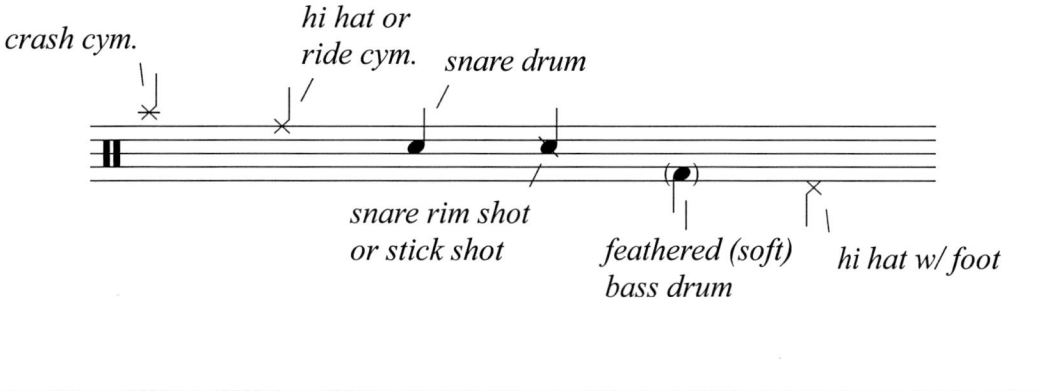

Notation notes:

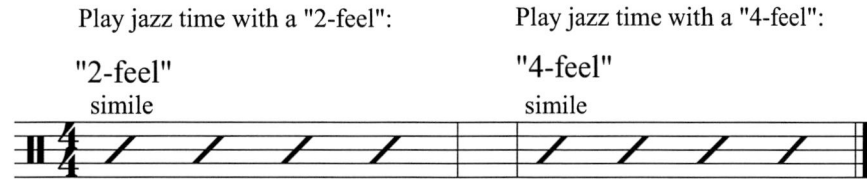

Suggested basic drum set part

Big Bertha

comp. by Duke Pearson
drum arr. by A. Hall

Jazz Time

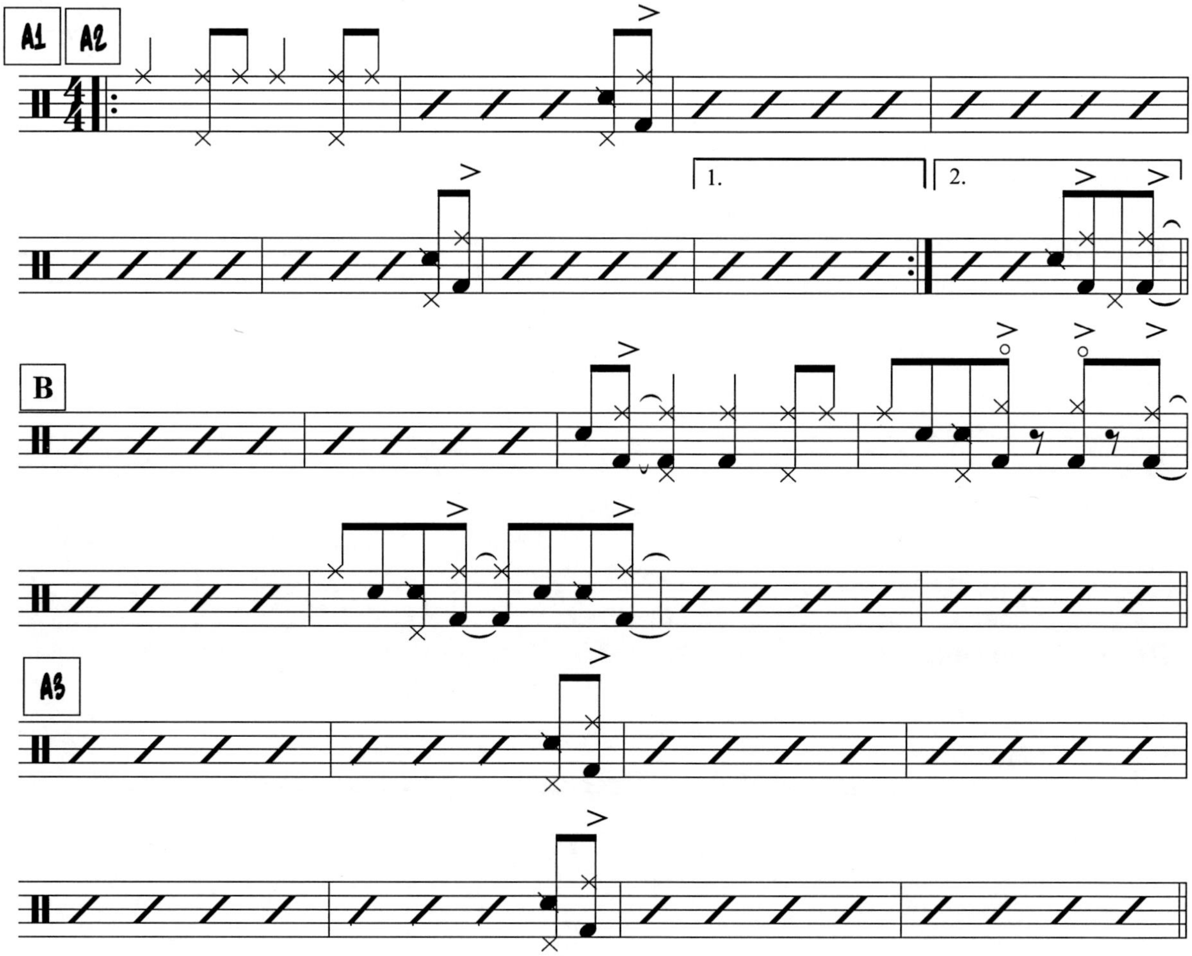

Fine

FOR SOLOS:

PLAY JAZZ TIME FREELY, INSTERACT AND HOLD THE PULSE
OVER A 32 BAR- AABA FORM.
WATCH FOR THE CUE TO "BACKGROUND FOR SOLOS"

ON CUE: BACKGROUND FOR SOLOS.

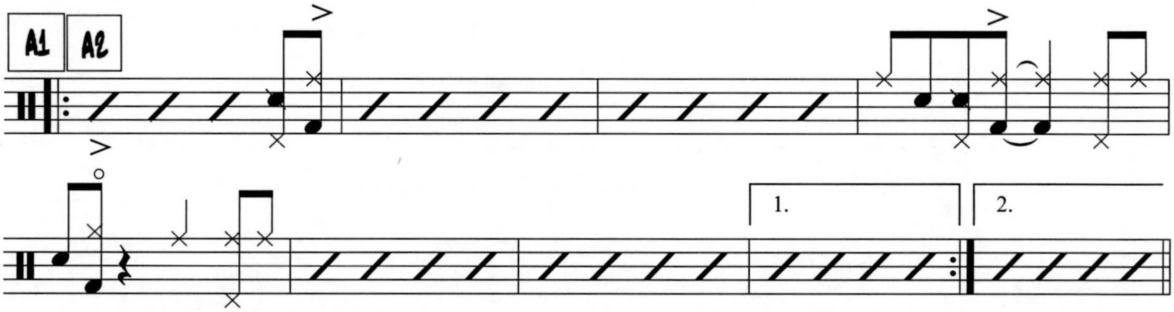

playthrough video - jazzdrumming.info/charts

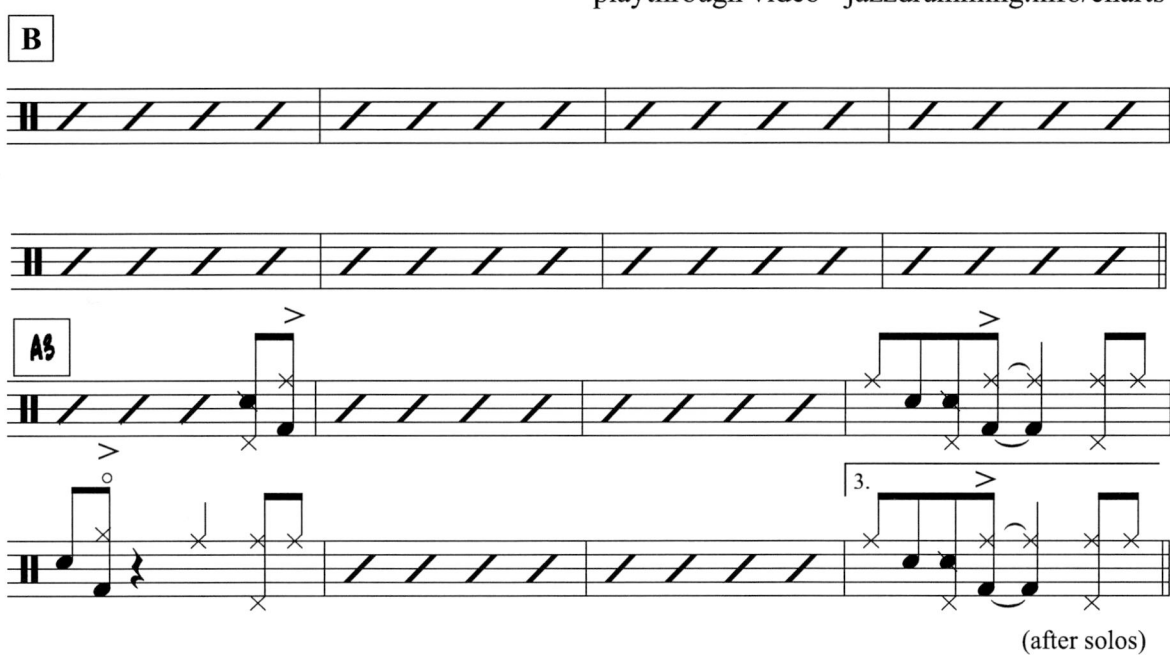

(after solos)

D.C. al Fine

Drum Set Legend:

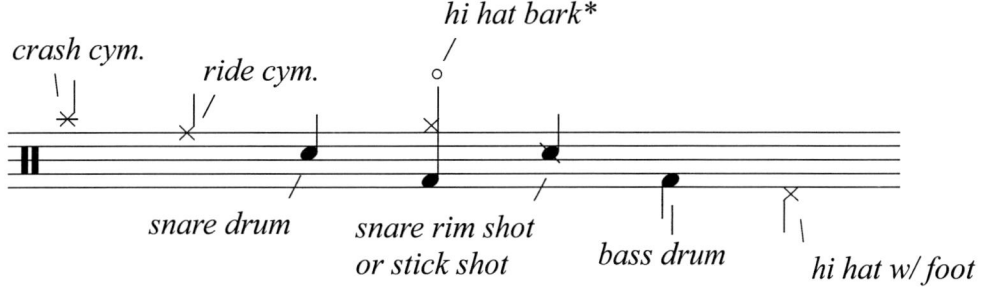

* strike slightly open hi hat (doubled with BD), then close immediatly.

Notation Notes:

Freely play jazz time, and catch this figure:

Section 2 — Drum Chart Supplement

Suggested basic drumset part

Jazz Time

Blue Seven

comp. by Sonny Rollins
drum arr. by A. Hall

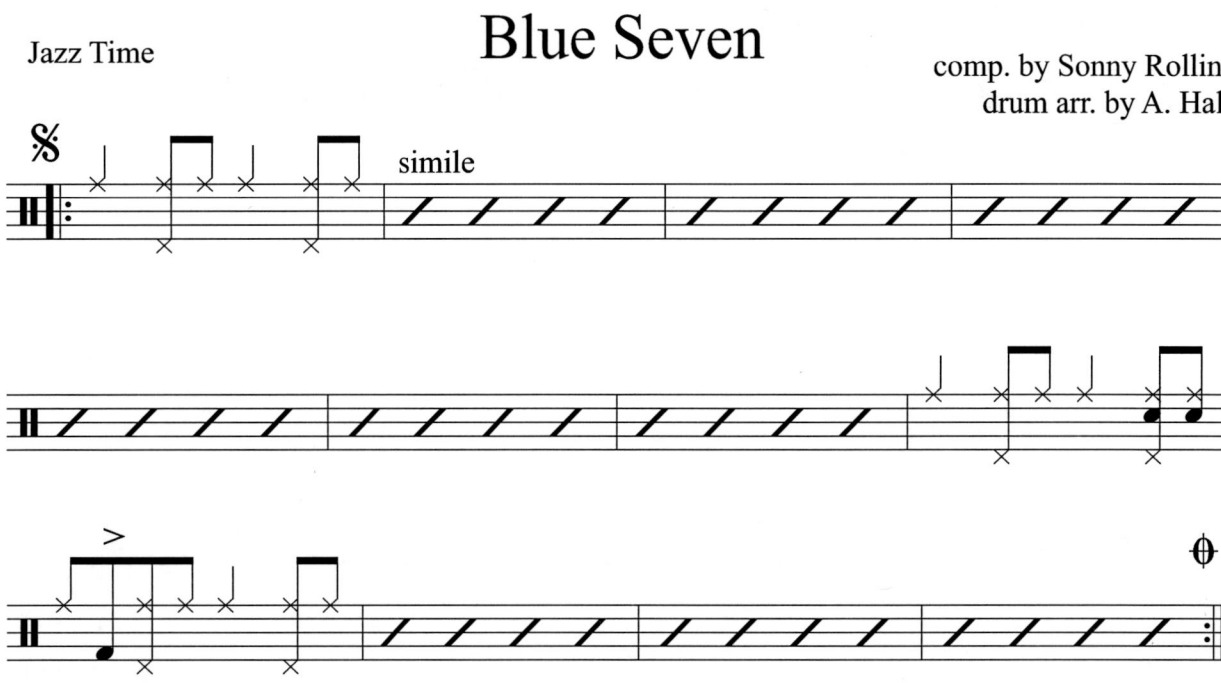

For Solos:
Play time freely in 12 bar phrases, listen, interact, hold the pulse.
Watch for the cue to "background for solos" and "shout chorus".

On Cue: Background for Solos

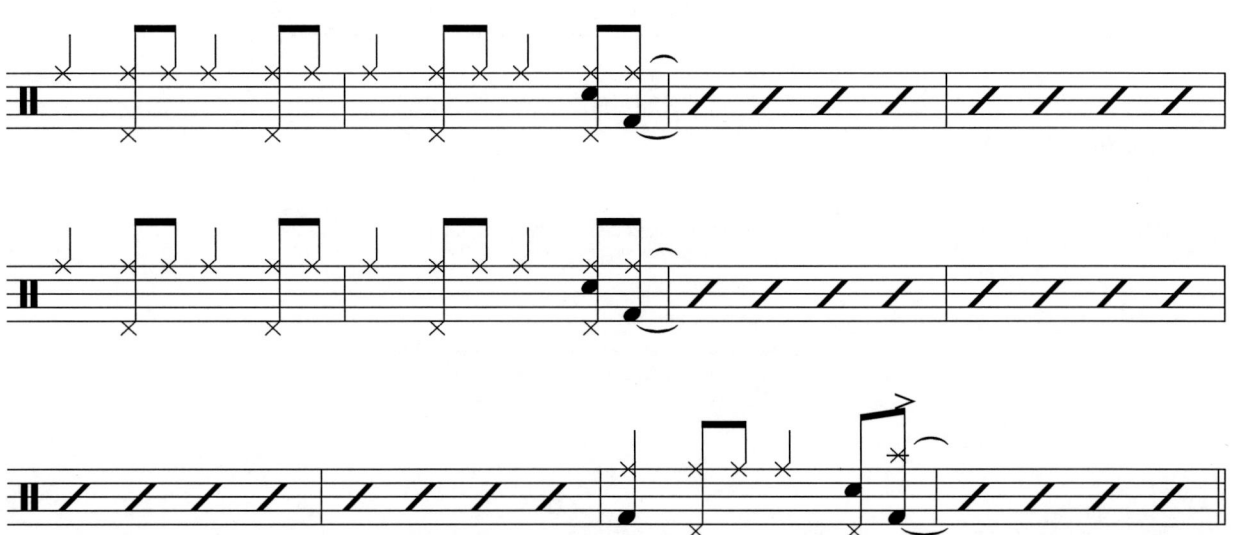

Shout chorus. Play after solos (optional)

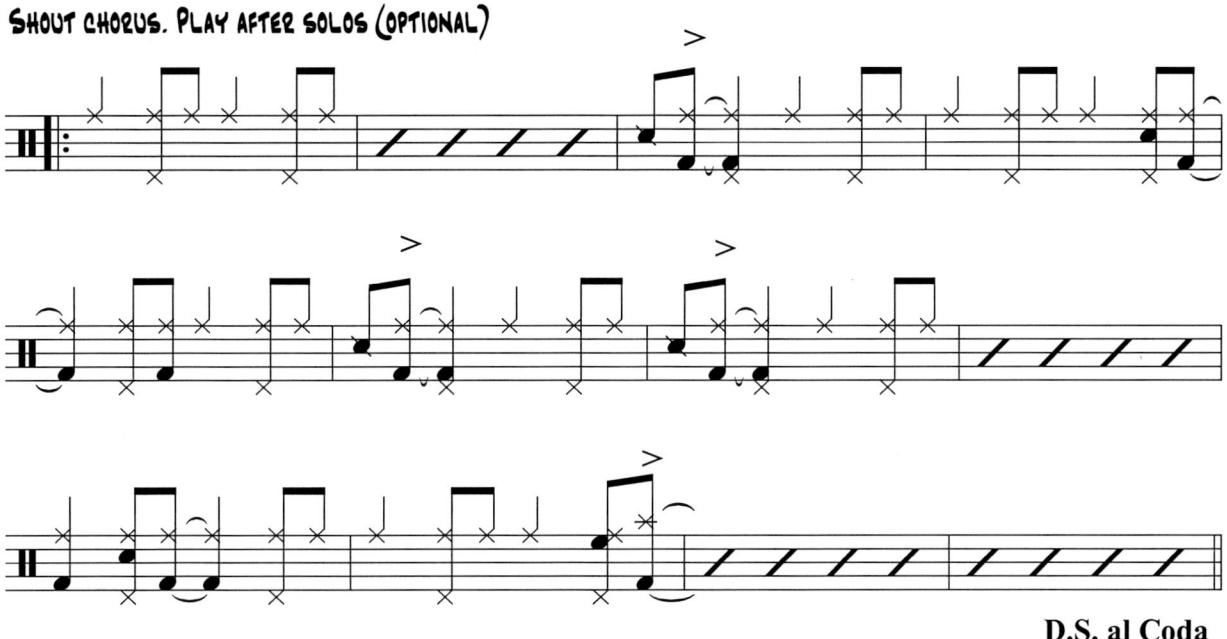

D.S. al Coda

Drum Set Legend:

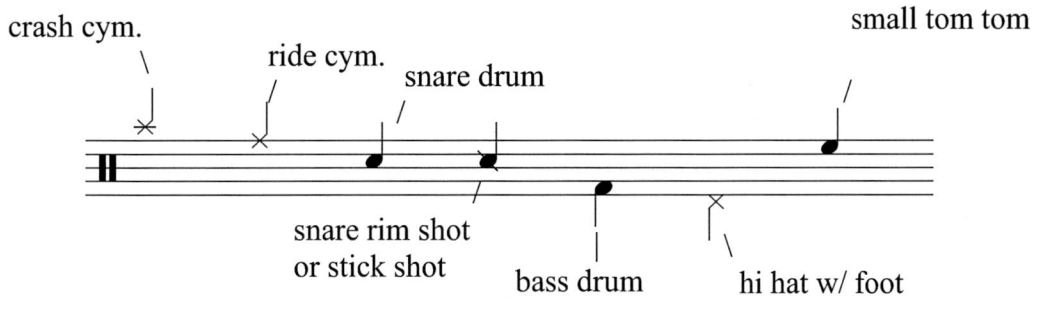

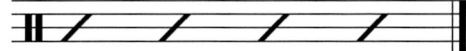

Notation notes:

These slashes mean play jazz time freely.

SECTION 2 — DRUM CHART SUPPLEMENT

Suggested basic drumset part

Blues by Five

comp. by Red Garland
drum arr. by A. Hall

jazz feel (swing 8ths)

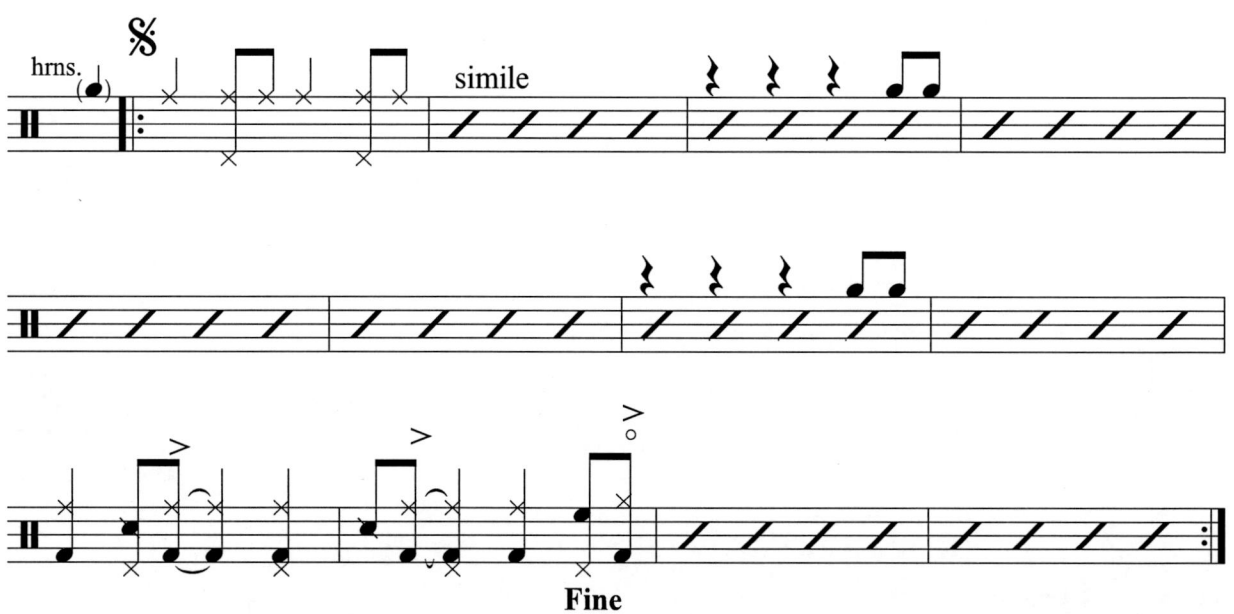

Fine

FOR SOLOS:
Play time freely in 12 bar phrases, listen, interact, hold the pulse.
Watch for the cue to "background for solos" and "shout chorus".

On Cue: Background for solos

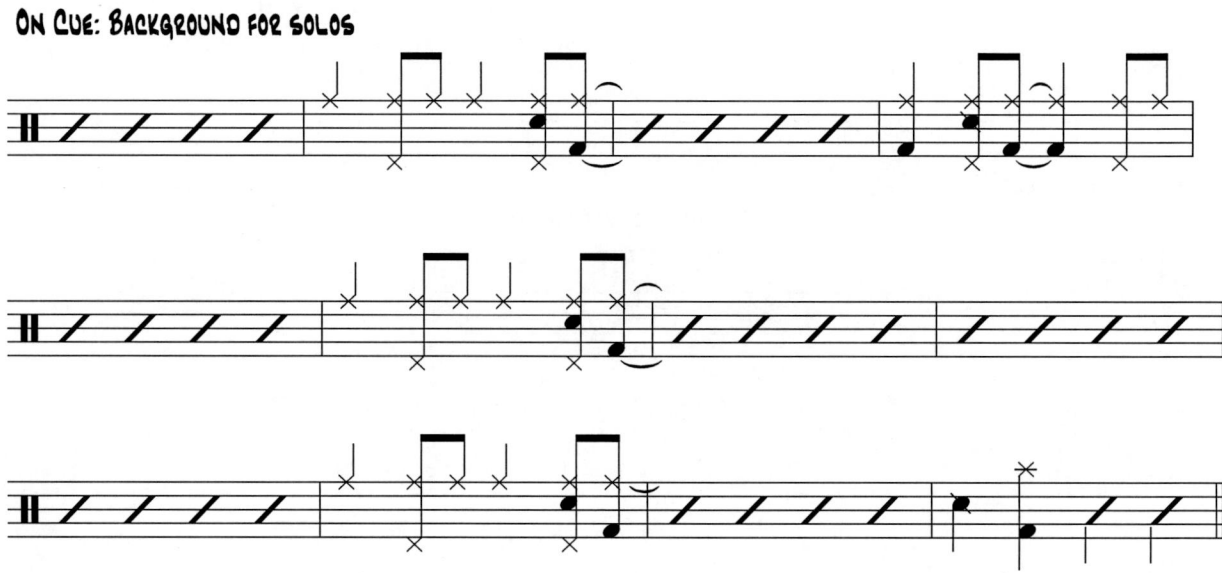

playthrough video - jazzdrumming.info/charts

SHOUT CHORUS. PLAY AFTER SOLOS (OPTIONAL)

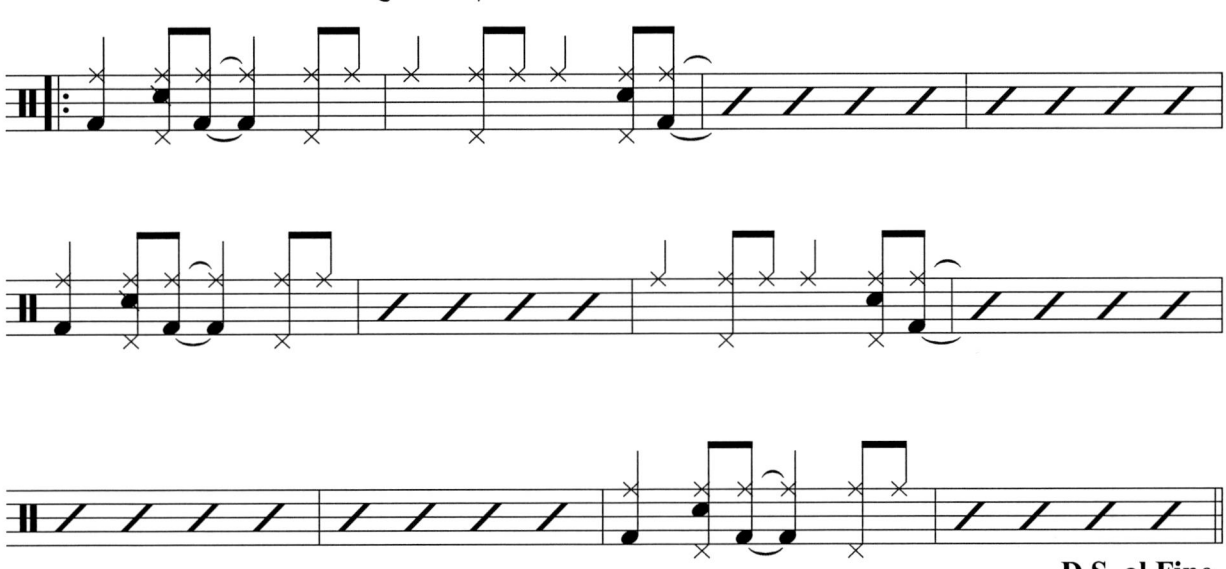

D.S. al Fine

Drum Set Legend:

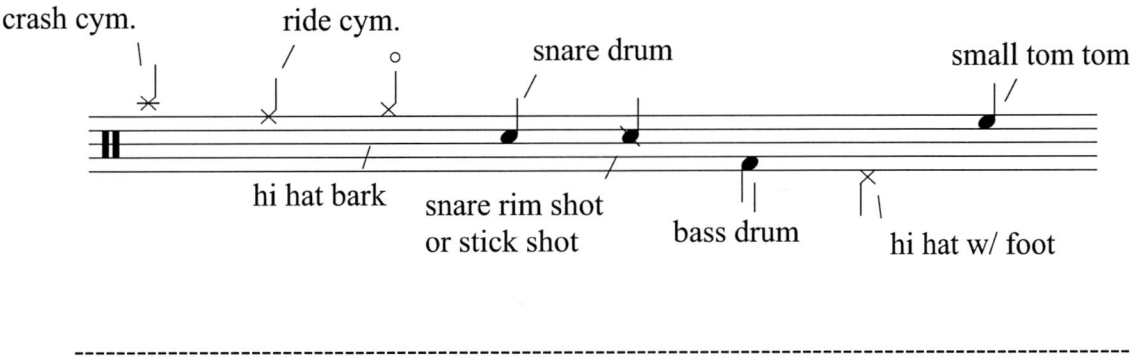

Notation notes:

Section 2 — Drum Chart Supplement

Suggested basic drum set part

Blues in the Closet

comp. by Oscar Pettiford
drum arr. by A. Hall

jazz time

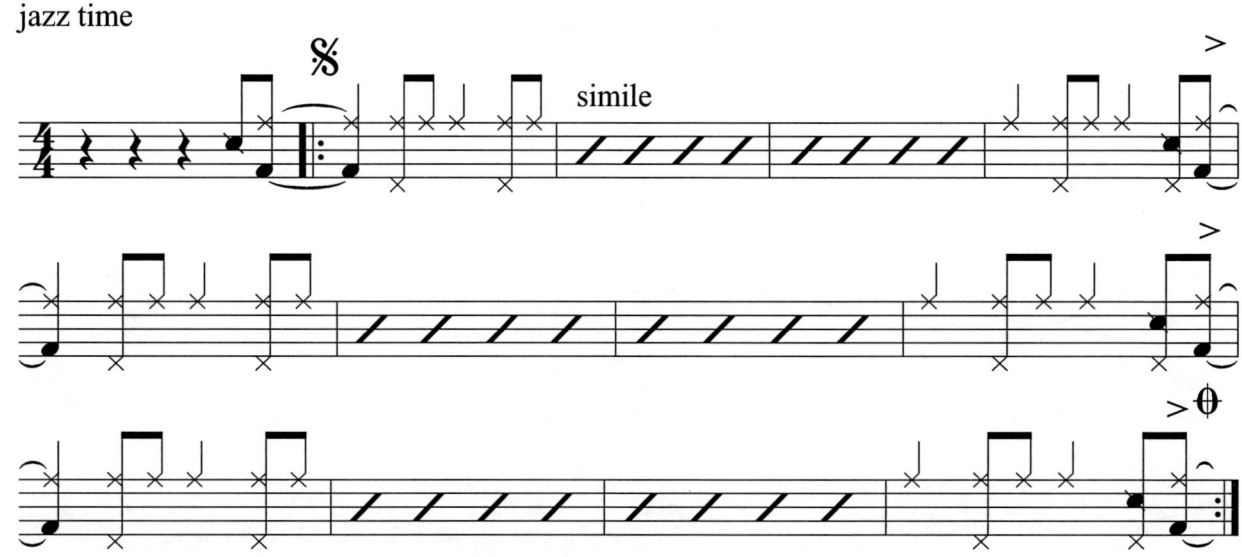

FOR SOLOS:
Play jazz time freely in 12 bar phrases, listen, interact, hold the pulse.
Watch for the cues to "background for solos" and "shout chorus".

fill...........

On Cue: Background for solos

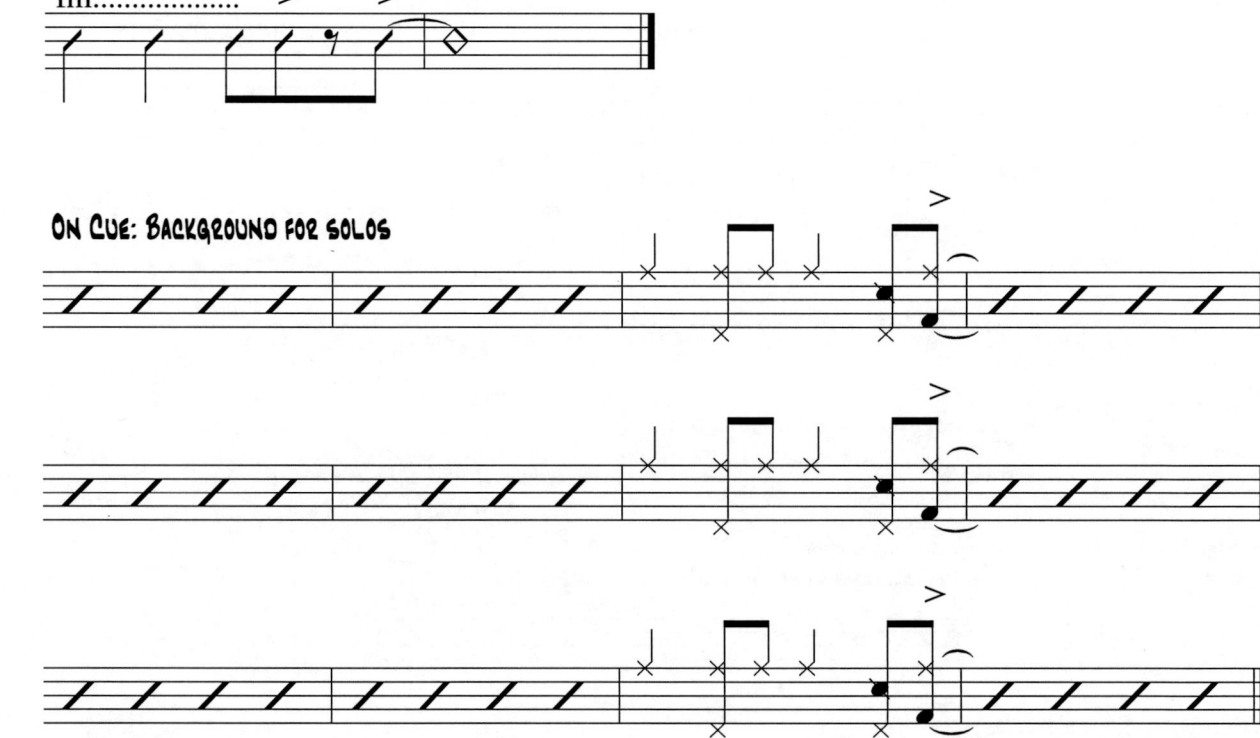

Drum Chart Supplement — Section 2

playthrough video - jazzdrumming.info/charts

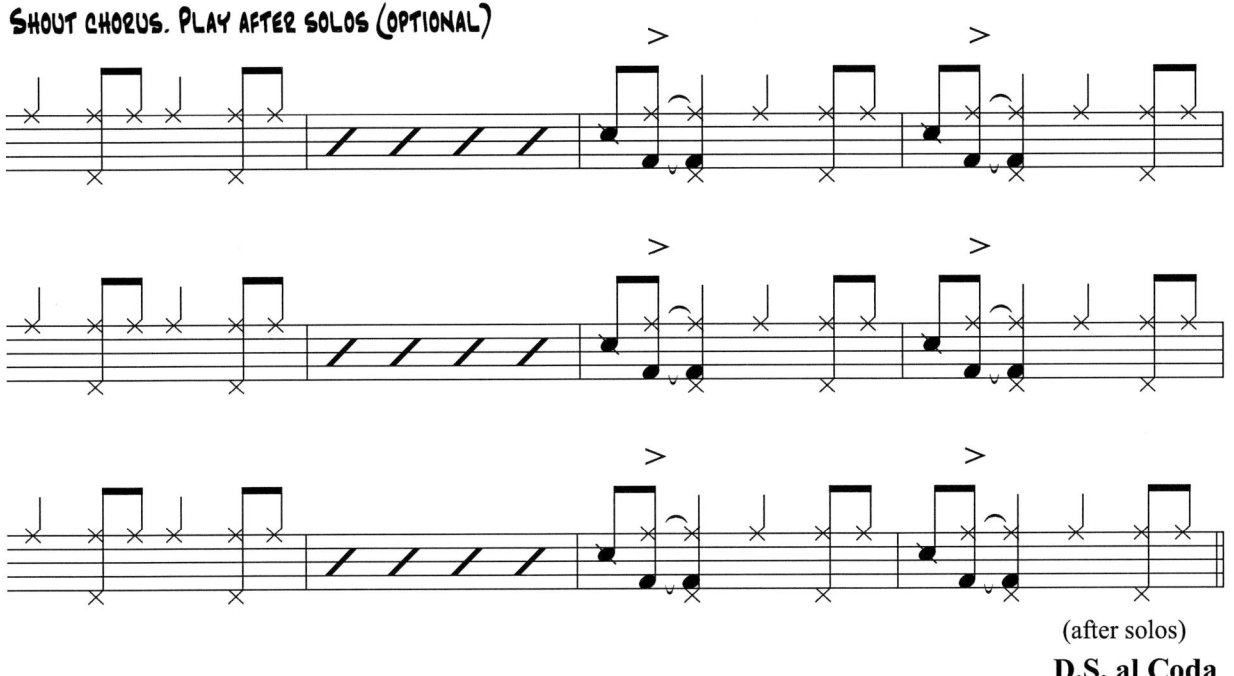

(after solos)
D.S. al Coda

Drum Set Legend:

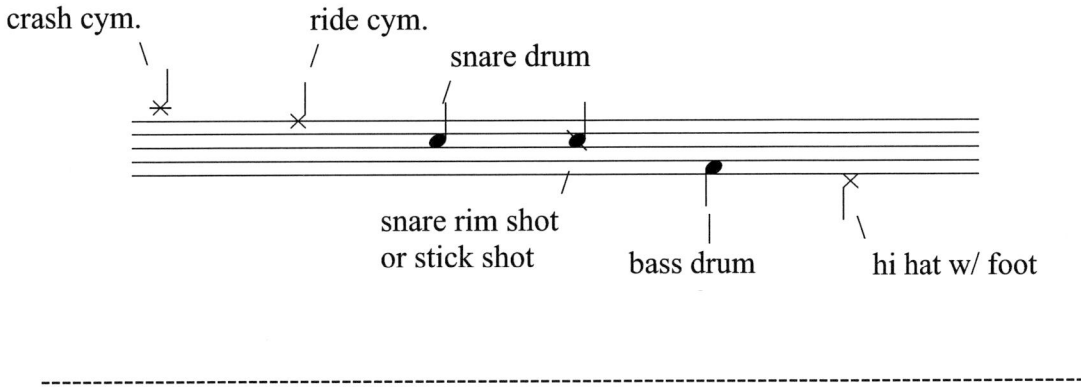

Notation notes:

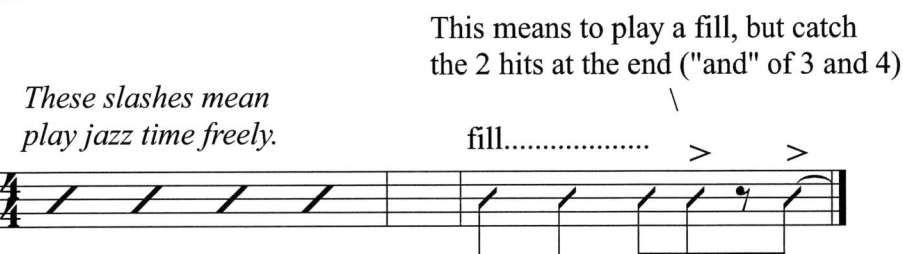

Section 2 — Drum Chart Supplement

Cold Duck Time

Suggested simplified drumset part

Composed by Eddie Harris
Drum arr. by Alan Hall

Straight 8th feel

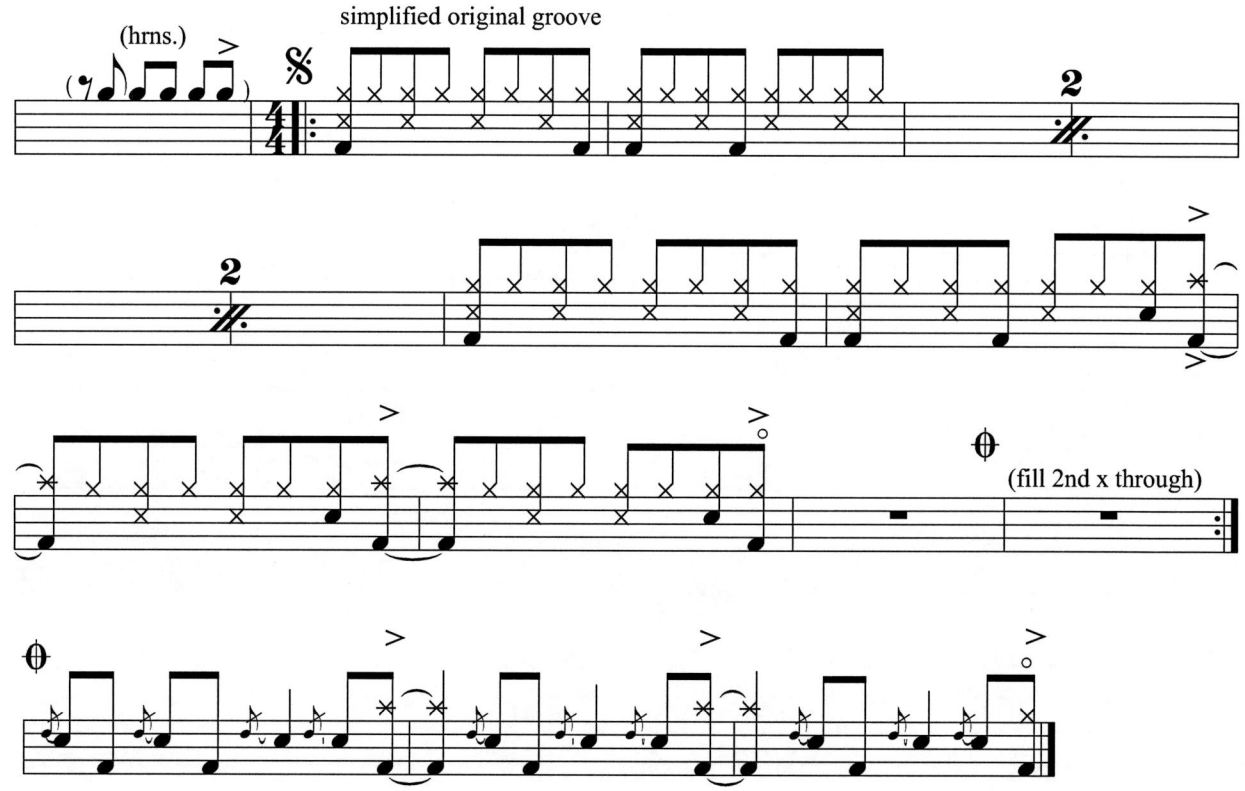

(suggested approach to set-ups and hits in this coda)

On Cue: Background for solos

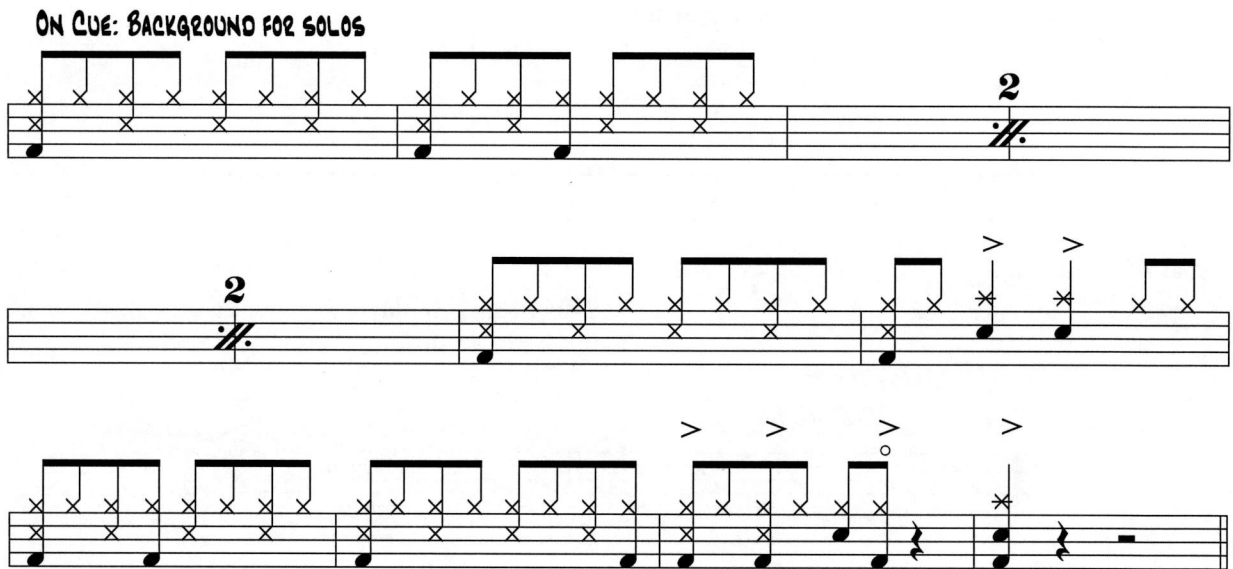

playthrough video - jazzdrumming.info/charts

Shout Chorus. Play after solos (optional)

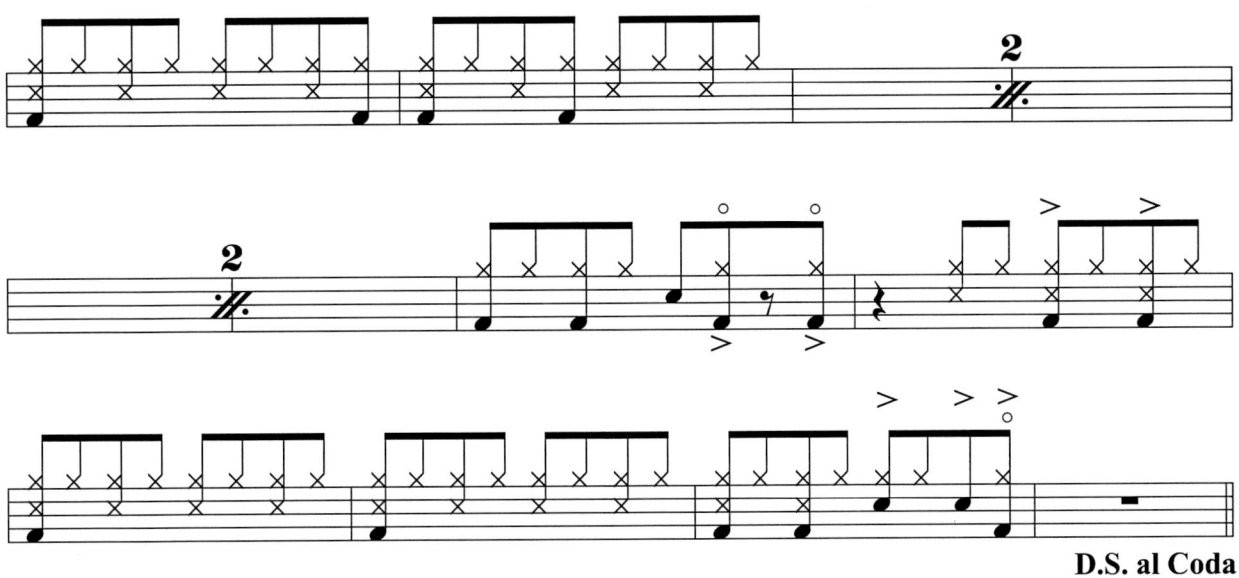

D.S. al Coda

Drum Set Legend

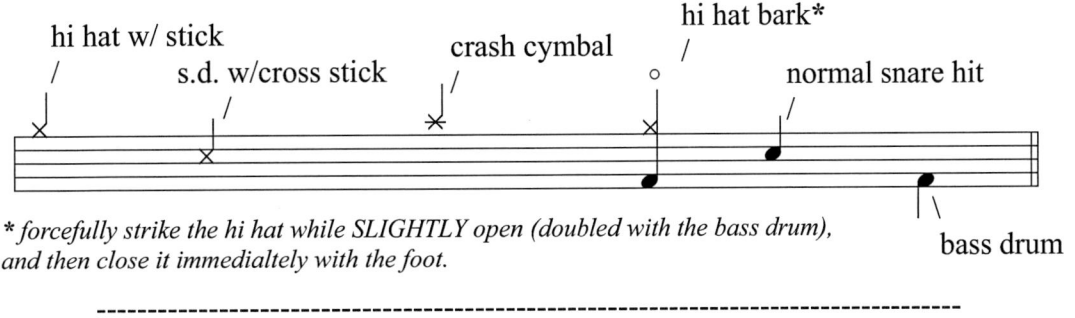

* forcefully strike the hi hat while SLIGHTLY open (doubled with the bass drum), and then close it immedialtely with the foot.

Notes:
- The groove here is suggested, but one can play a rock type groove as well, as long as you still catch all accents.

- If you choose to play something like this written groove, you may vary the snare cross stick hits, and bass drum hits, like on the original recording. Some variation on the grooves in Jazz is generally fine.

- **Important: If the bass player is playing a bass line other than the sample bass line, you should vary your bass drum rhythm to reflect that bass line rhythm.**

Contemplation

Suggested basic drum set part

comp. by McCoy Tyner
drum arr. by Alan Hall

Elvin Jones type Jazz Waltz

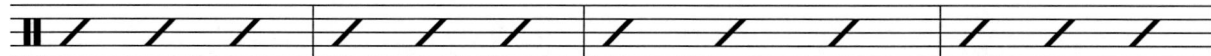

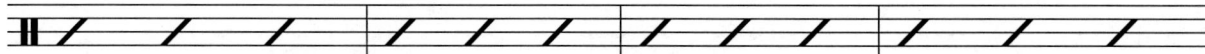

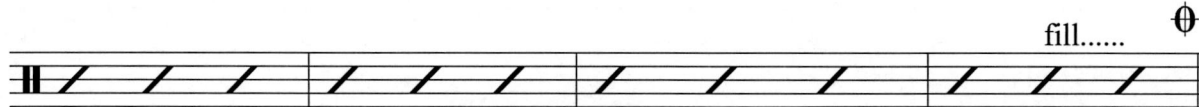

For Solos:
Play jazz shuffle time freely in 16 bar phrases, listen, interact, hold the pulse.
Watch for the cue to "background for solos" and "Shout Chorus"

On Cue: Bascкground for solos

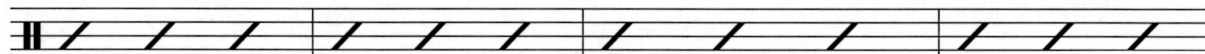

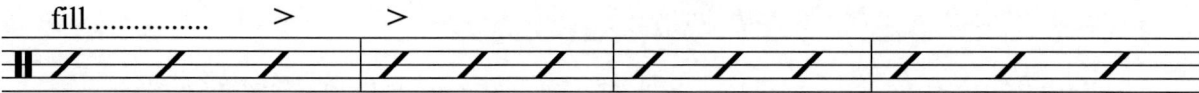

Drum Chart Supplement

playthrough video - jazzdrumming.info/charts

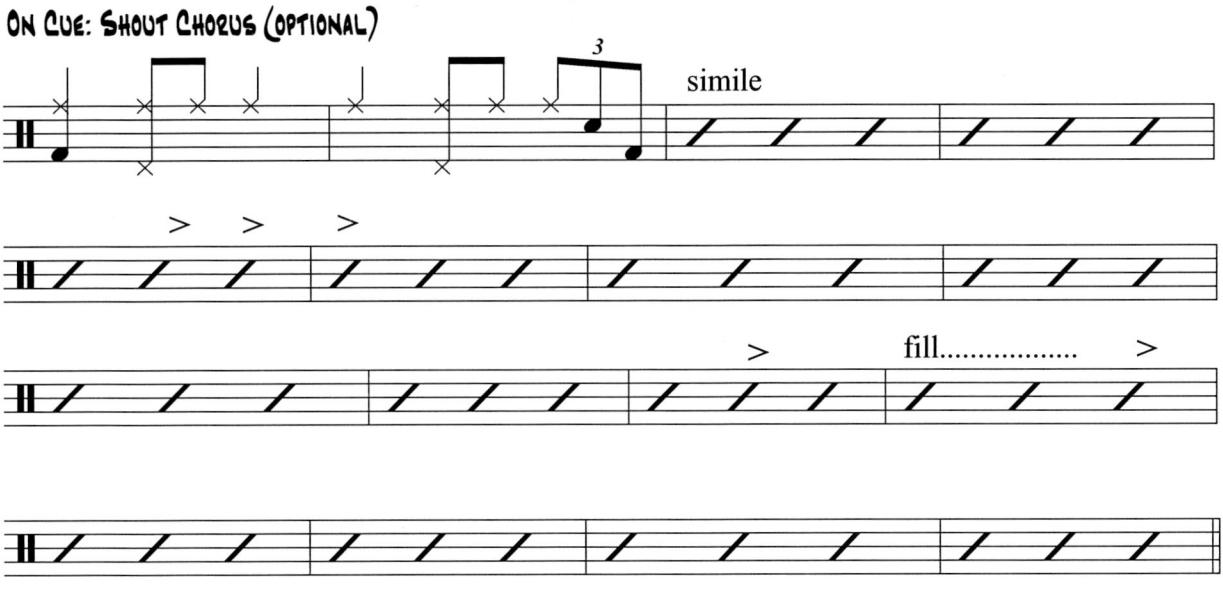

D.C. al Coda

Drum Set Legend:

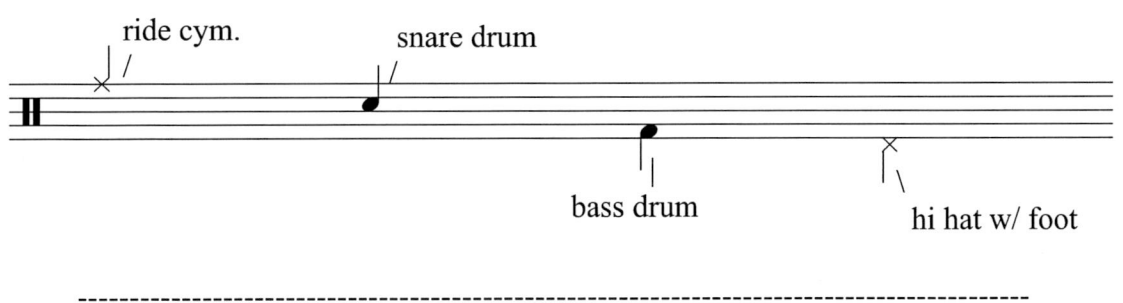

Notation Notes:

SECTION 2 — Drum Chart Supplement

Suggested basic drumset part

Doxy

comp. by Sonny Rollins
drum arr. by Alan Hall

Jazz Time

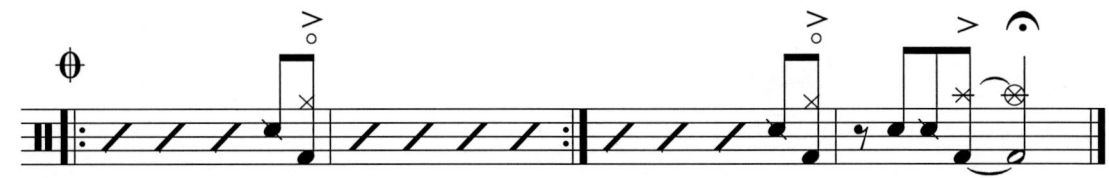

FOR SOLOS:
Play time freely in 16 bar phrases, listen, interact, hold the pulse.
Watch for the cue to "background for solos"

DRUM CHART SUPPLEMENT — SECTION 2

playthrough video - jazzdrumming.info/charts

On Cue, Background for Solos

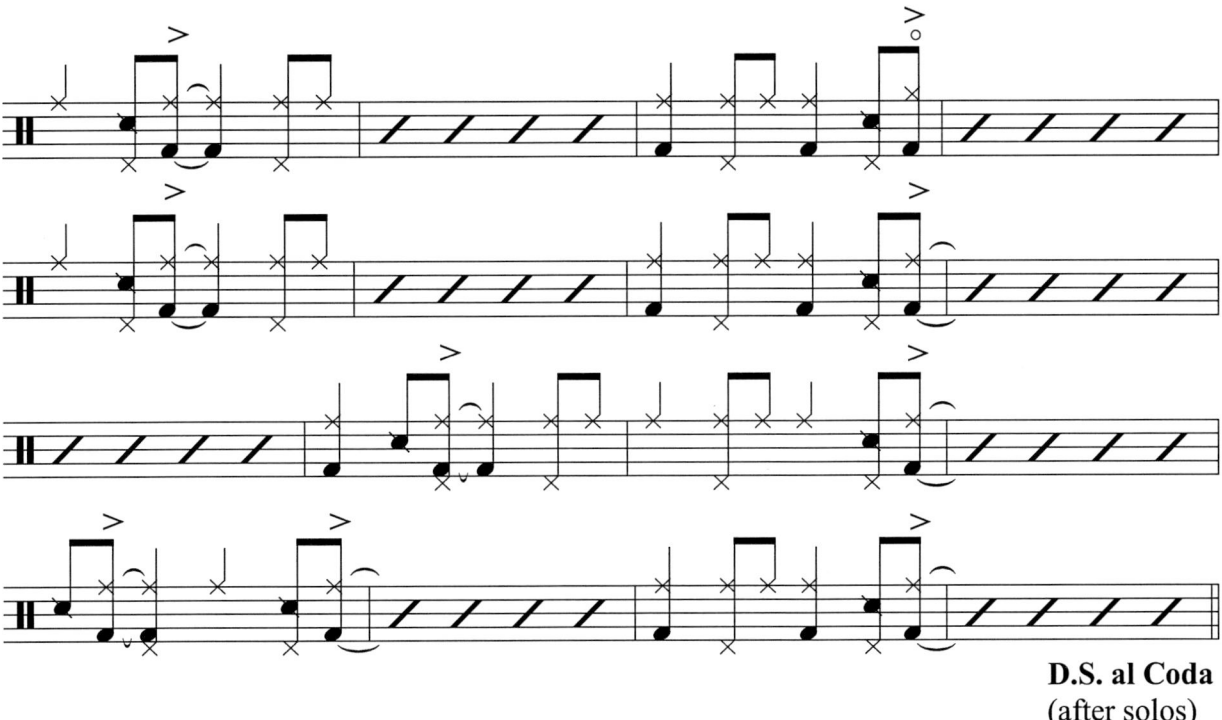

D.S. al Coda
(after solos)

Drum Set Legend:

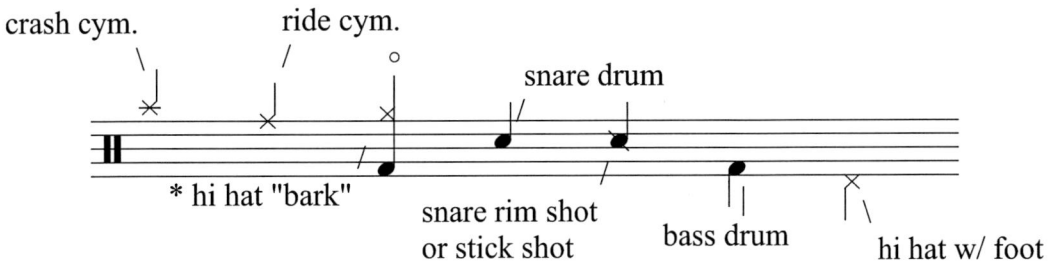

* *strike hi hat while slightly open (double it with bass drum), then close hi hat immediately*

Notation Notes:

Play jazz time freely.

Play time, but catch this accent too:

Edward Lee

Suggested basic drumset part

comp. by Harold Mabern
drum arr. by A. Hall

jazz time

FOR SOLOS:
PLAY JAZZ OR TIME FREELY, INTERACT AND HOLD THE PULSE
OVER A 32 BAR- AABA FORM.
WATCH FOR THE CUE TO "BACKGROUND FOR SOLOS"

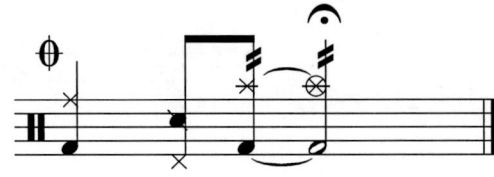

Drum Chart Supplement — Section 2

playthrough video - jazzdrumming.info/charts

ON CUE: BACKGROUND FOR SOLOS.

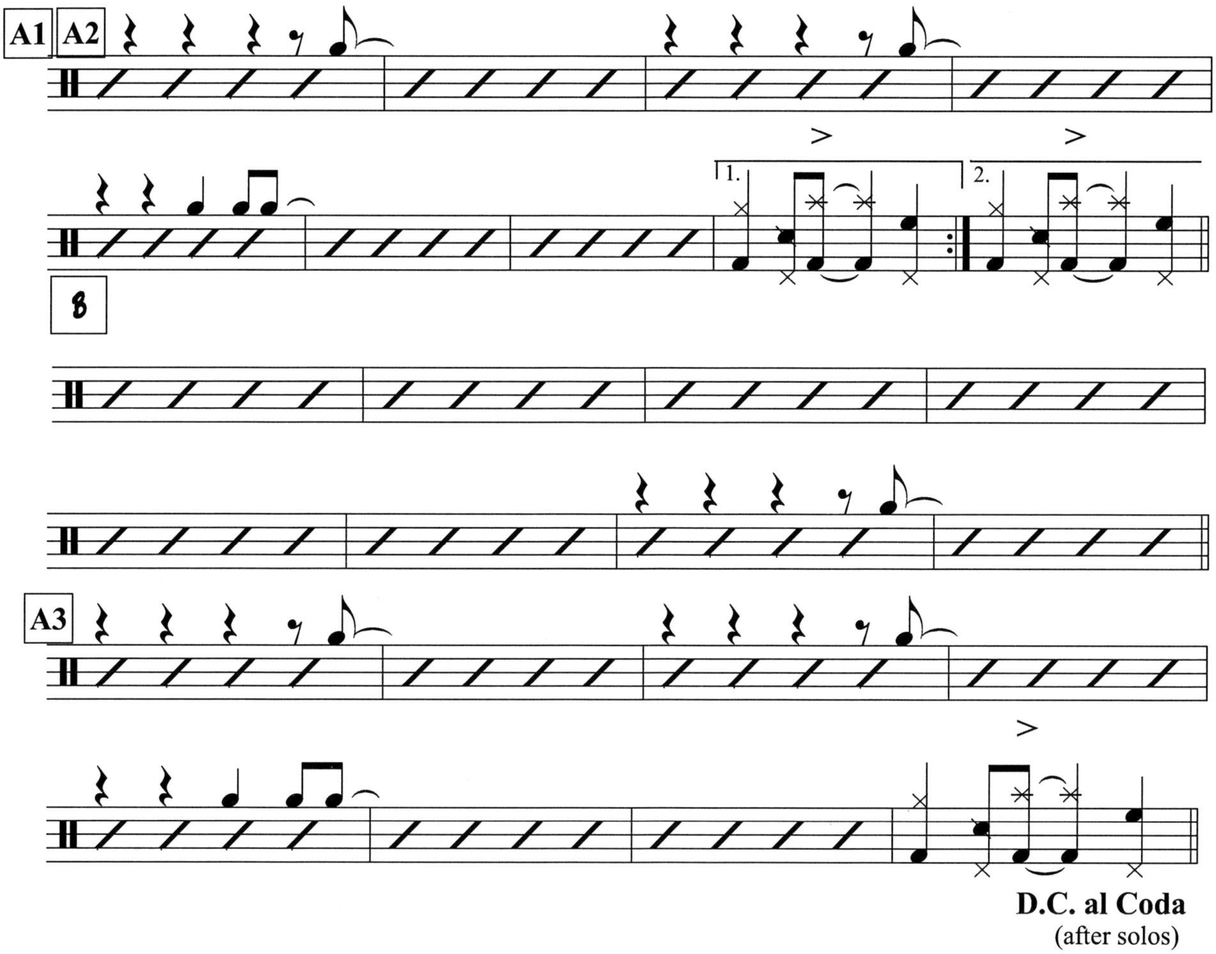

[Sheet music: A1/A2, B, A3 sections with D.C. al Coda (after solos)]

Drum Set Legend:

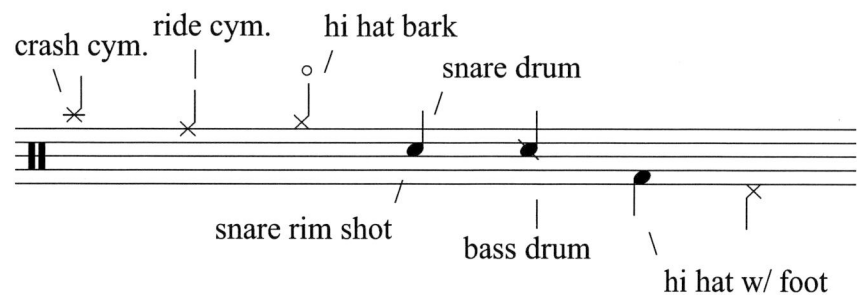

Notation Note:

27

SECTION 2 — Drum Chart Supplement

Suggested basic drumset part

Equinox

Jazz Time

comp. by John Coltrane
drum arr. by A. Hall

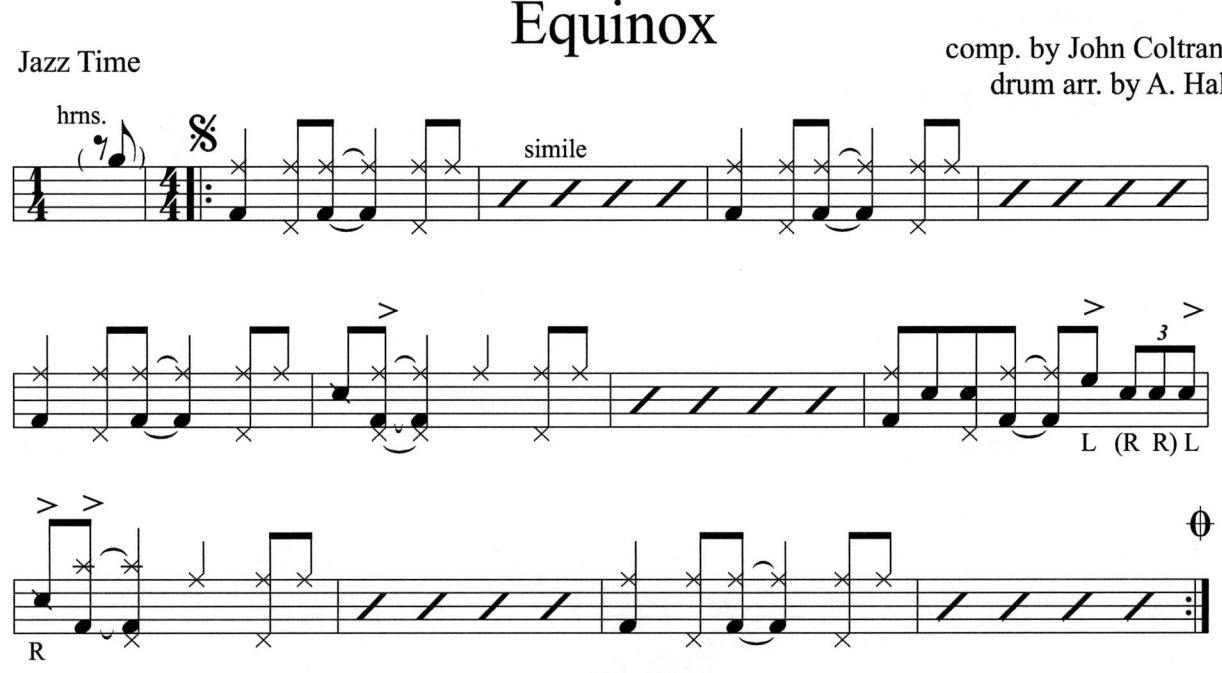

FOR SOLOS:
Play jazz time freely in 12 bar phrases, listen, interact, hold the pulse.
Watch for the cue to "background for solos" and "shout chorus".

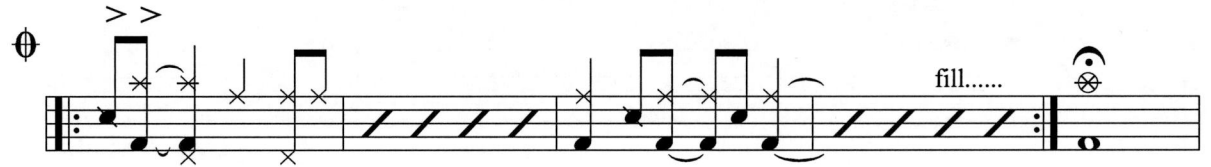

On Cue: Background for solos

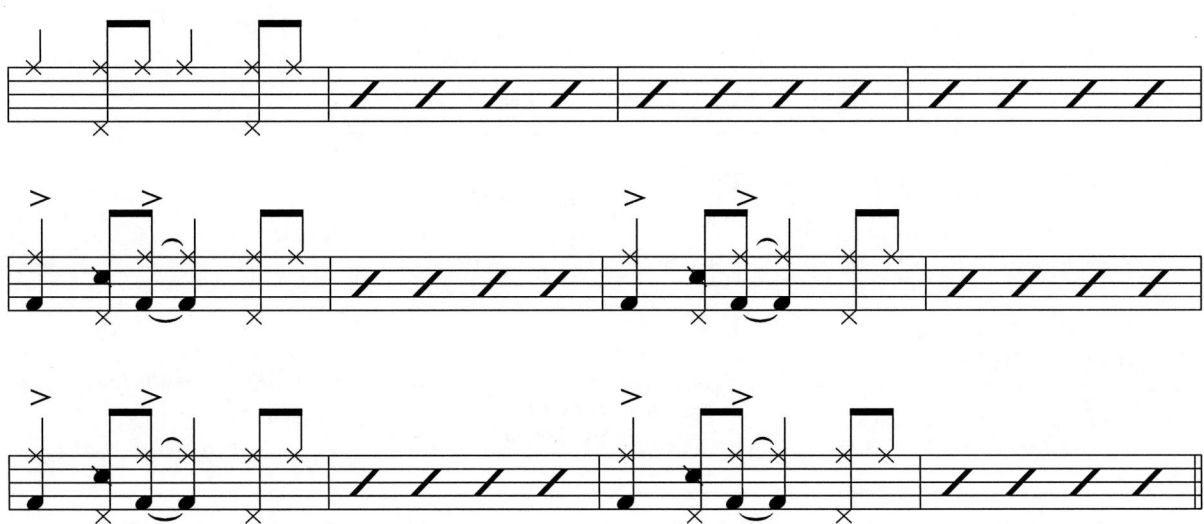

Drum Chart Supplement

Section 2

playthrough video - jazzdrumming.info/charts

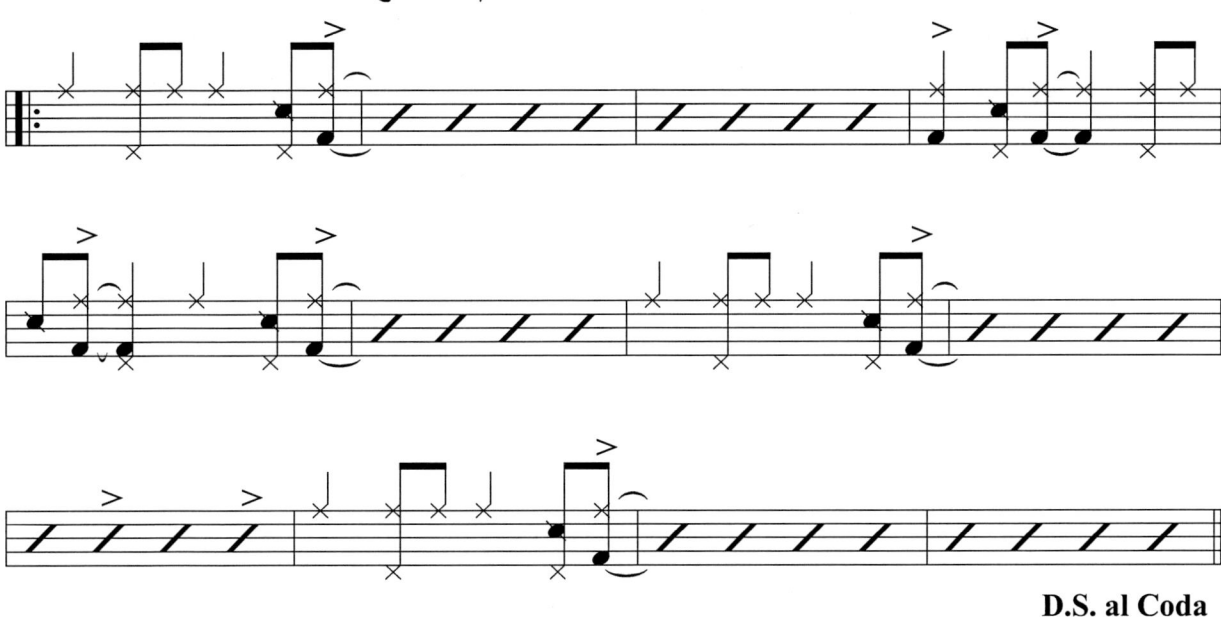

D.S. al Coda

Drum Set Legend:

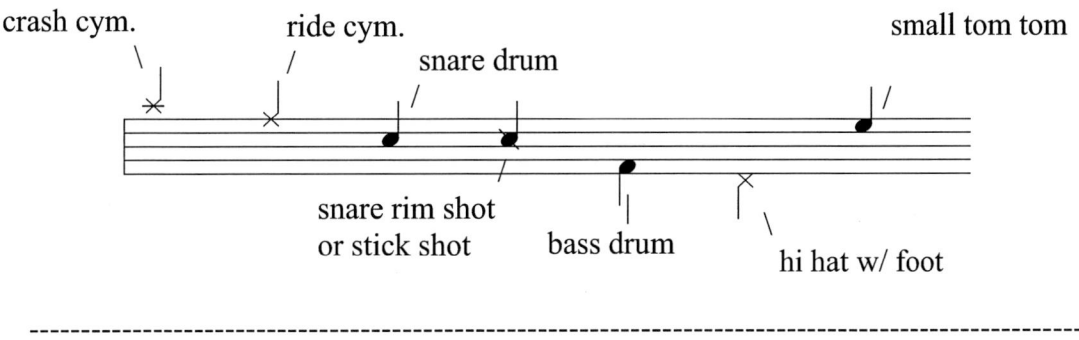

Notation notes:

Section 2 — Drum Chart Supplement

Suggested basic drumset part

Freedom Jazz Dance

1/2 feel Swing Funk*

comp. by Eddie Harris
drum arr. by Alan Hall

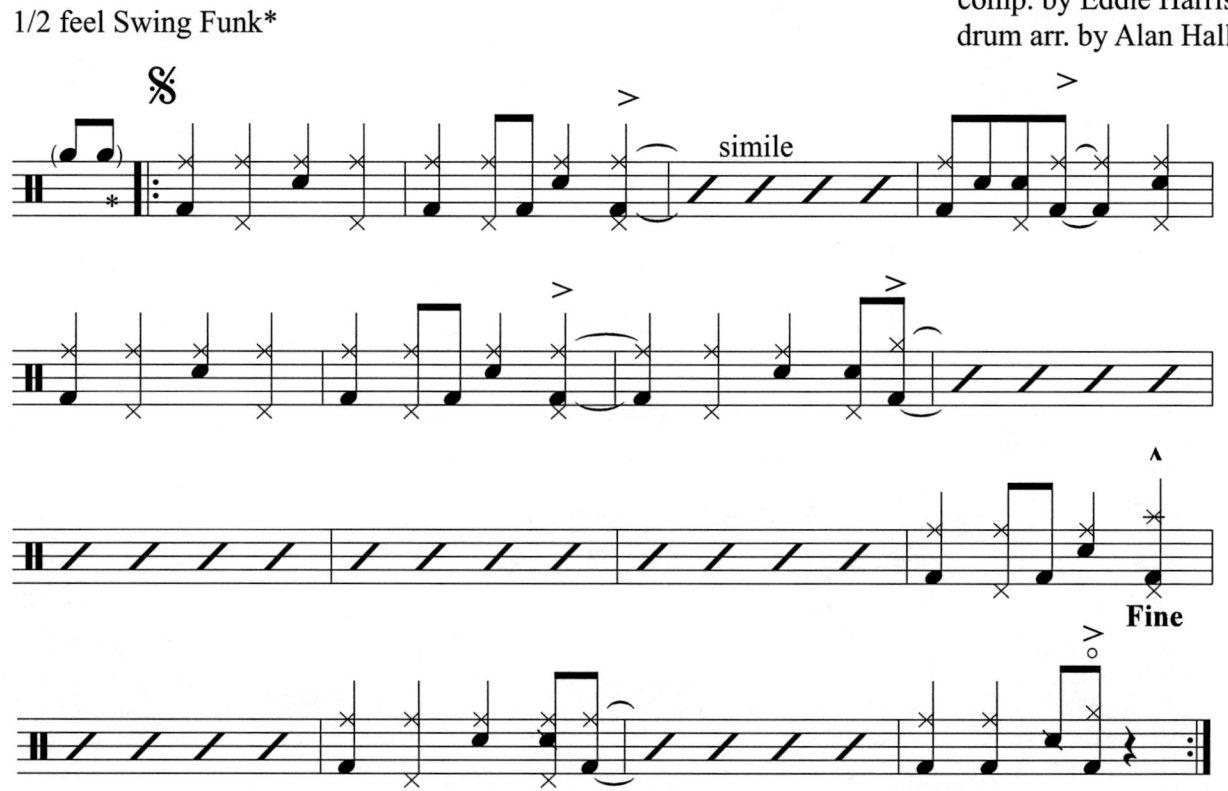

FOR SOLOS:
PLAY A LOOSE 1/2 SWIMNG FUNK GROOVE FREELY IN 16 BAR PHRASES, LISTEN, INTERACT, HOLD THE PULSE.
WATCH FOR THE CUE TO "BACKGROUND FOR SOLOS" AND "SHOUT CHORUS"

ON CUE: BASCKGROUND FOR SOLOS

simile

playthrough video - jazzdrumming.info/charts

On Cue: Shout Chorus (optional)

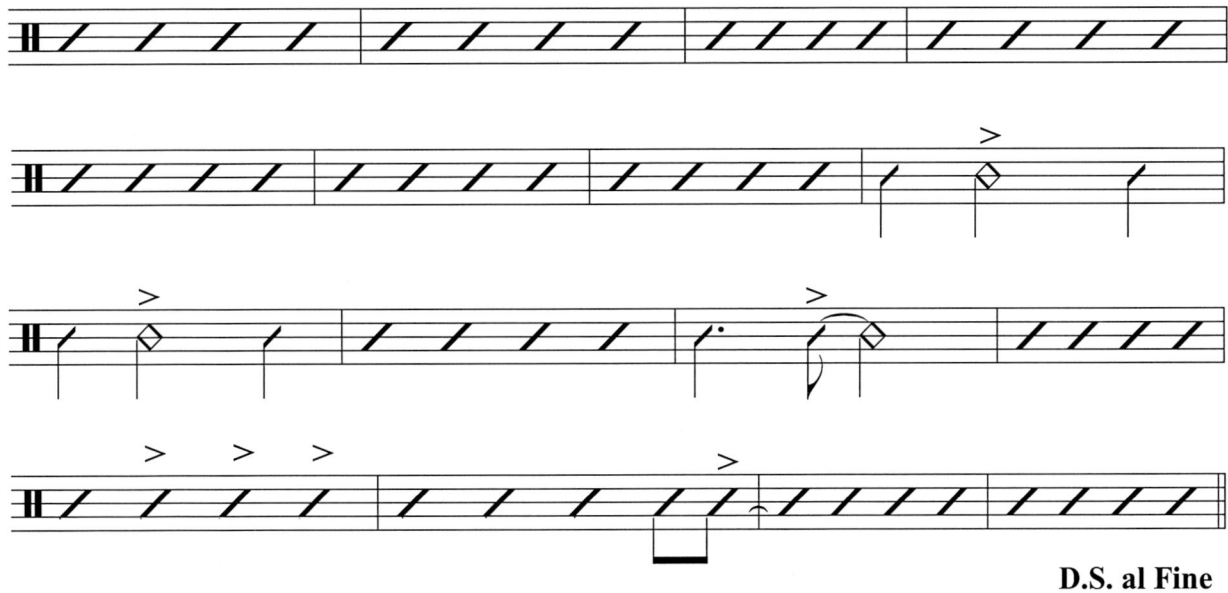

D.S. al Fine

Drum Set Legend:

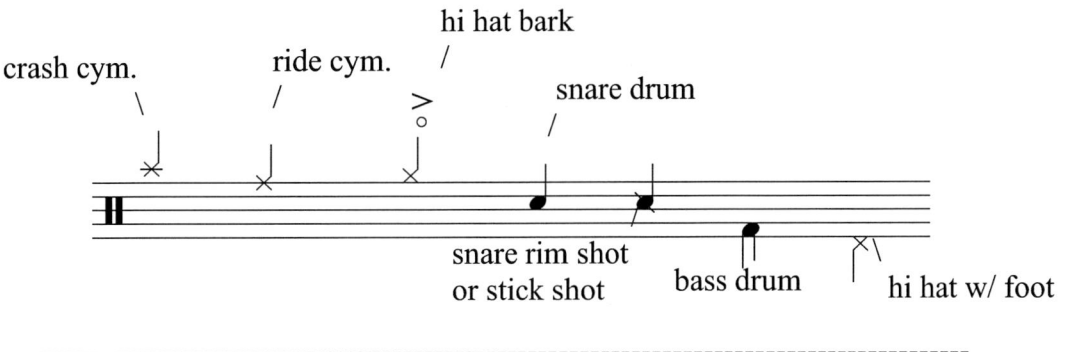

Notation Notes:

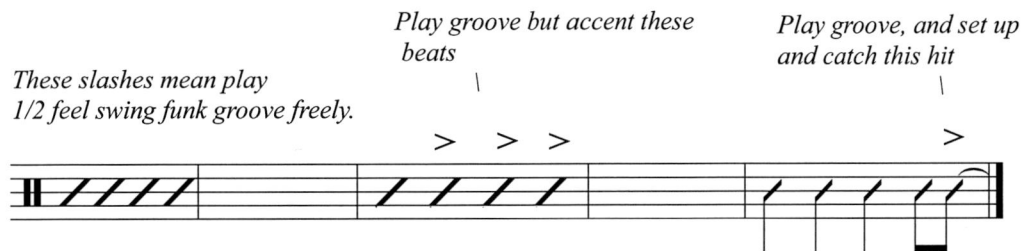

*note - this tune has been played with many different types of grooves, so stay open to other approaches.

SECTION 2 — Drum Chart Supplement

Suggested basic drumset part

Gingerbread Boy

Modern Jazz

comp. by Jimmy Heath
drum arr. by Alan Hall

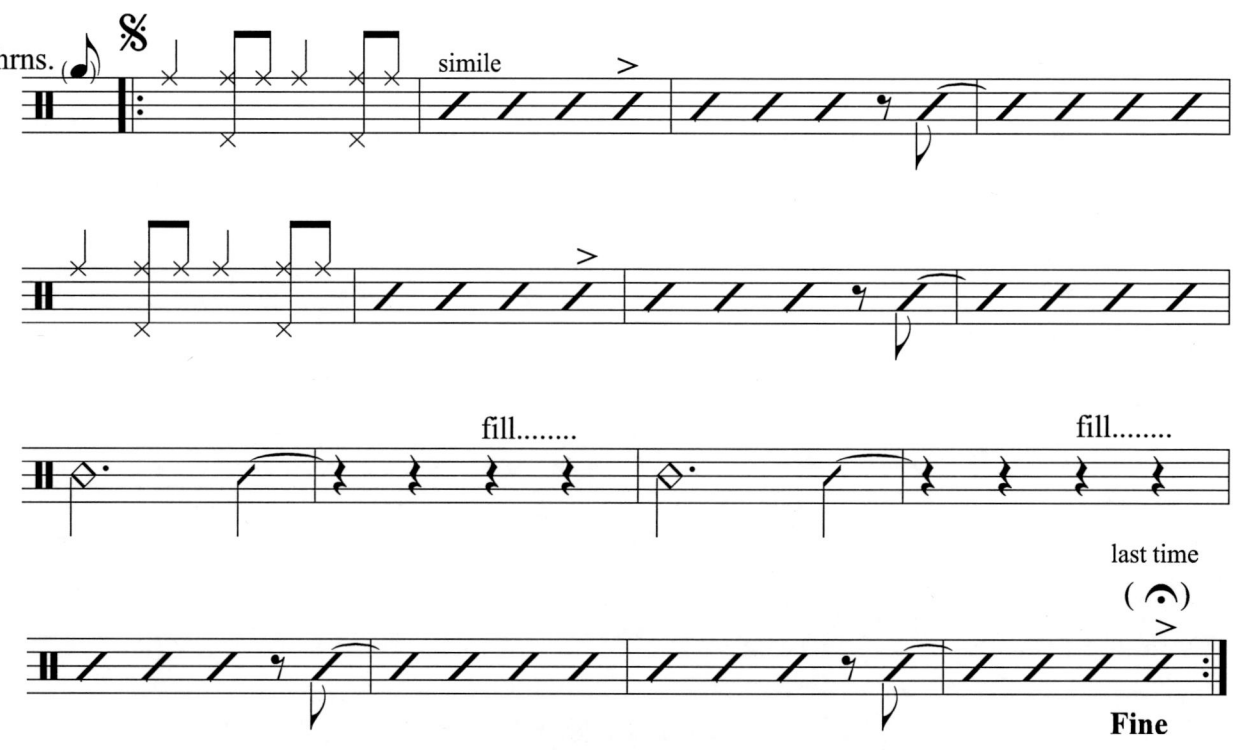

FOR SOLOS:
Play jazz time freely in a 12 bar blues form, listen, interact, hold the pulse.
Watch for the cue to "background for solos" and "Shout Chorus"

On Cue: Basckground for solos

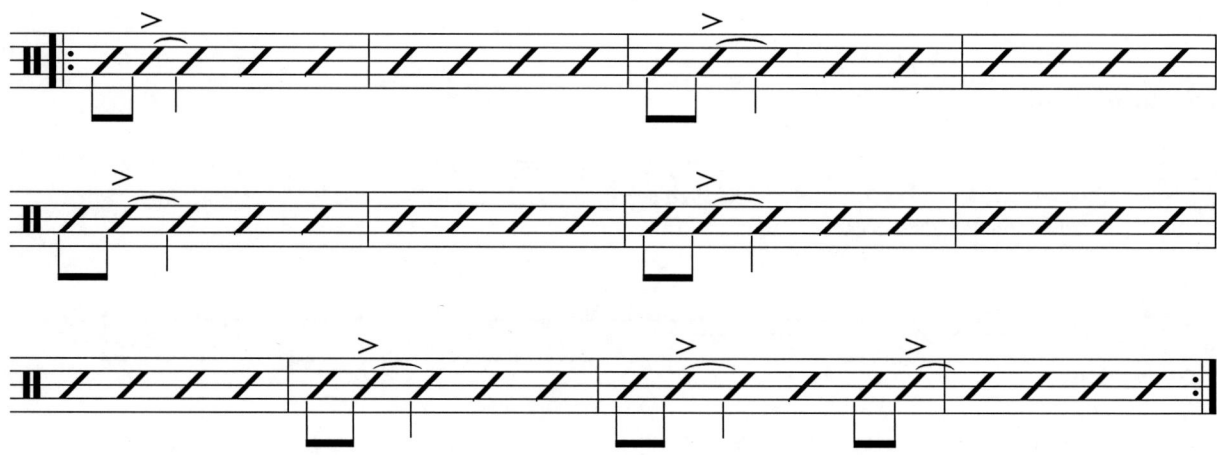

ON CUE: SHOUT CHORUS (OPTIONAL)

playthrough video - jazzdrumming.info/charts

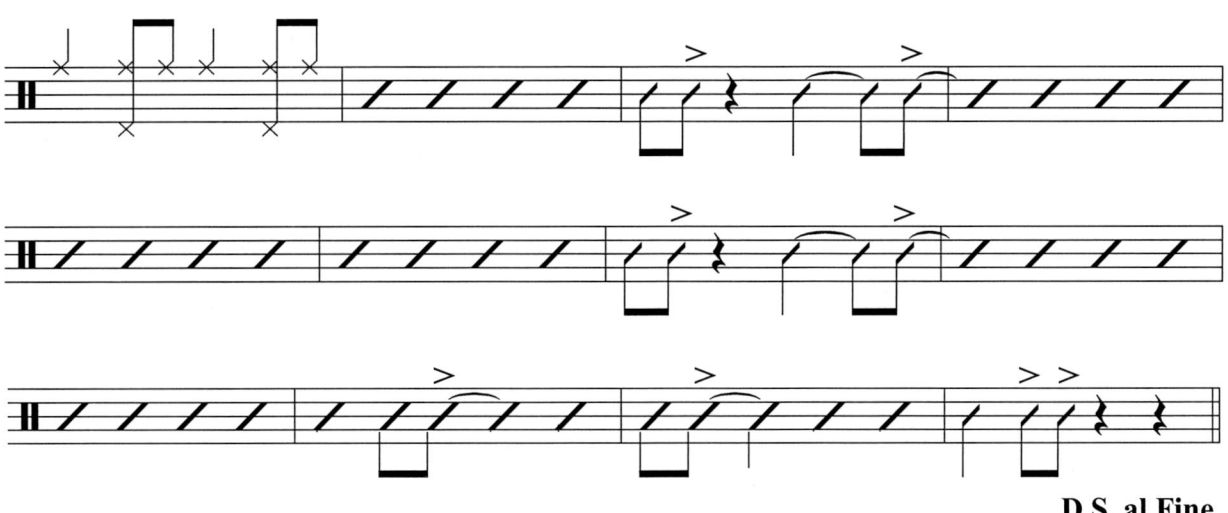

D.S. al Fine

Drum Set Legend:

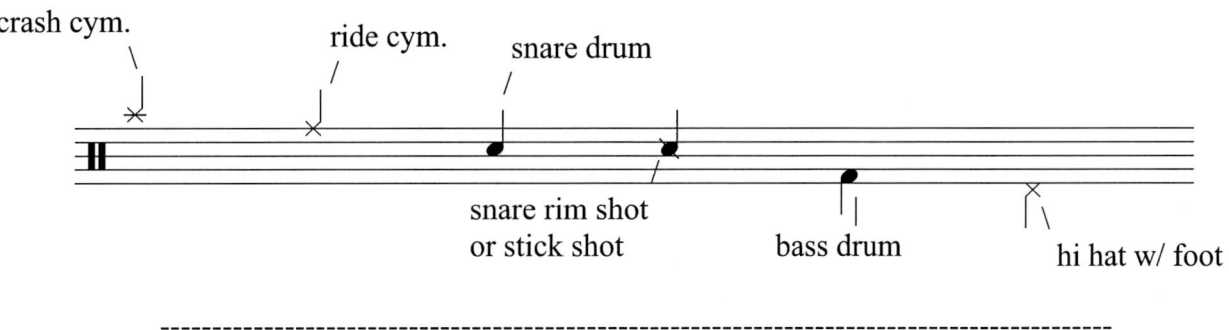

Notation Notes:

These slashes mean play jazz time freely.

Play time, but accent this beat.

Catch the 2 hits, then add a fill.

Play time, but also set-up and catch this hit

Groove Merchant

Suggested basic drum set part

comp. by Jerome Richardson
drum arr. by Alan Hall

"jazz shuffle"

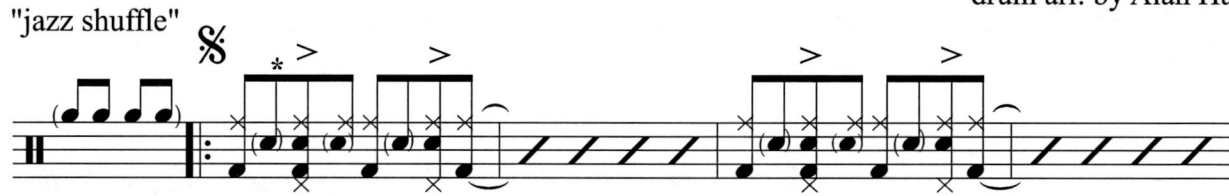

* Drop notes in parenthesis if they're too hard to play confortably.
Otherwise, play them very softly (ghosted).

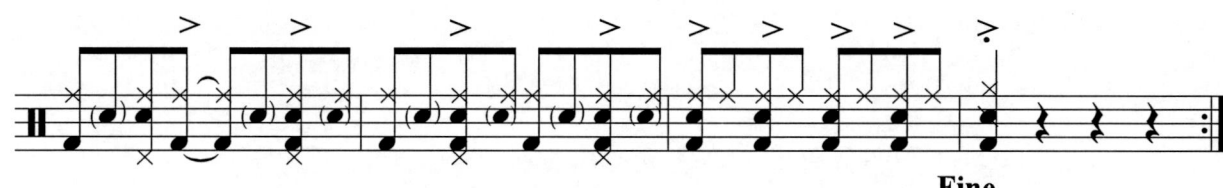

Fine

FOR SOLOS:
Play jazz shuffle time freely in 16 bar phrases, listen, interact, hold the pulse.
Watch for the cue to "background for solos" and "Shout Chorus"

On Cue: Basckground for solos

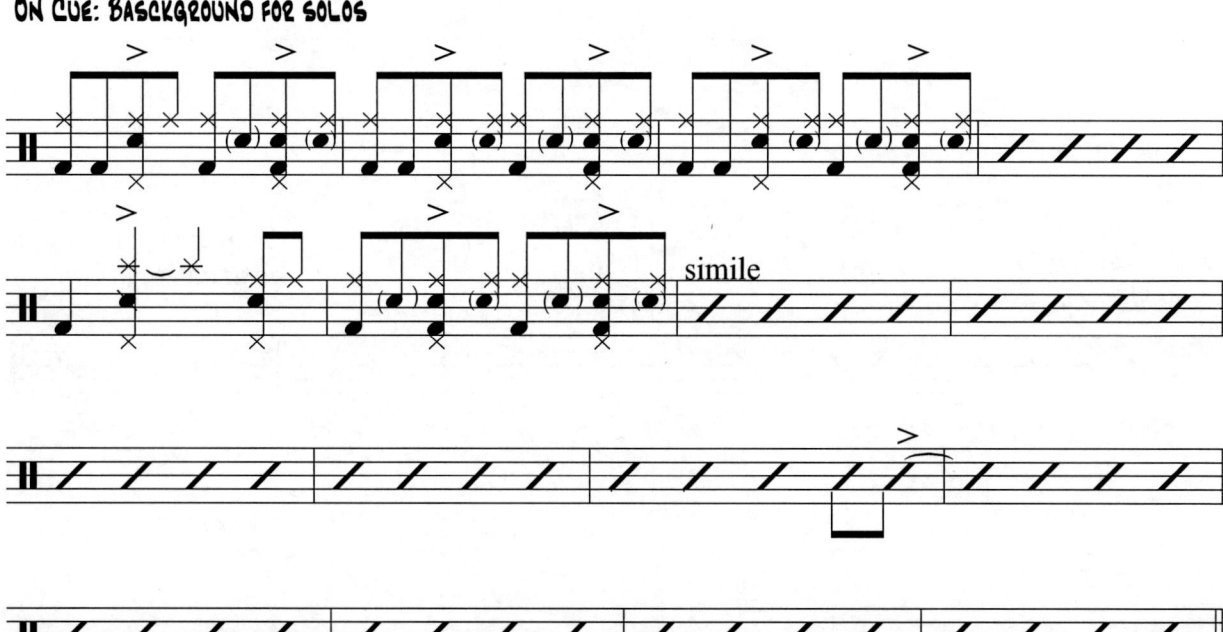

Drum Chart Supplement

Section 2

playthrough video - jazzdrumming.info/charts

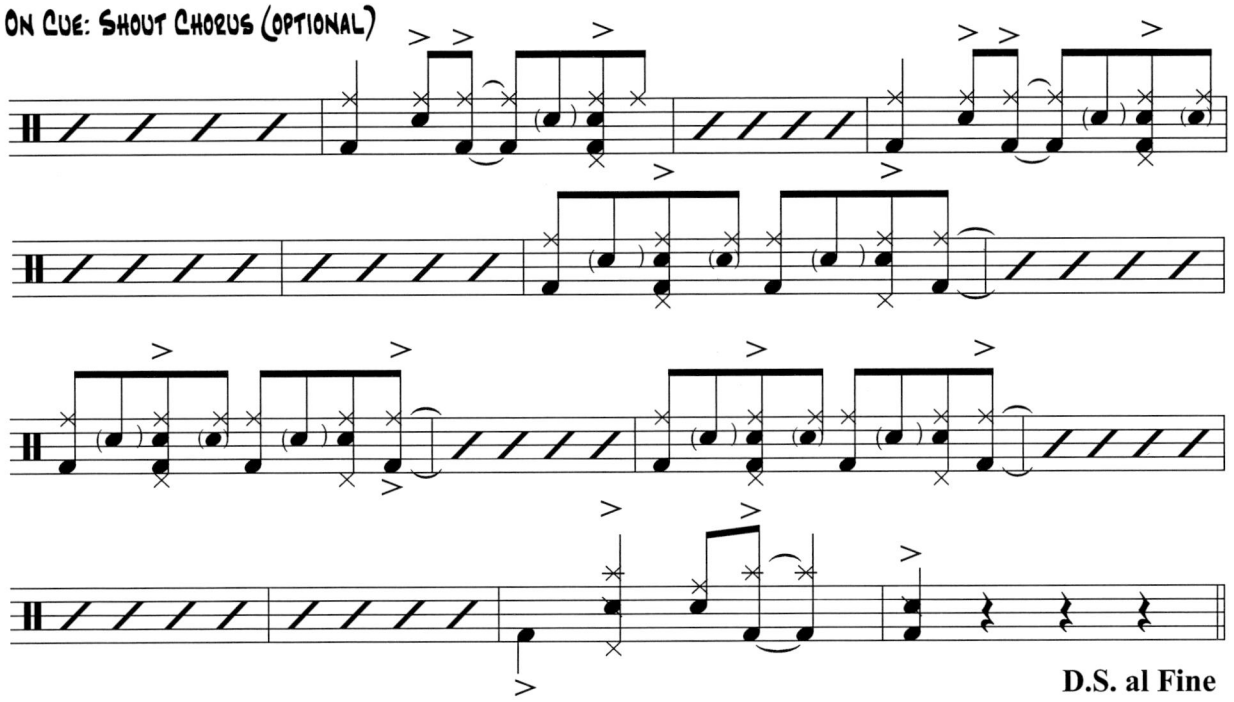

D.S. al Fine

Drum Set Legend:

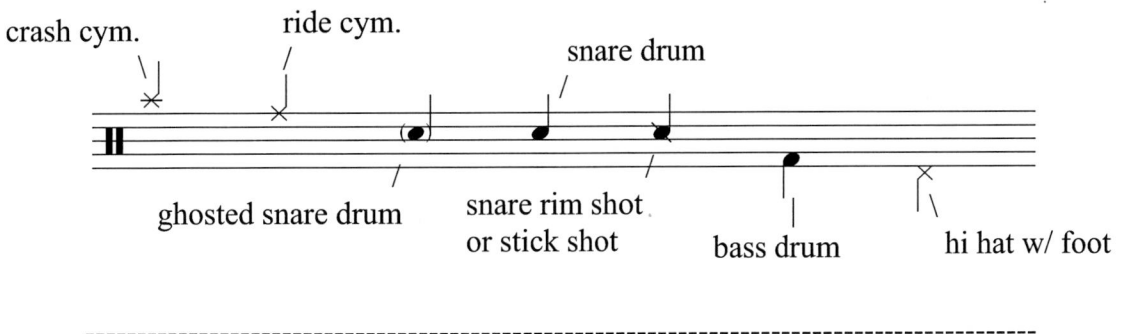

Notation Notes:

These slashes mean play jazz shuffle time freely.

Slash and rhythmic notation means play time, but catch this rhythm also.

Section 2 — Drum Chart Supplement

Suggested basic drumset part

Jive Samba

Bossa Nova type groove

comp. by Nat Adderly
drum arr. by A. Hall

FOR SOLOS:
Continue with the basic groove over a 32 bar form, AABB form.
Support, interact and hold the pulse.
Watch for the cue to "background for solos"

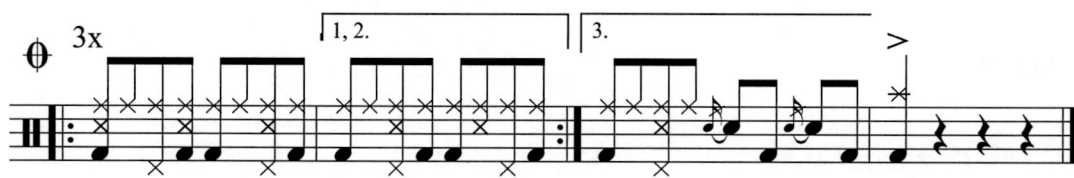

* This groove above is from the album, "Cannonball Adderly: The Best of Capital Years"
This has also been recorded with a cha cha groove.

ON CUE: BACKGROUND FOR SOLOS.

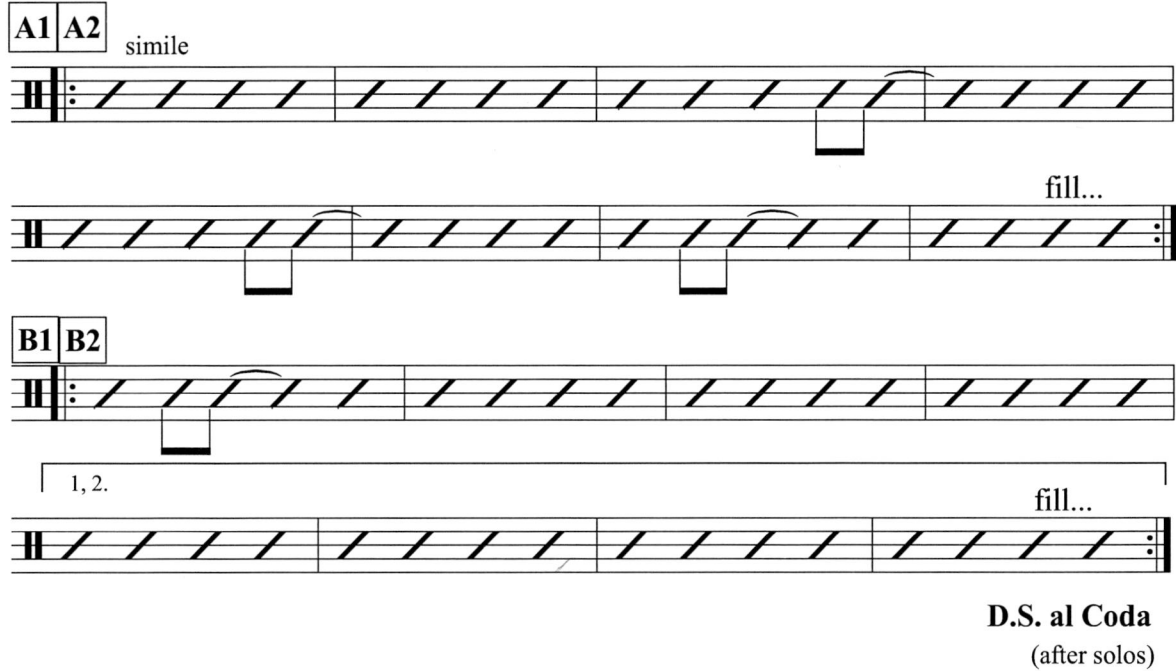

D.S. al Coda
(after solos)

Drum Set Legend:

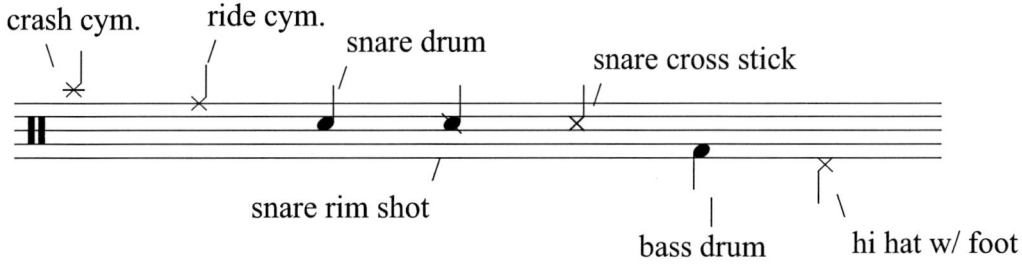

Notation Note:

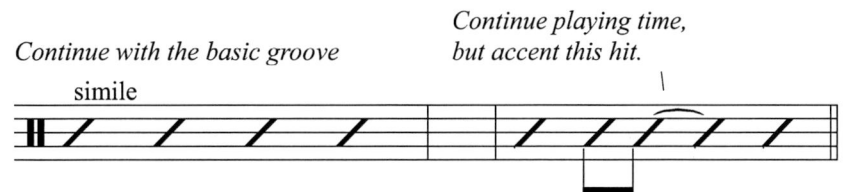

SECTION 2 — Drum Chart Supplement

Suggested basic drum set part

Jo Jo Calypso

comp. by Jim Nadel
drum arr. by Alan Hall

Jazz Calypso Beat

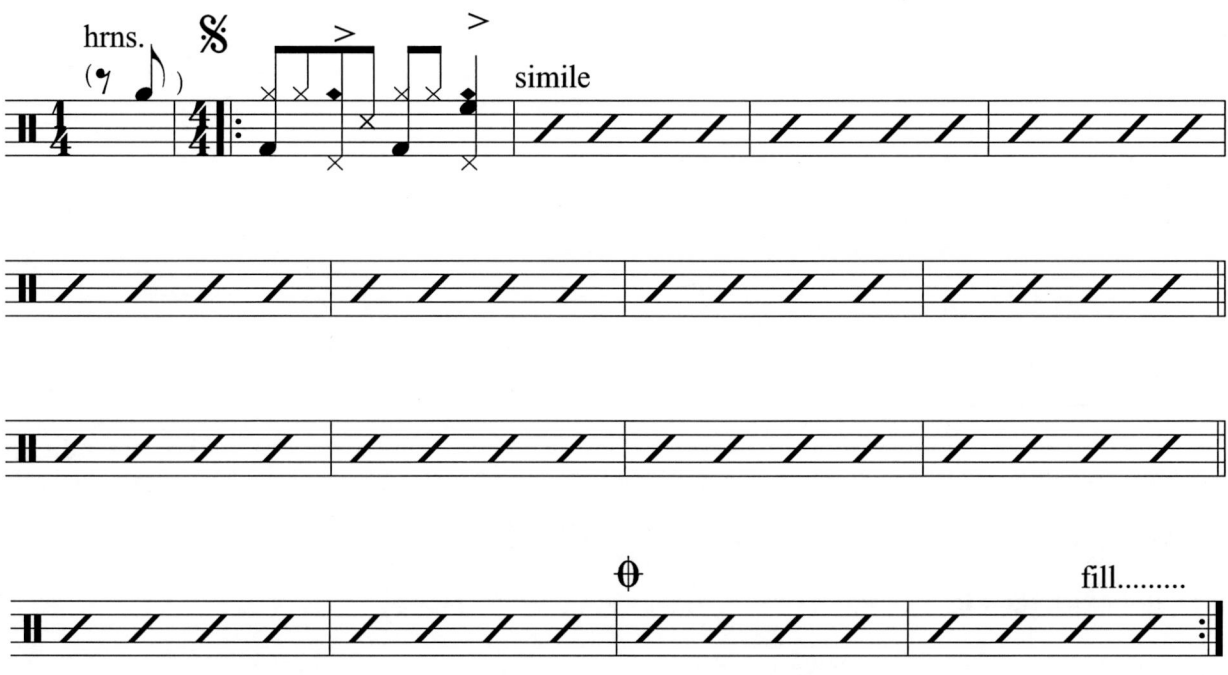

FOR SOLOS:
Play time freely in 16 bar phrases, listen, interact, hold the pulse.
Watch for the cue to "background for solos"

On Cue: Background Section

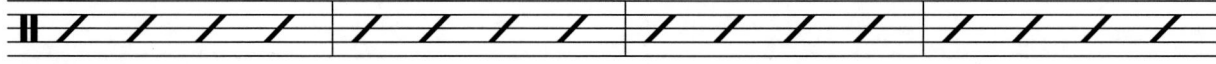

Drum Chart Supplement

SECTION 2

playthrough video - jazzdrumming.info/charts   groove video - jazzdrumming.info/more

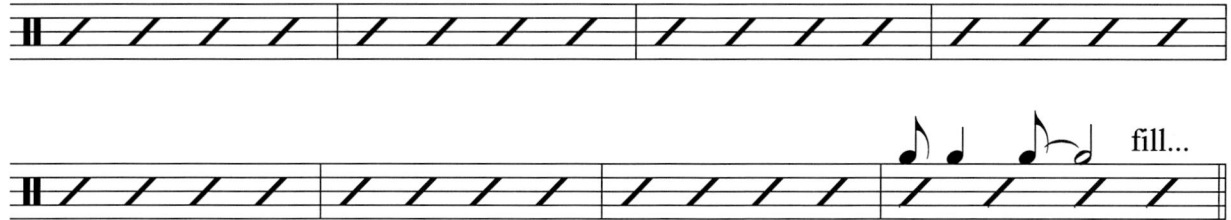

Shout Chorus. Play after solos (optional)

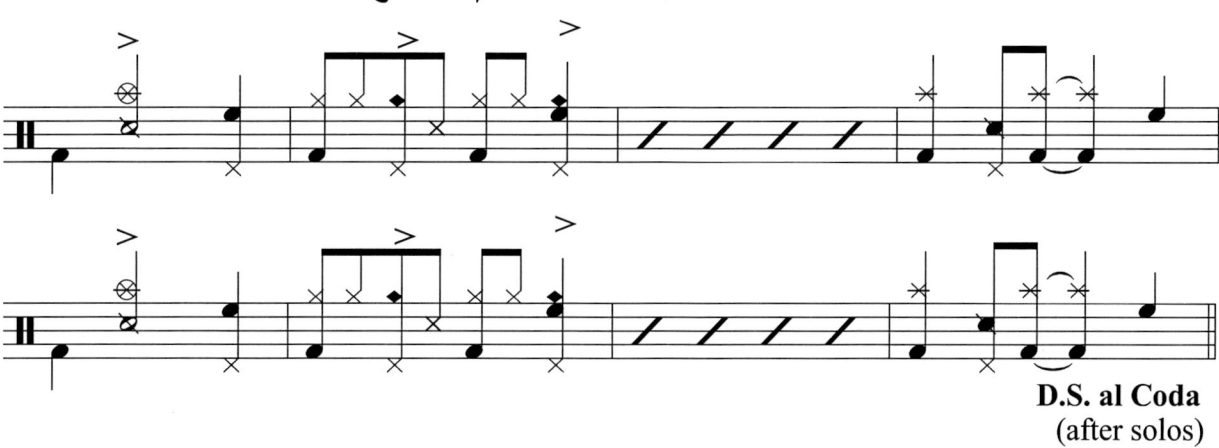

D.S. al Coda
(after solos)

Drum Set Legend:

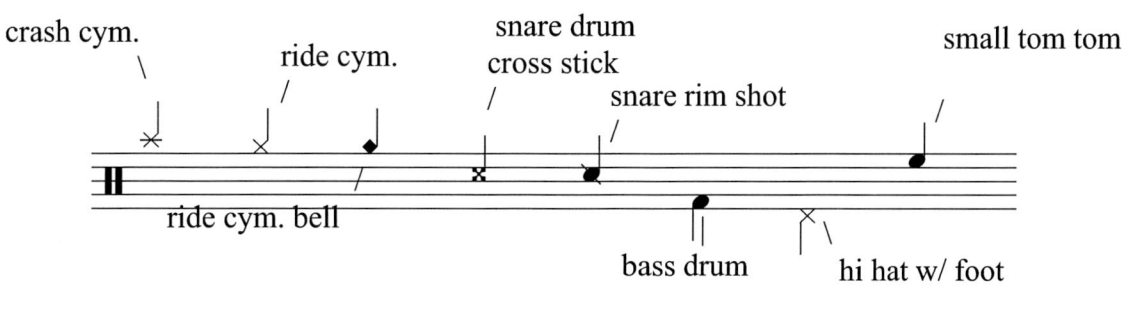

Notation Notes:

SECTION 2 — Drum Chart Supplement

Suggested basic drumset part

The Jody Grind

comp. by Horace Silver
drum arr. by A. Hall

Straight 8th feel
(soul jazz groove)

FOR SOLOS:
Play a soul jazz groove freely, in 12 bar phrases, listen, interact, hold the pulse.
Watch for the cue to "background for solos" and "shout chorus".

On Cue: Background for solos

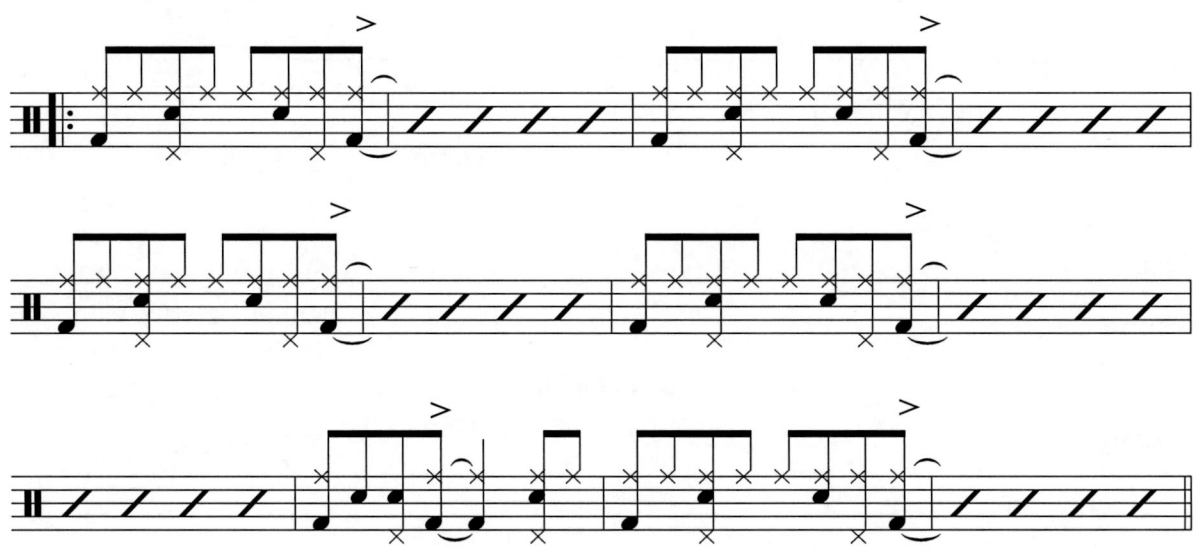

playthrough video - jazzdrumming.info/charts

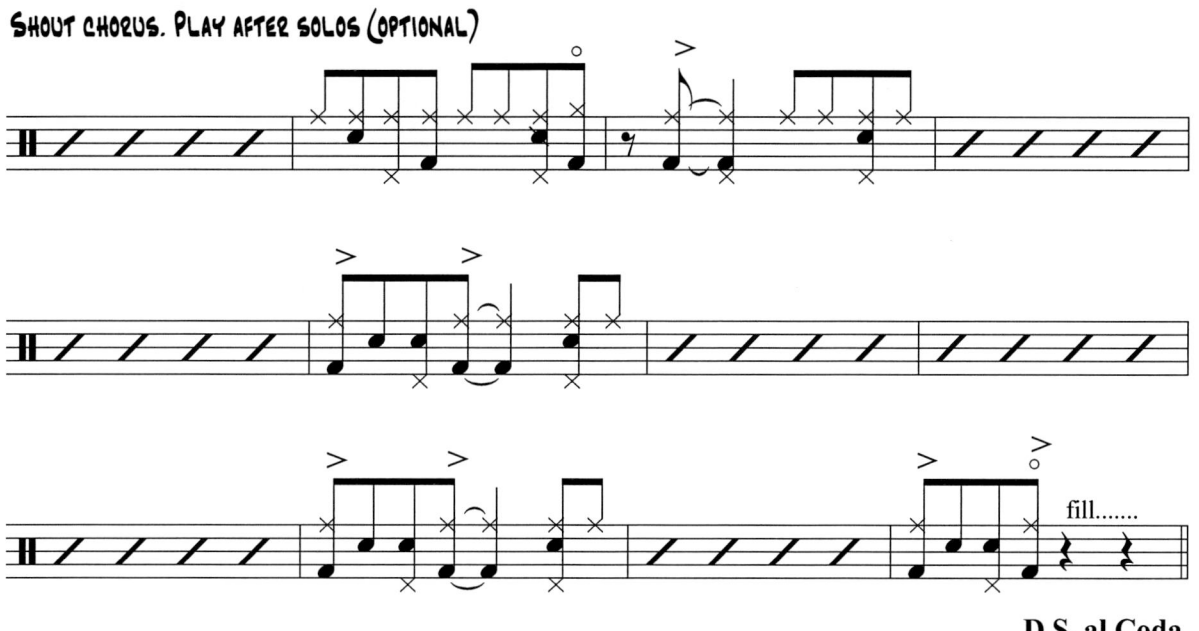

D.S. al Coda

Drum Set Legend:

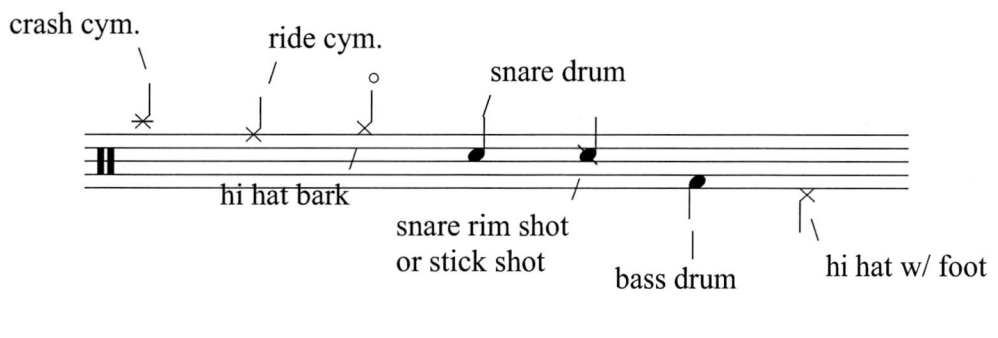

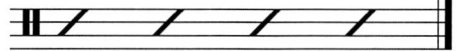

Notation notes:

These slashes mean soul jazz time freely.

Suggested basic drum set part

Killer Joe

comp. by Benny Golson
drum arr. by A. Hall

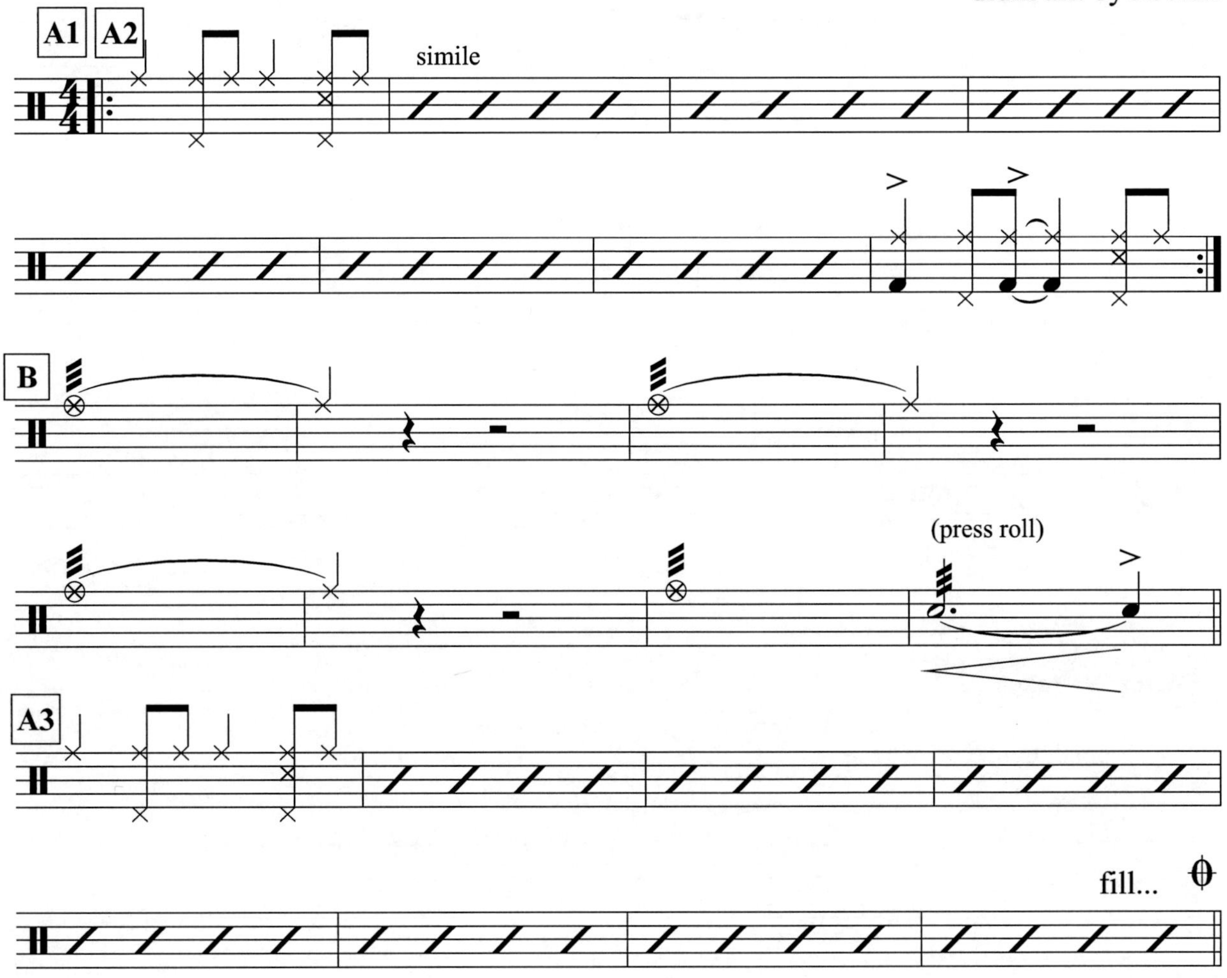

FOR SOLOS:
THIS IS GENERALLY PLAYED AS A PATTERN-BASED DRUM PART: HOLD THE DRUM COMPING PATTERN THROUGHOUT,
AABA FORM
WATCH FOR THE CUE TO "BACKGROUND FOR SOLOS"

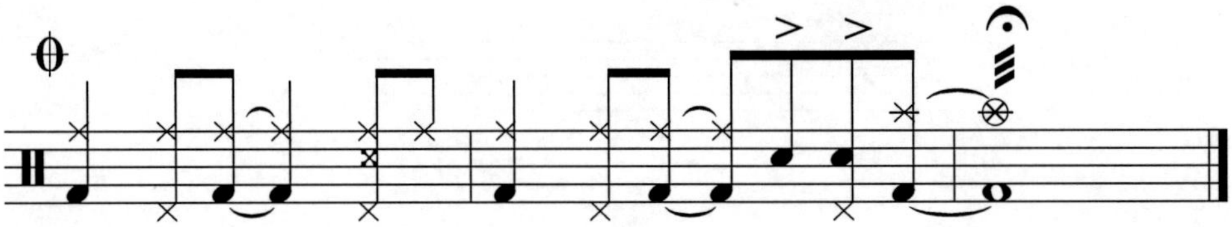

playthrough video - jazzdrumming.info/charts

ON CUE: BACKGROUND FOR SOLOS.

D.C. al Coda
(after solos)

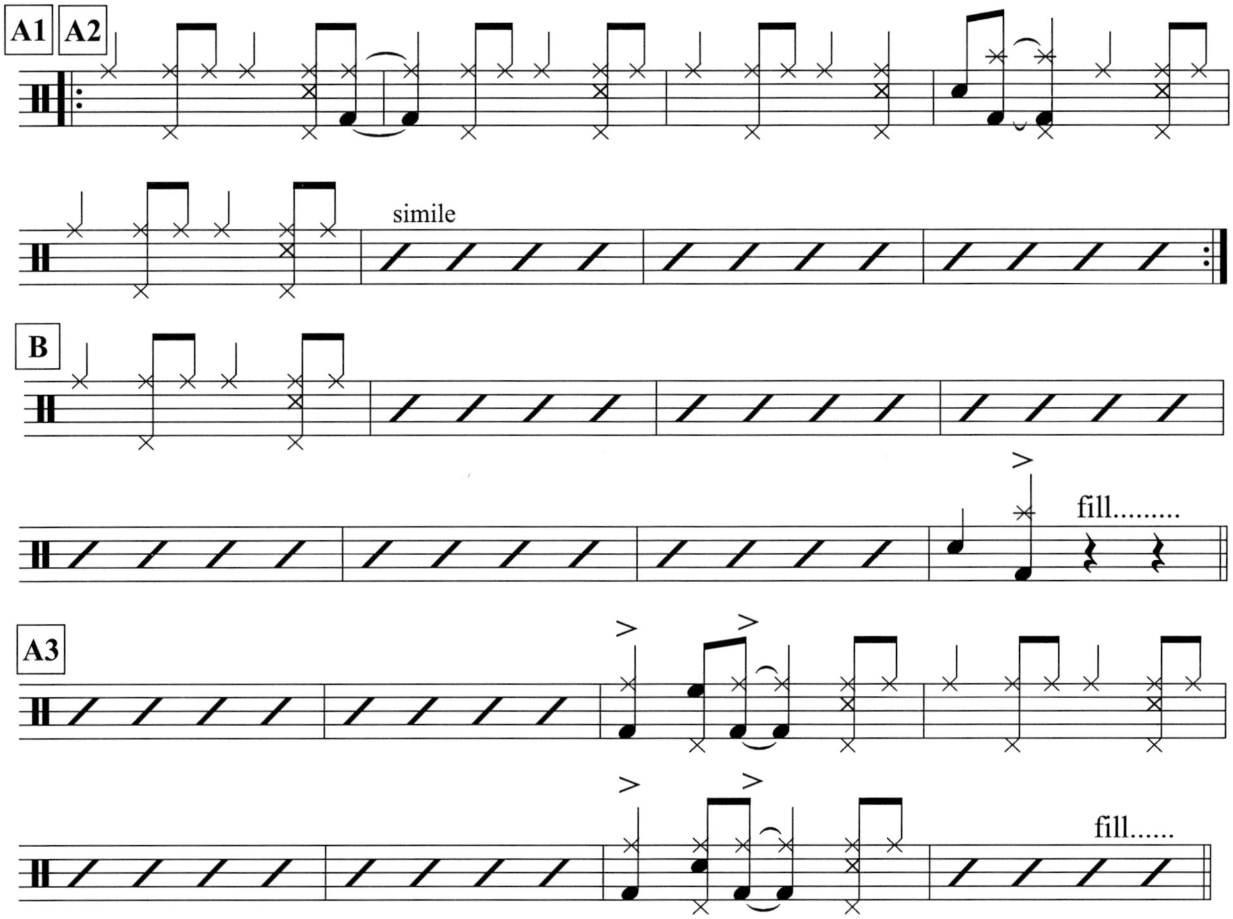

Drum Set Legend:

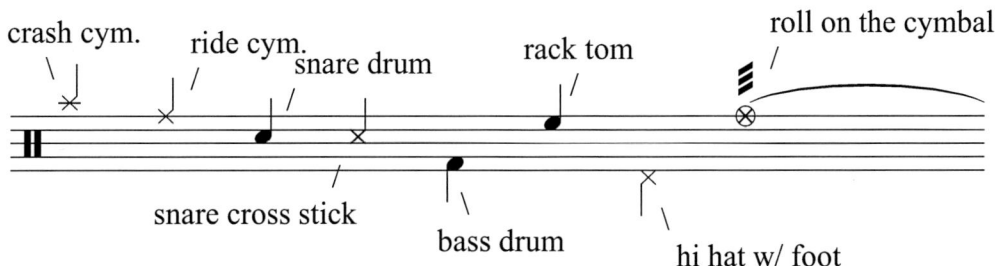

Listen Here

Suggested basic drumset part

funky cha cha type groove*

comp. by Eddie Harris
drum arr. by Alan Hall

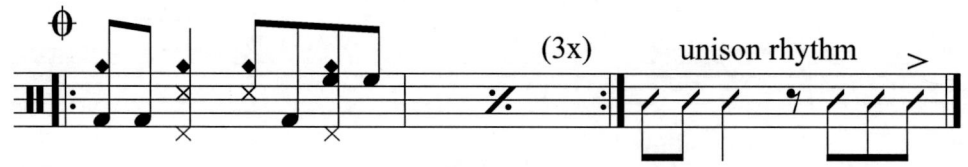

* based on Richard Smith's groove from "The Electrifying Eddie Harris" version.

playthrough video - jazzdrumming.info/charts

On Cue: Background for solos.

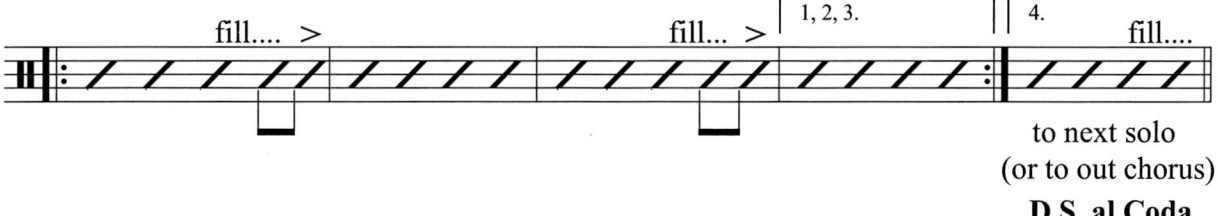

to next solo
(or to out chorus)
D.S. al Coda

Drum Set Legend:

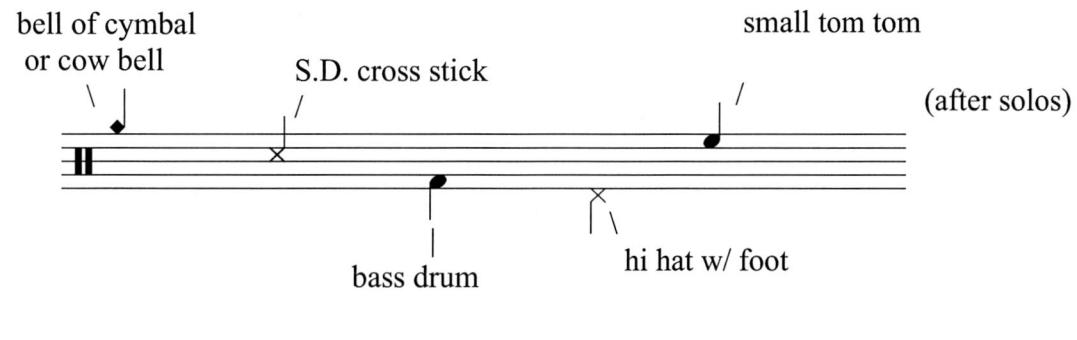

(after solos)

Notation Notes:

Little Sunflower

Suggested basic drum set part

comp. by Freddie Hubbard
drum arr. by Alan Hall

Jazz Bossa Type Groove
(straight 8th feel)

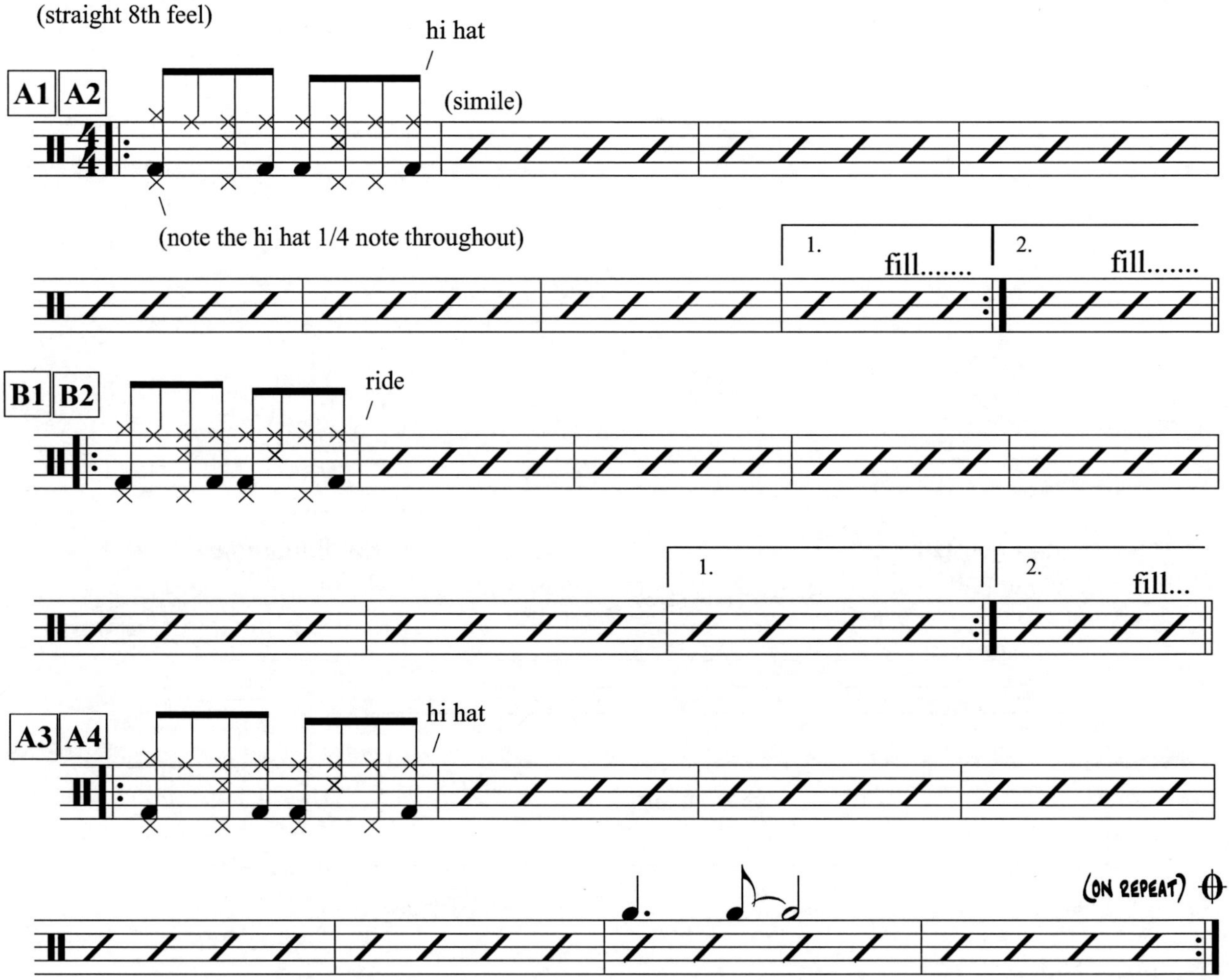

FOR SOLOS:
Play a varied jazz bossa type groove, listen, interact, hold the pulse,
keep the form: 48 bars (A A B B A A)
Watch for the cue to "Background for Solos"

On Cue: Background for Solos

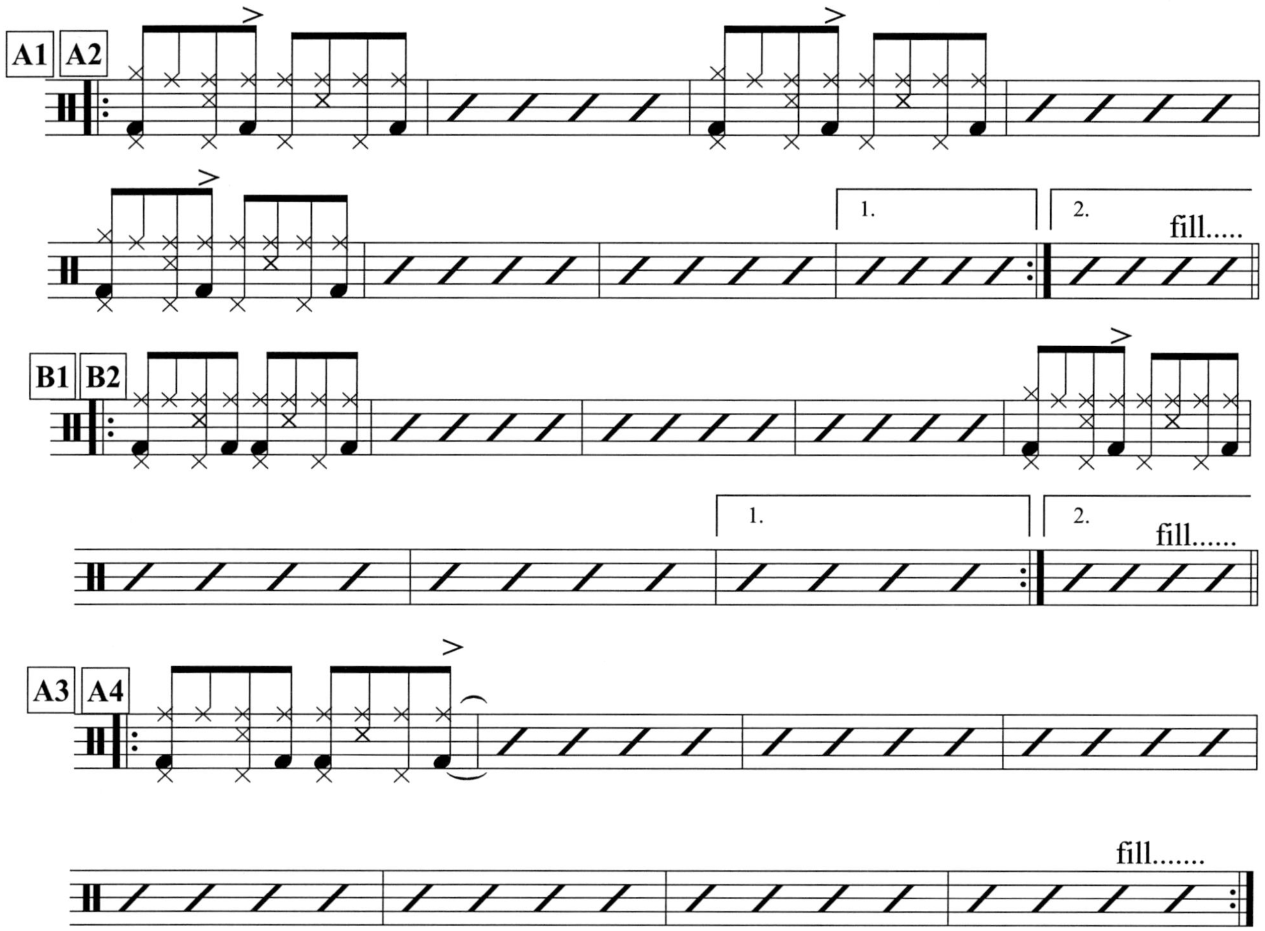

(musical notation for sections A1/A2, B1/B2, A3/A4 with repeats and 1st/2nd endings)

fill.......
(after solos)
D.C. al Coda

Drum Set Legend:

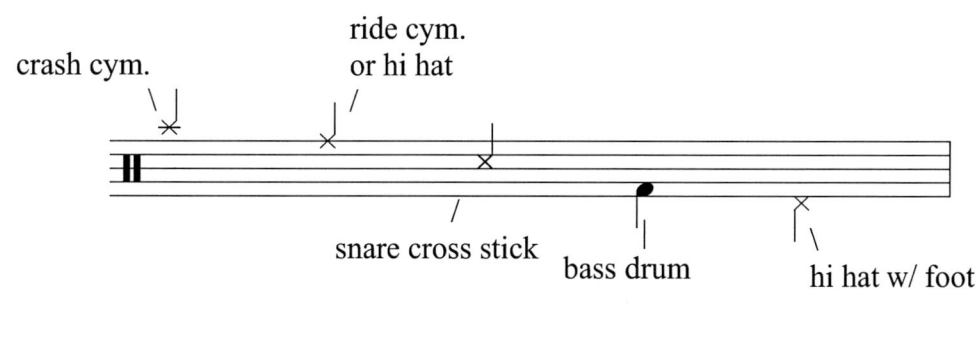

crash cym. — ride cym. or hi hat — snare cross stick — bass drum — hi hat w/ foot

Notation Notes:

These slashes mean play jazz bossa freely

Play the groove, then improvise a brief fill on the drums
fill.........

Suggested basic drumset part

Mercy, Mercy, Mercy

comp. by Joe Zawinul
drum arr. by Alan Hall

Funk Rock
(with a straight 8th feel)

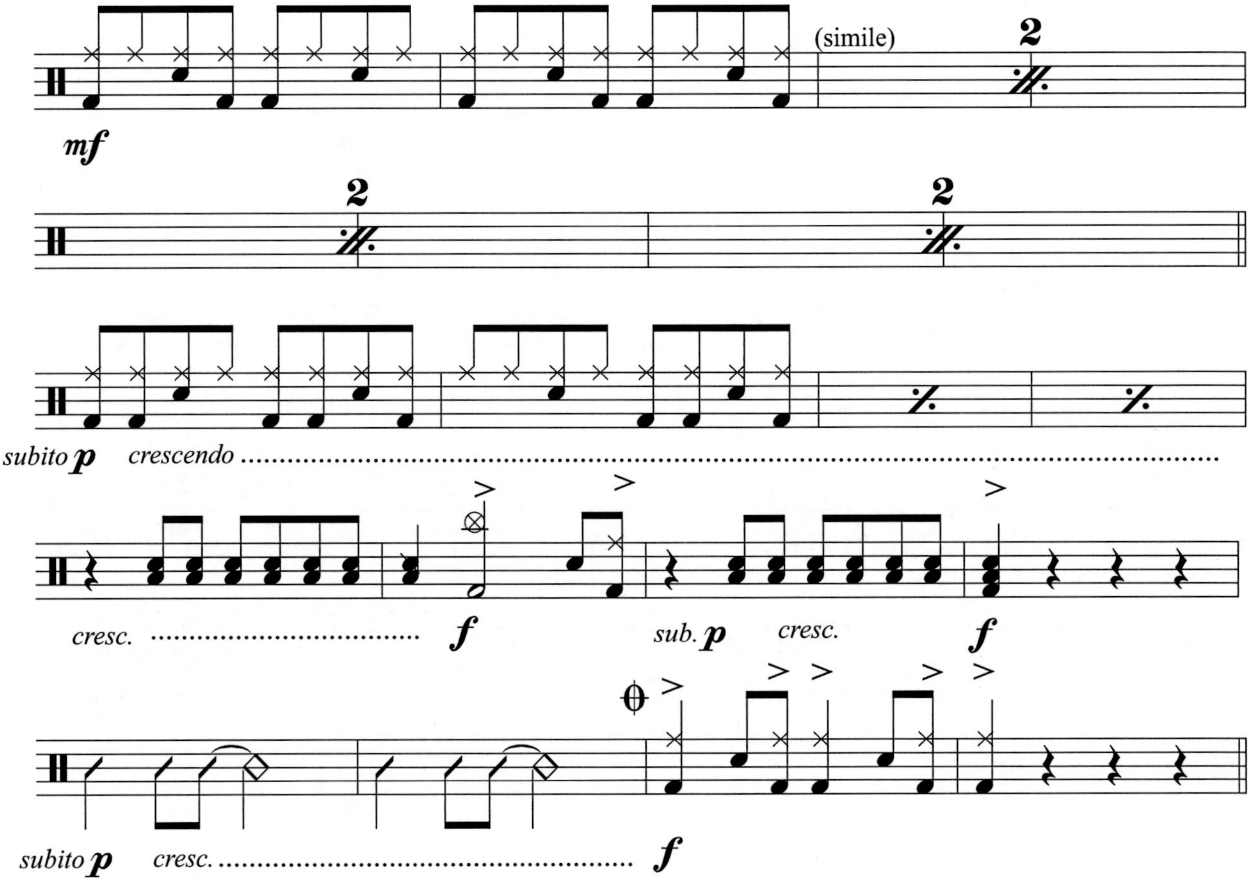

FOR SOLOS:
Play a loose, funk type groove, in a 20 bar form, listen, interact, hold the pulse.
Watch for the cue to "background for solos"

Drum Chart Supplement — Section 2

playthrough video – jazzdrumming.info/charts

On Cue: Backgroud for solos.

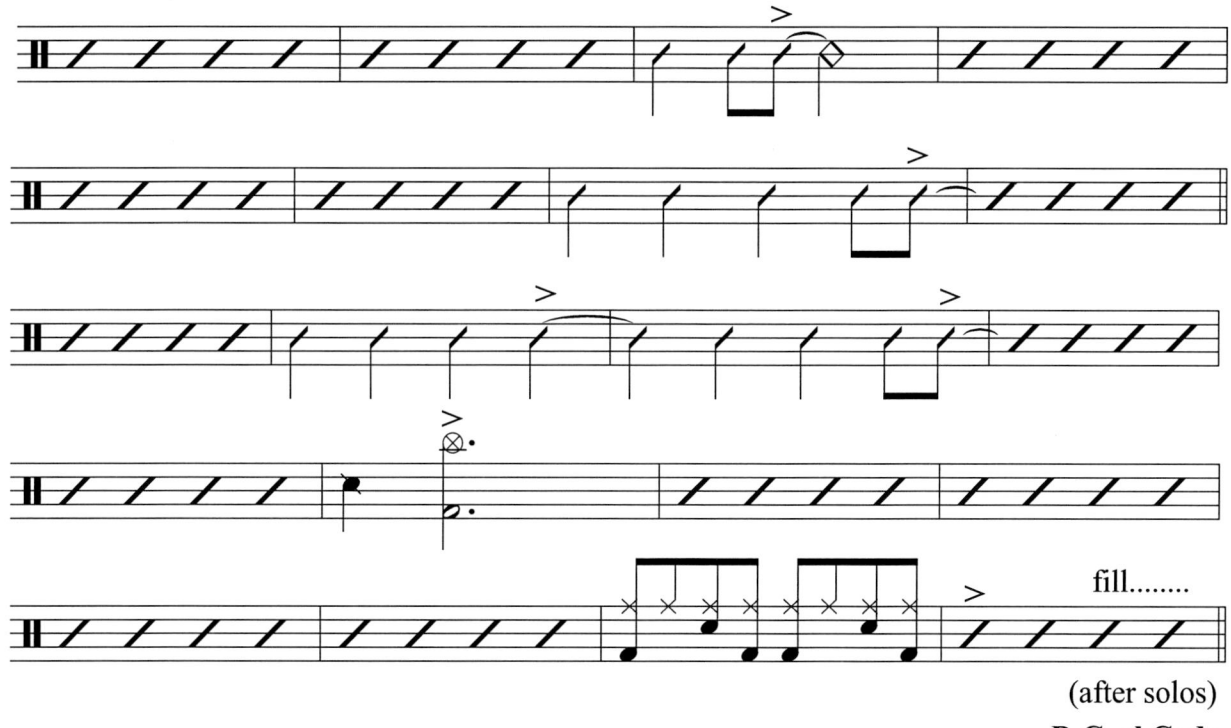

(after solos)
D.C. al Coda

Drum Set Legend:

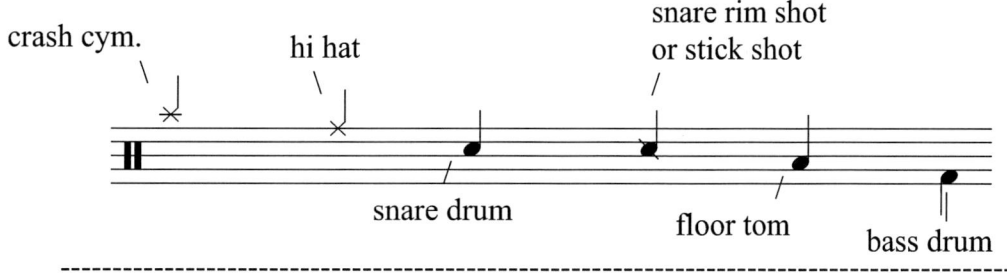

Notation Notes:

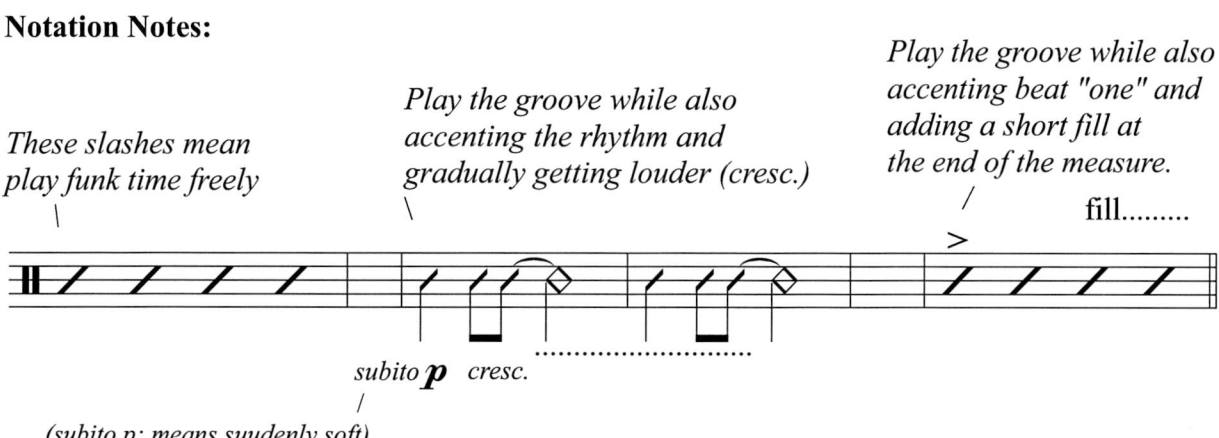

(subito p: means suudenly soft)

Section 2 — Drum Chart Supplement

Suggested basic drumset part

Midnight Waltz

comp. by Cedar Walton
drum arr. by Alan Hall

Jazz Waltz

For Solos:
Play a loose jazz waltz over a 24 bar blues form. Listen, interact, hold the pulse.
Watch for the cue to "Shout Chorus"

50

Drum Chart Supplement — Section 2

playthrough video – jazzdrumming.info/more

On Cue: Shout Chorus

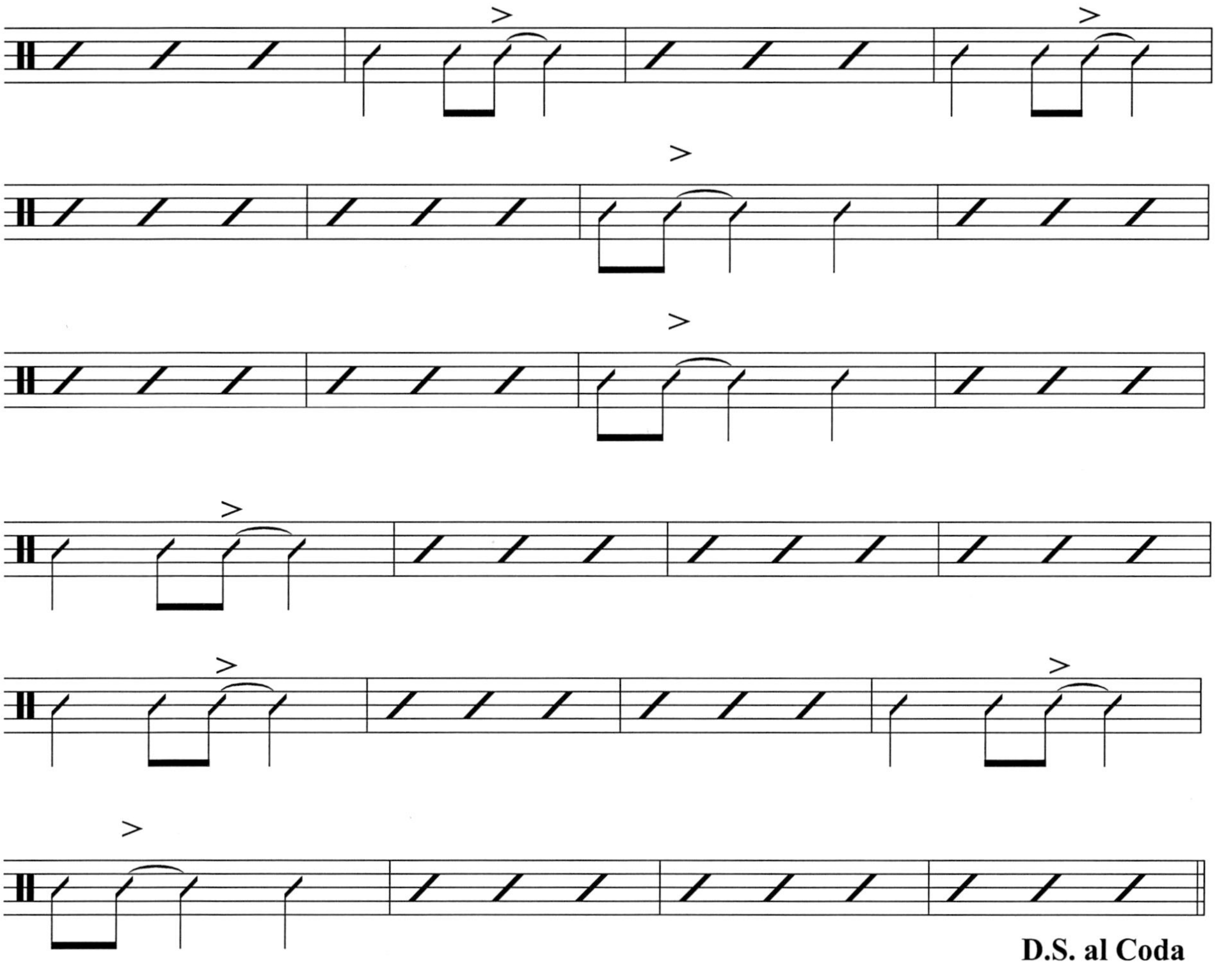

[musical notation: 6 lines of jazz waltz shout chorus chart with slashes and accented figures]

D.S. al Coda

Drum Set Legend:

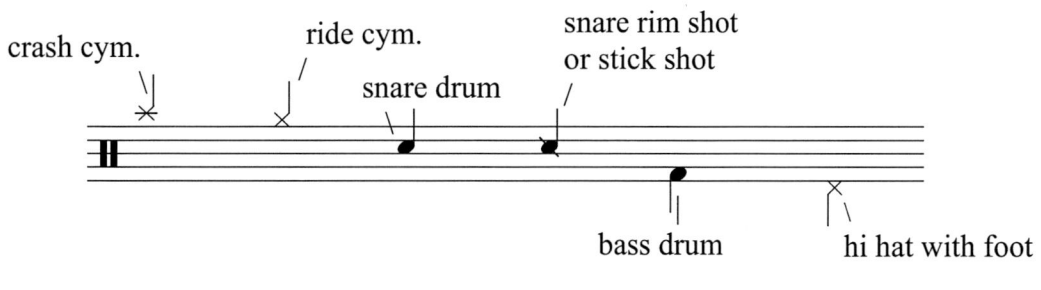

Notation Notes:

These slashes mean play jazz waltz time freely

Continue to play waltz time, but also push this rhythmic accent

SECTION 2 — DRUM CHART SUPPLEMENT

Suggested basic drumset part

Mr. P.C.

comp. by John Coltrane
drum arr. by A. Hall

Jazz Time

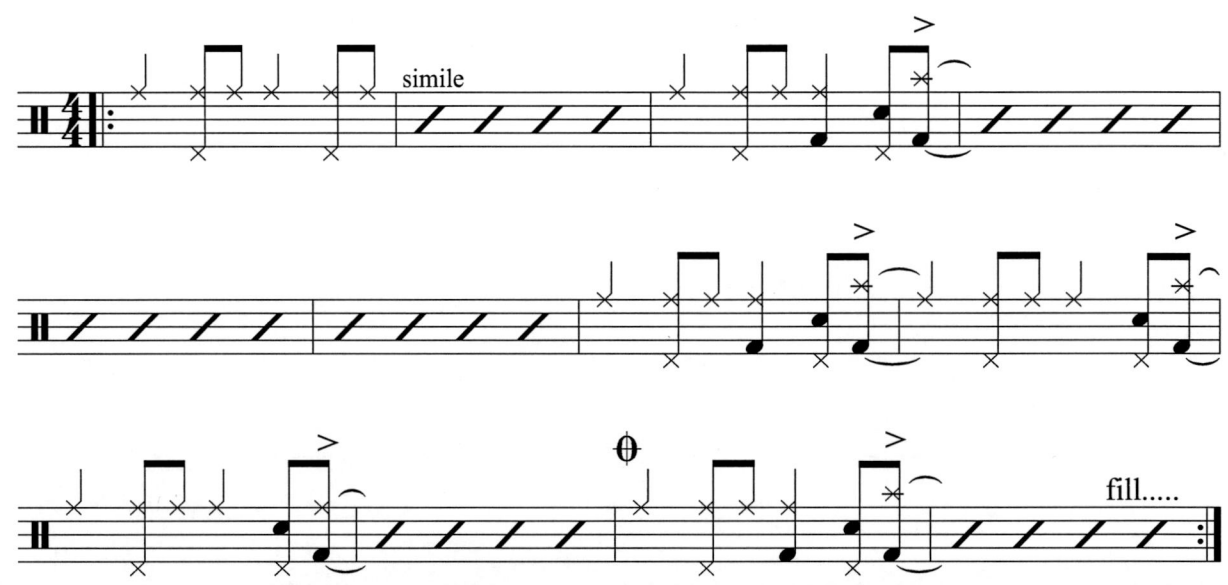

FOR SOLOS:
Play time freely in 12 bar phrases, listen, interact, hold the pulse.
Watch for the cue to "background for solos" and "shout chorus".

On Cue: Background for solos

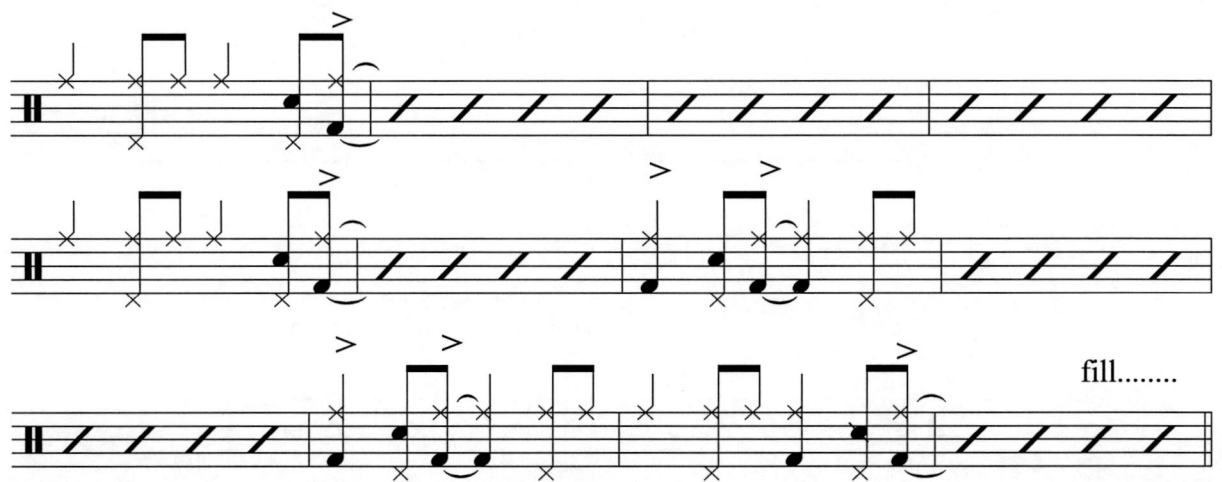

playthrough video - jazzdrumming.info/charts

SHOUT CHORUS. PLAY AFTER SOLOS (OPTIONAL)

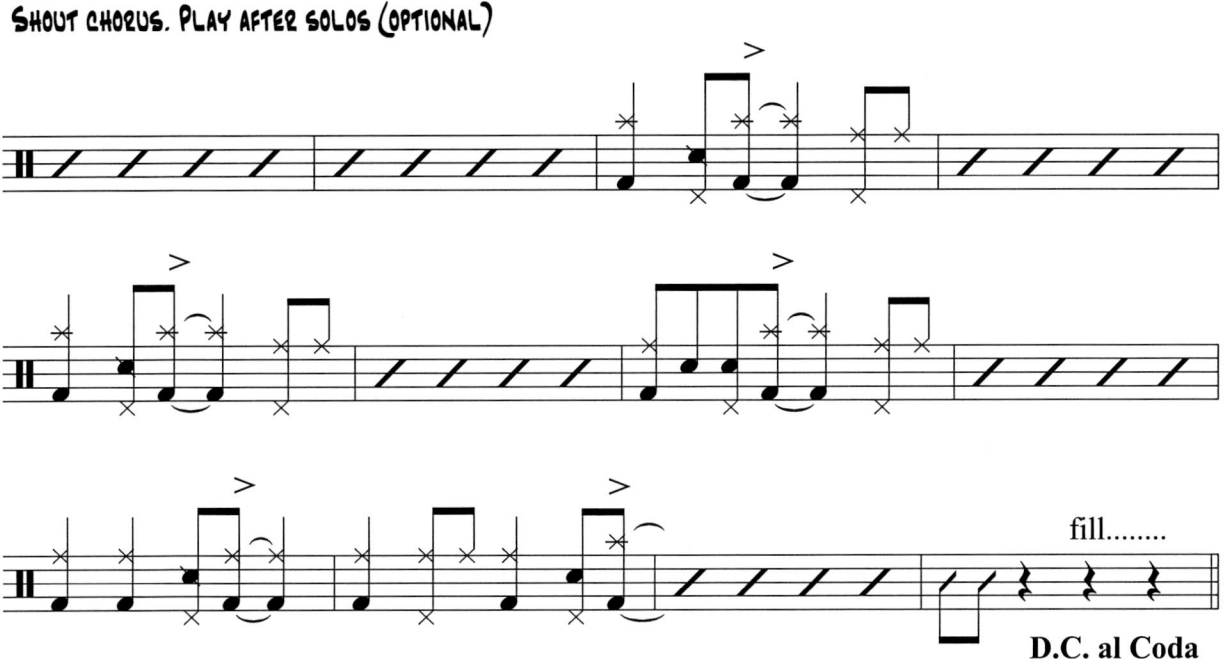

D.C. al Coda

Drum Set Legend:

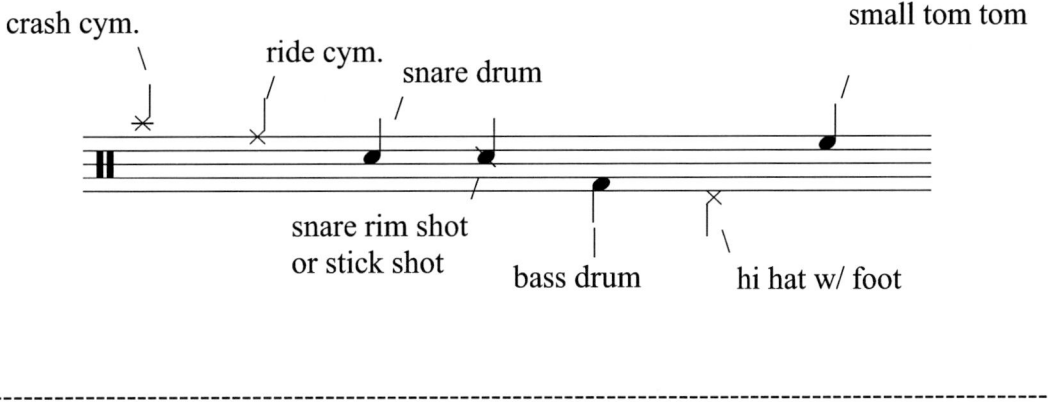

Notation notes:

These slashes mean play jazz time freely.

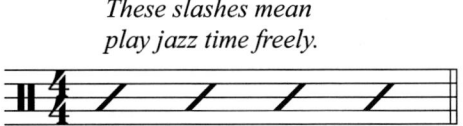

SECTION 2 — DRUM CHART SUPPLEMENT

Suggested basic drumset part

One for Daddy-O

comp. by Nat Adderly
drum arr. by A. Hall

Very Cool "2 - feel"

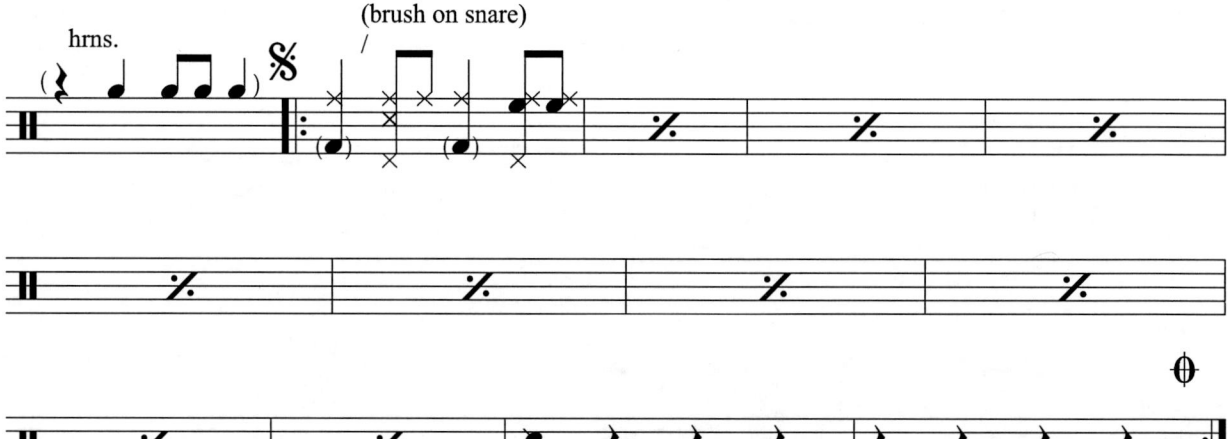

FOR SOLOS:
RIGHT HAND SWITCH TO A 4 - FEEL ON THE RIDE CYMBAL, IN 12 BAR PHRASES, LISTEN, HOLD THE PULSE.
WATCH FOR THE CUE TO "BACKGROUND FOR SOLOS" AND "SHOUT CHORUS".

ON CUE: BACKGROUND FOR SOLOS

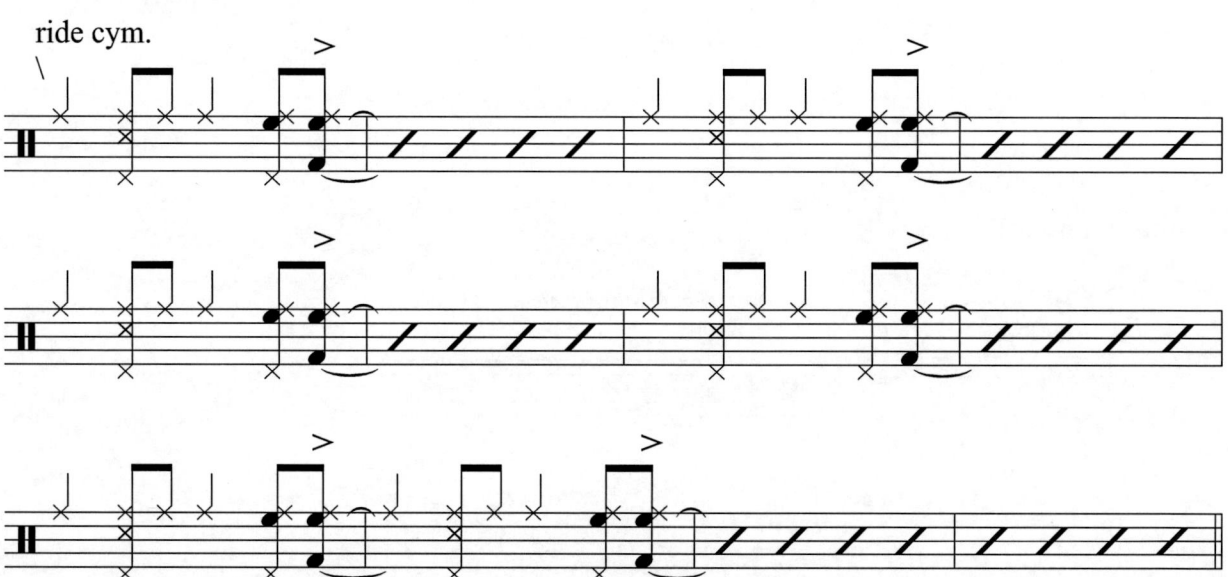

Drum Chart Supplement — Section 2

playthrough video - jazzdrumming.info/charts

Shout Chorus. Play after solos (optional)

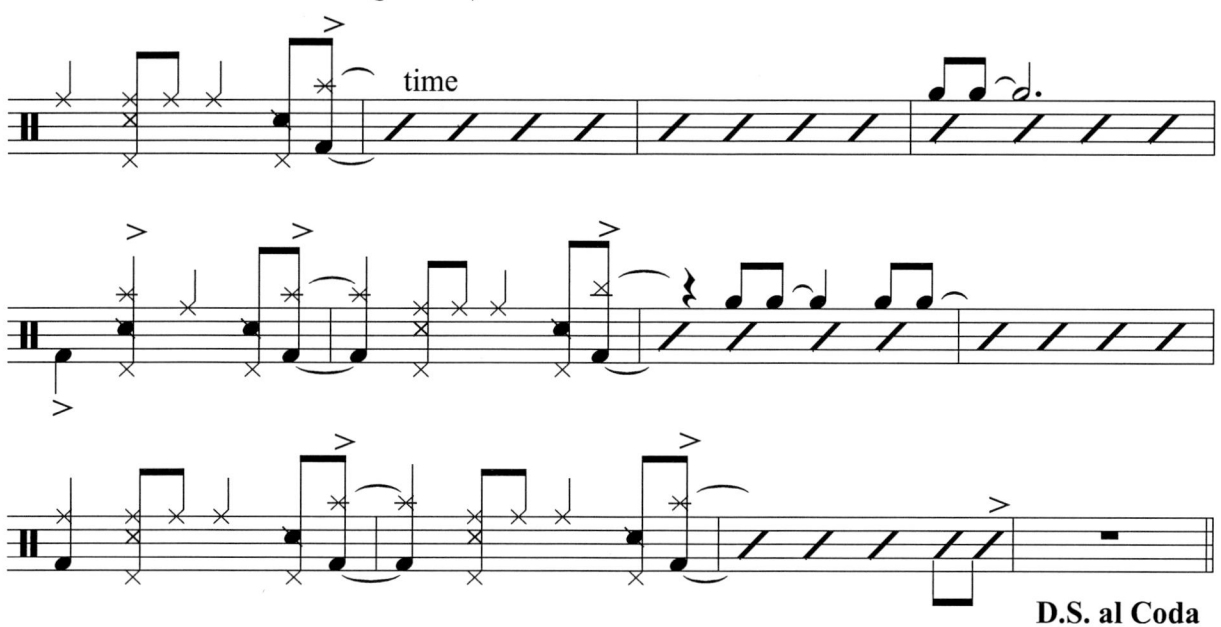

D.S. al Coda

Drum Set Legend:

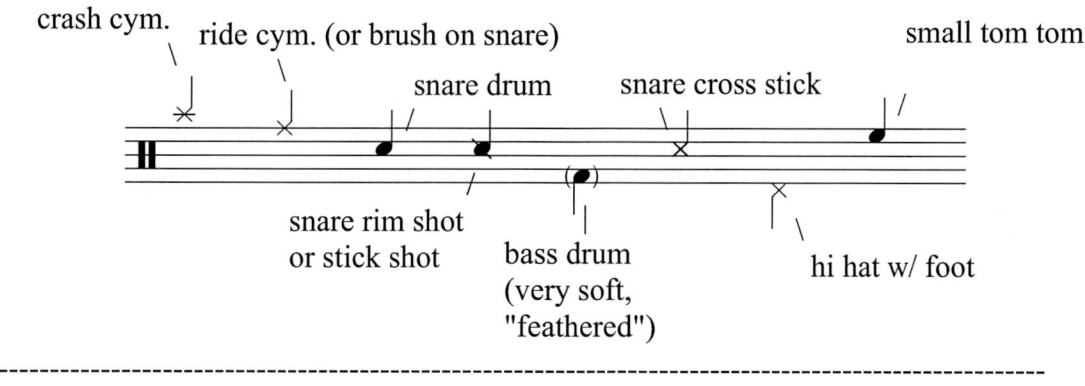

Notation Notes:

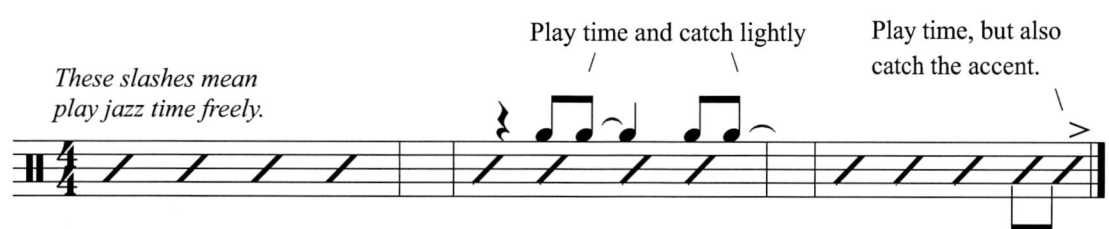

55

SECTION 2 — Drum Chart Supplement

Suggested basic drumset part

Red's Good Groove

jazz 8th feel

comp. by Red Garland
drum arr. by A. Hall

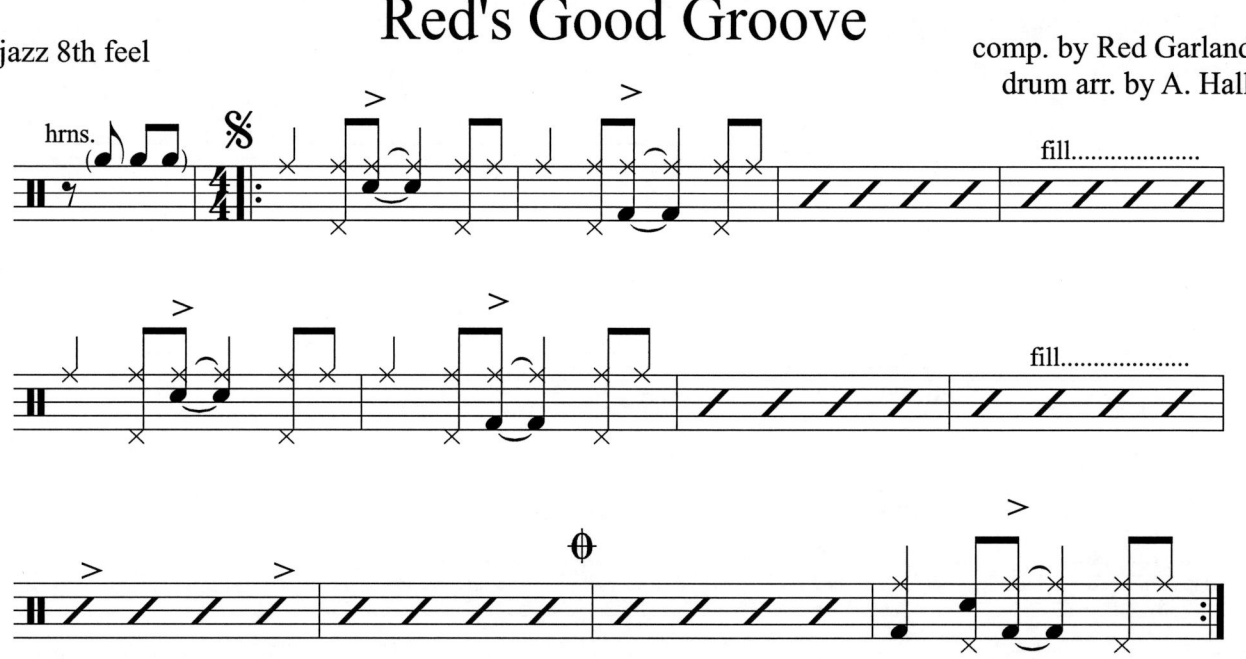

FOR SOLOS:
Play time freely in 12 bar phrases, listen, interact, hold the pulse.
Watch for the cue to "background for solos" and "shout chorus".

On Cue: Background for solos

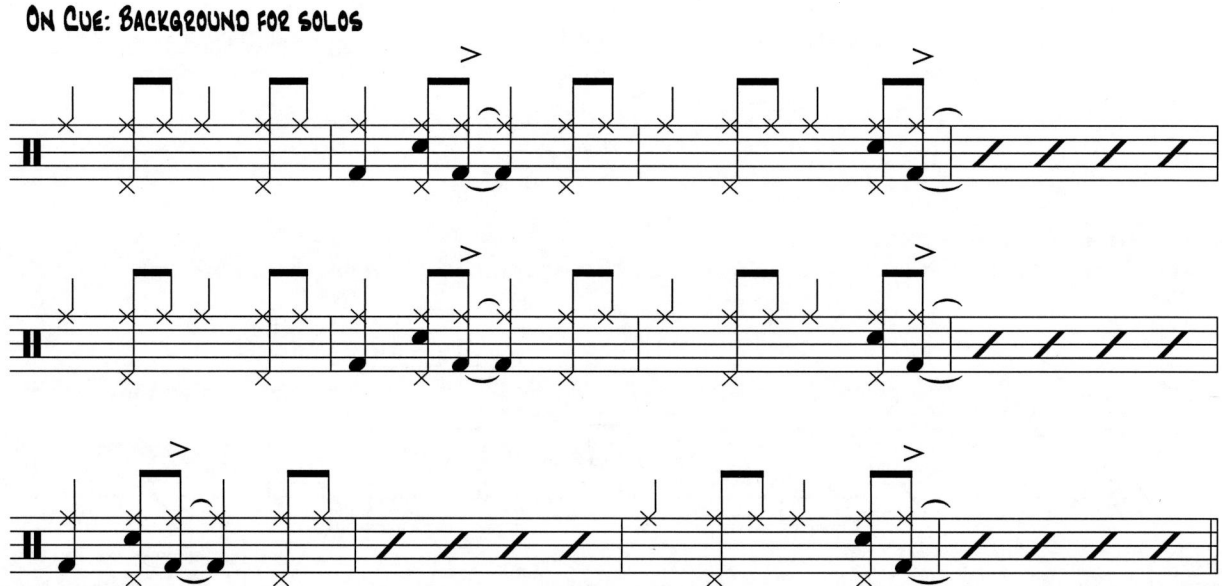

Drum Chart Supplement

SECTION 2

playthrough video - jazzdrumming.info/charts

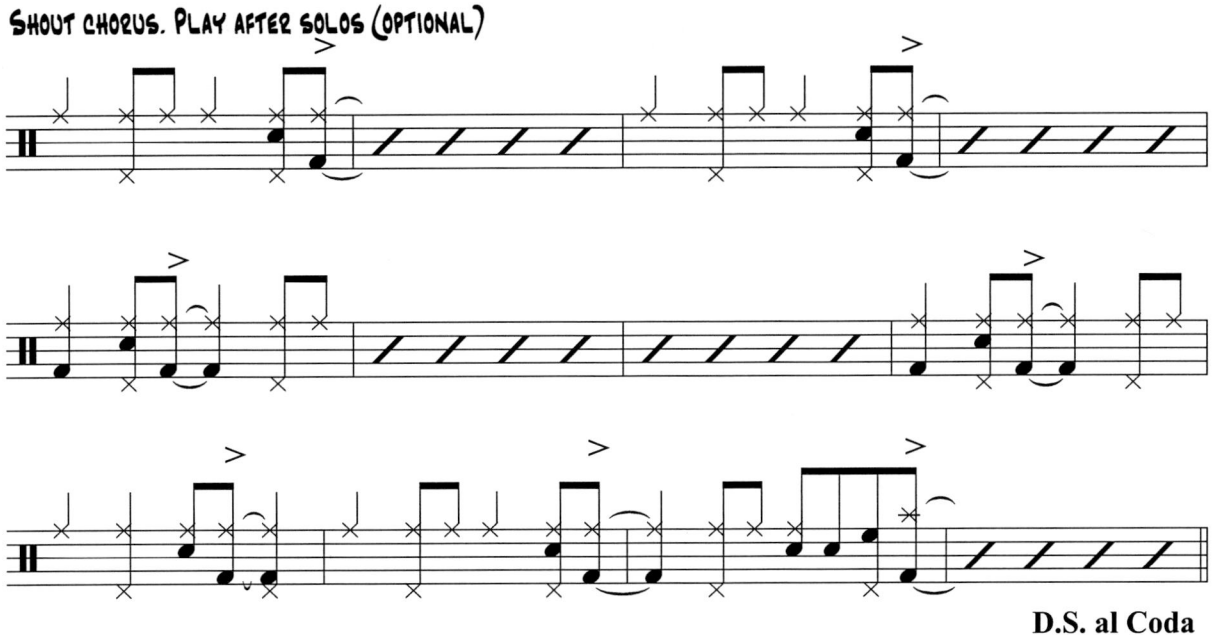

Shout chorus. Play after solos (optional)

D.S. al Coda

Drum Set Legend:

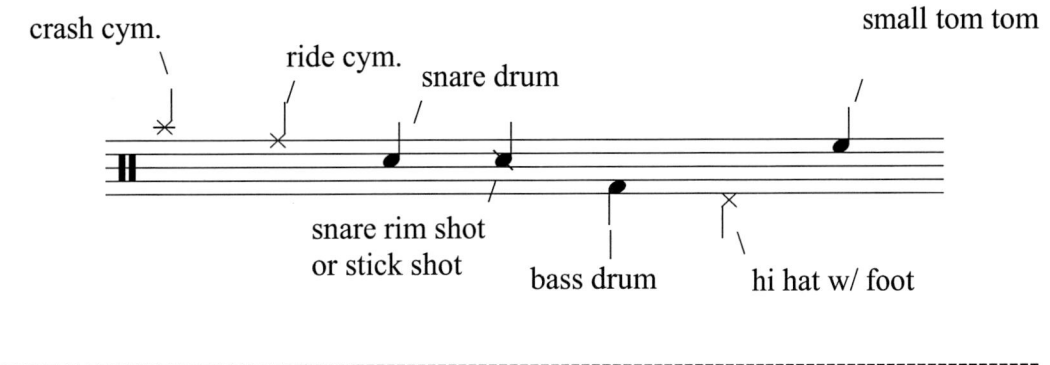

crash cym.
ride cym.
snare drum
small tom tom
snare rim shot or stick shot
bass drum
hi hat w/ foot

Notation notes:

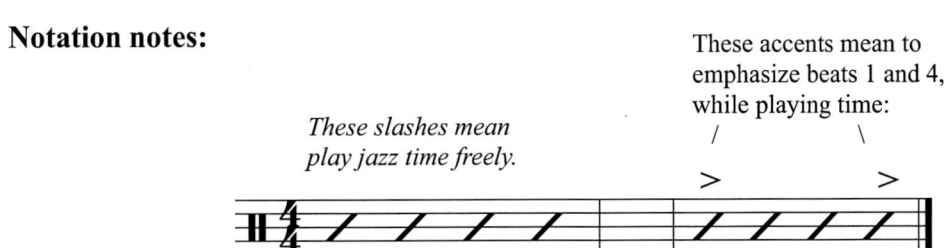

These slashes mean play jazz time freely.

These accents mean to emphasize beats 1 and 4, while playing time:

57

Section 2 — Drum Chart Supplement

Suggested basic drumset part

Revelation

comp. by Kenny Barron
drum arr. by A. Hall

Jazz Time

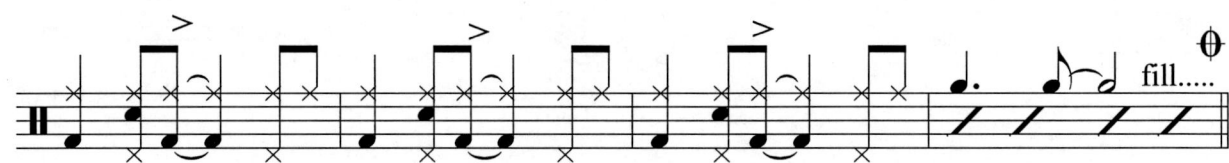

FOR SOLOS:
Play time freely in 12 bar phrases, listen, interact, hold the pulse.
Watch for the cue to "background for solos" and "shout chorus".

ON CUE: BACKGROUND FOR SOLOS

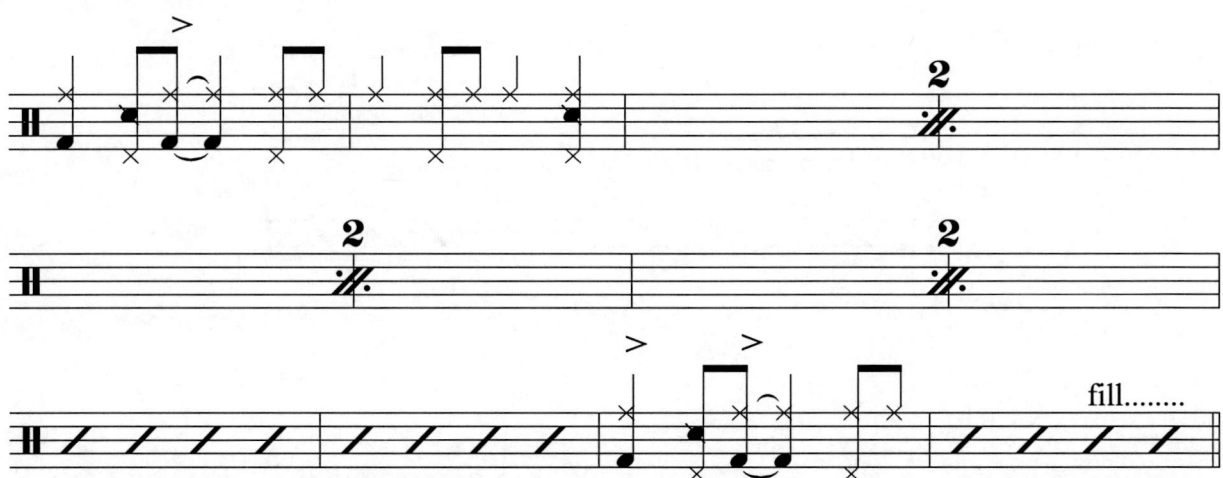

58

playthrough video - jazzdrumming.info/charts

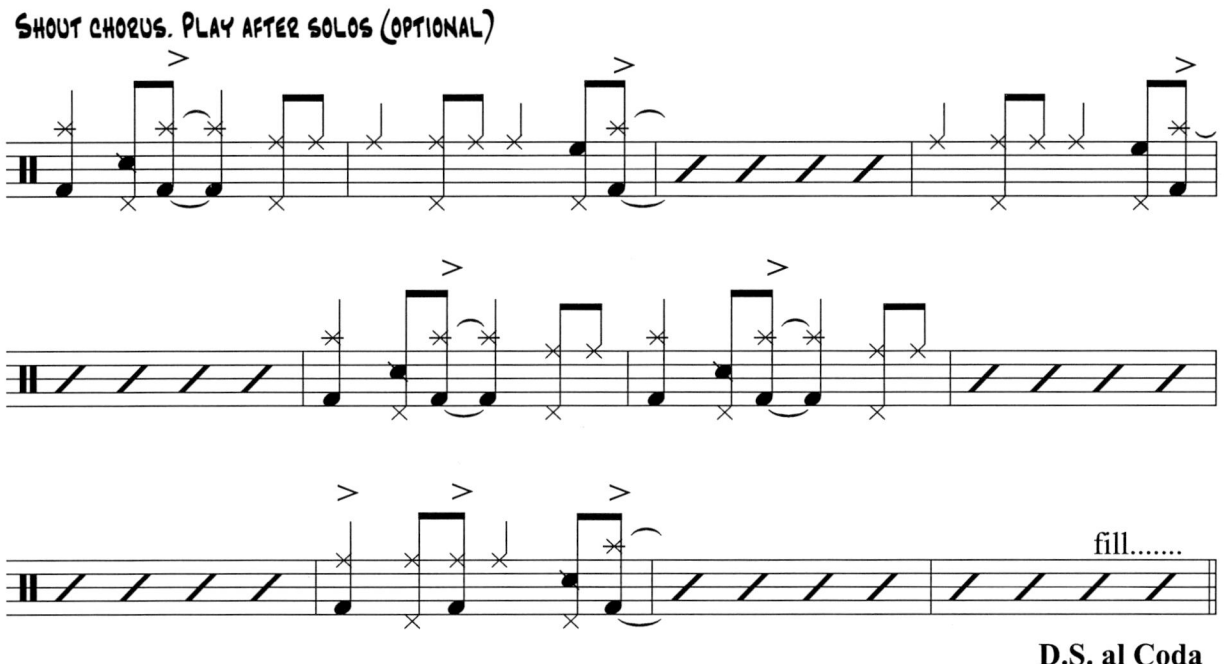

D.S. al Coda

Drum Set Legend:

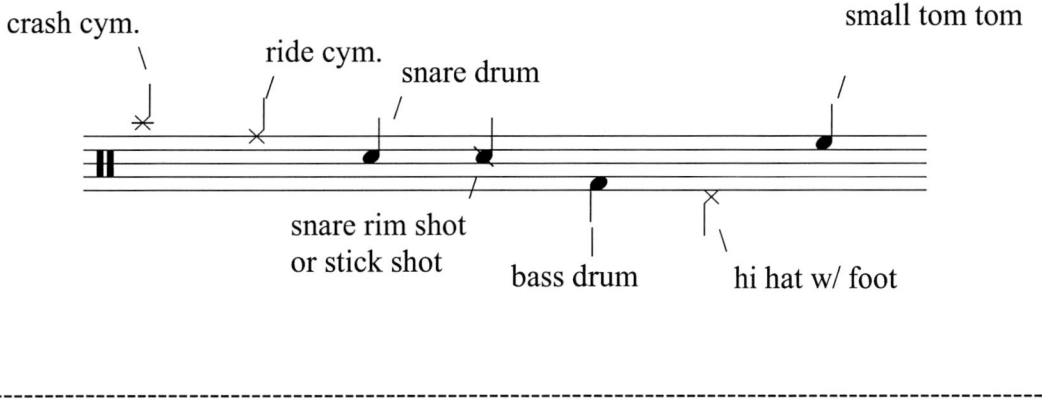

Notation notes:

These slashes mean play jazz time freely.

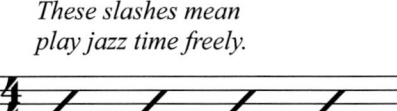

Suggested basic drumset part

Road Song

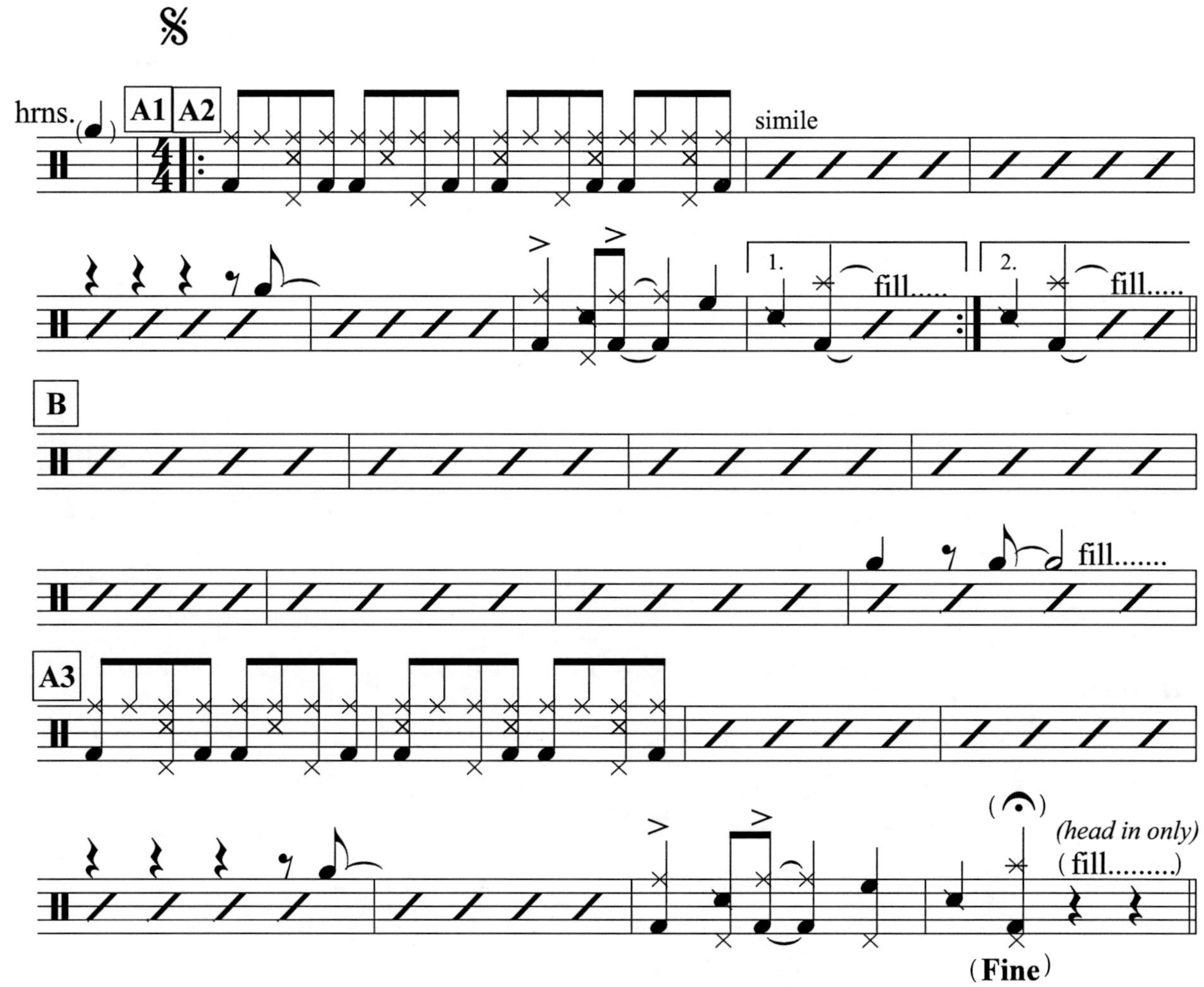

comp. by Wes Montgomery
drum arr. by A. Hall

Jazz Bossa Nova

FOR SOLOS:

PLAY JAZZ BOSSA FREELY, INTERACT, HOLD THE PULSE
AND KEEP THE 32 BAR - AABA FORM.
WATCH FOR THE CUE TO "BACKGROUND FOR SOLOS"

ON CUE: BACKGROUND FOR SOLOS

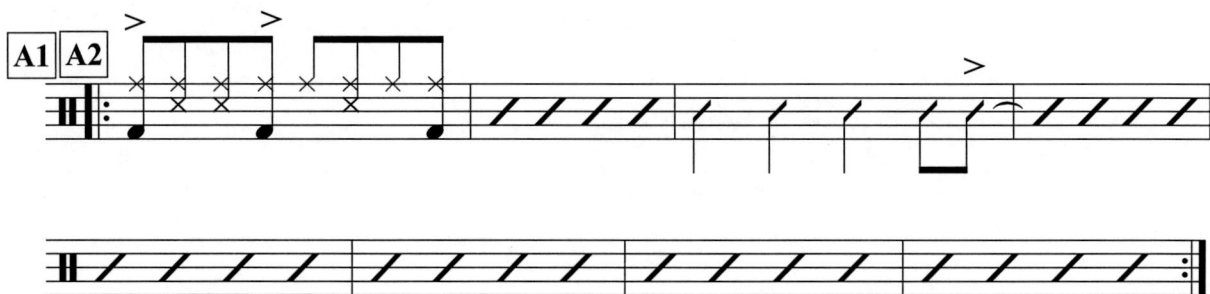

Drum Chart Supplement

playthrough video - jazzdrumming.info/charts

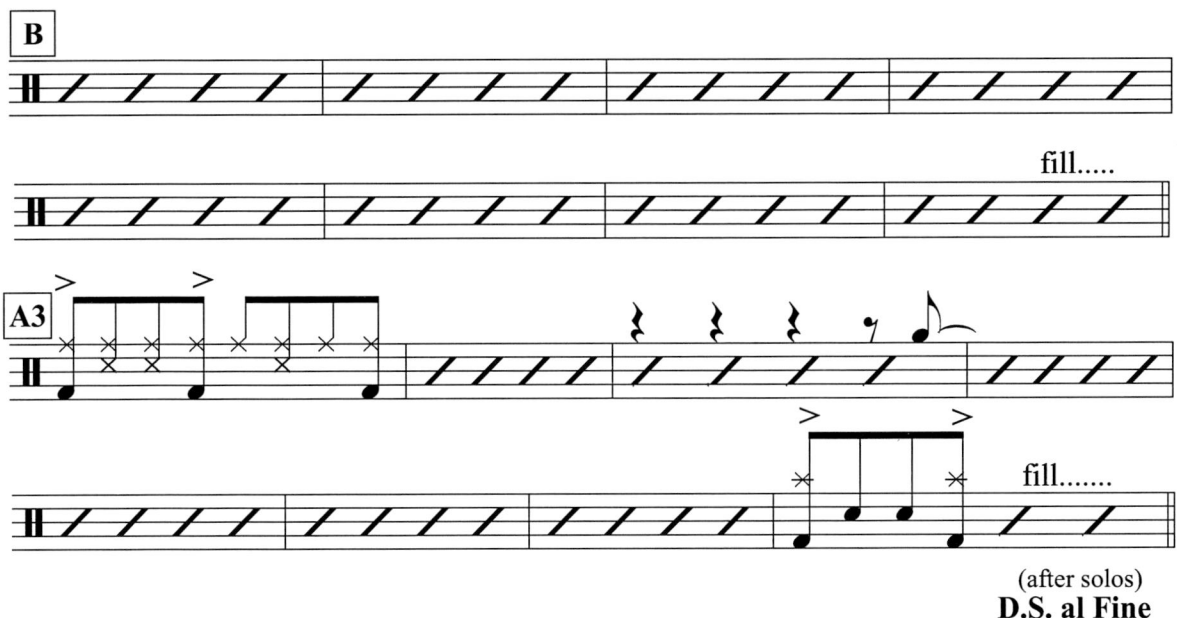

(after solos)
D.S. al Fine

Drum Set Legend:

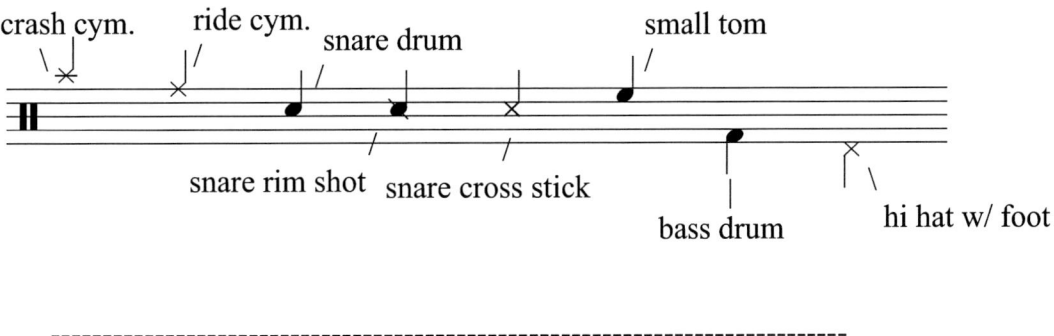

Notation Notes:

61

SECTION 2 — DRUM CHART SUPPLEMENT

Suggested basic drumset part

Short Stuff

comp. by Cedar Walton
drumset arr. by A. Hall

4/4 swing feel
(or 2 feel, like original)

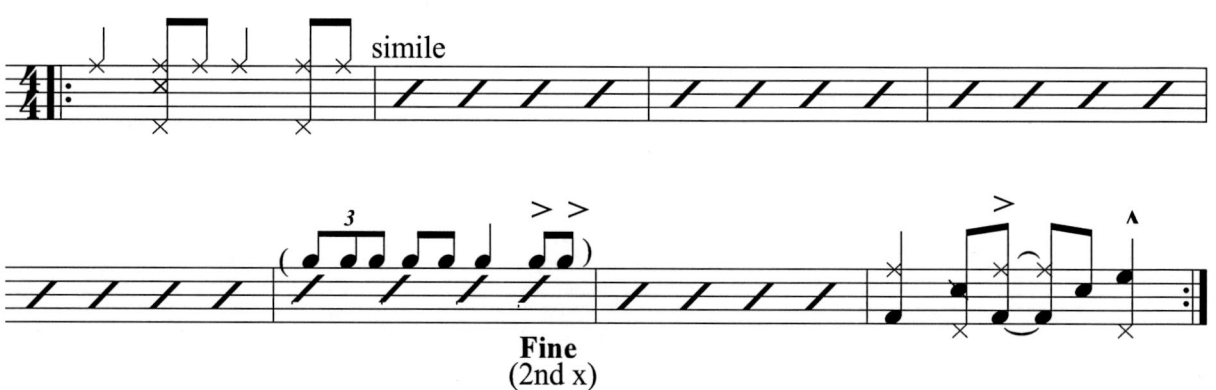

Fine
(2nd x)

FOR SOLOS:
Play time freely in 8 bar phrases, listen, interact, hold the pulse.
Watch for the cues to "background for solos" and "shout chorus".

4/4 feel (if bass player is "walking")

IN CUE: Background for solos

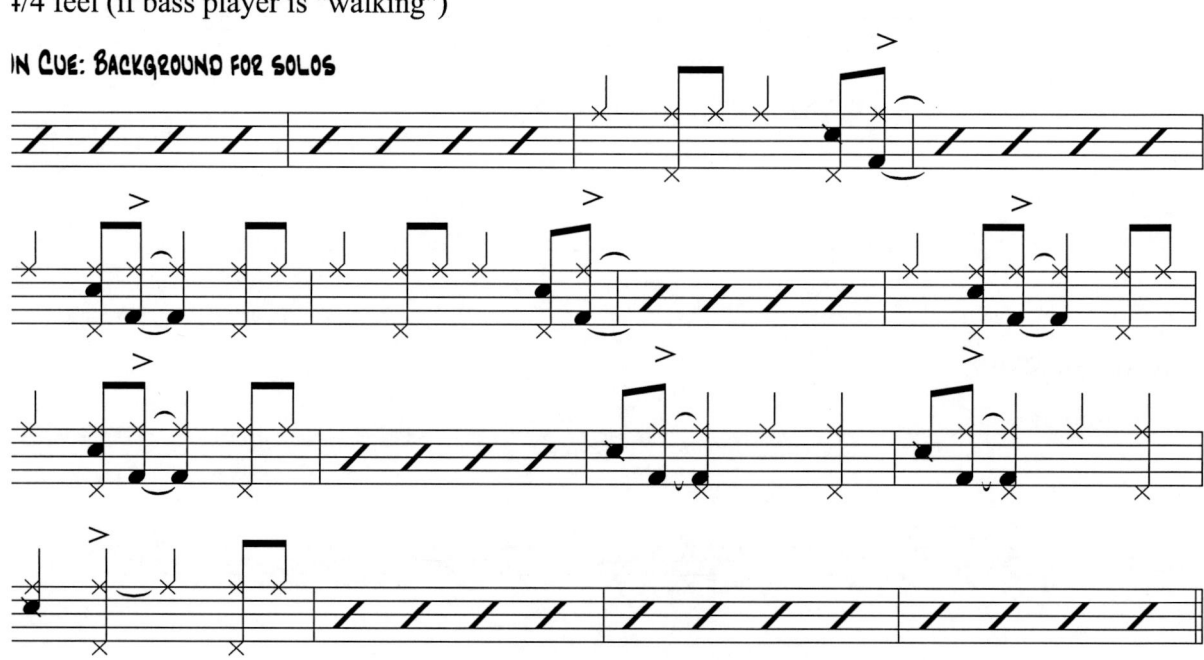

62

Drum Chart Supplement — Section 2

playthrough video – jazzdrumming.info/charts

SHOUT CHORUS. PLAY AFTER SOLOS (OPTIONAL)

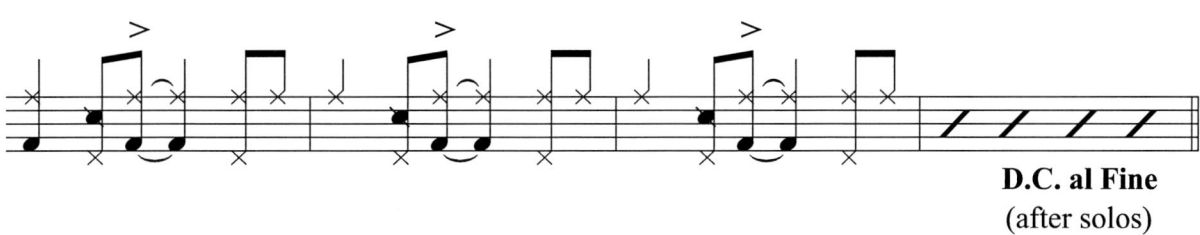

D.C. al Fine
(after solos)

Drum Set Legend:

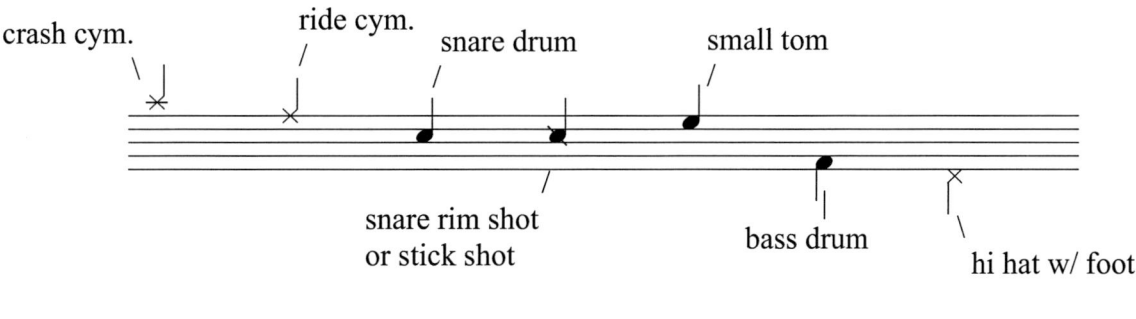

Notation notes:

(These are cue notes which indicate a rhythm played by the horns)

These slashes mean / play jazz time freely.

Fine

This "Fine" indicates that the ending rhythms of the tune are the the 8th notes above

Suggested simplified drumset part

Shoshana

comp. Mark Levine
drum arr. Alan Hall

Jazz Mambo*

piano intro montuno

(use a groove from the groove samples on the following page)

(use different groove from above)

For Solos, play over the A section. The B section is cued
as an interlude between soloists.
Watch for the cue to "Backgrounds for solos"

On cue: background for solos.

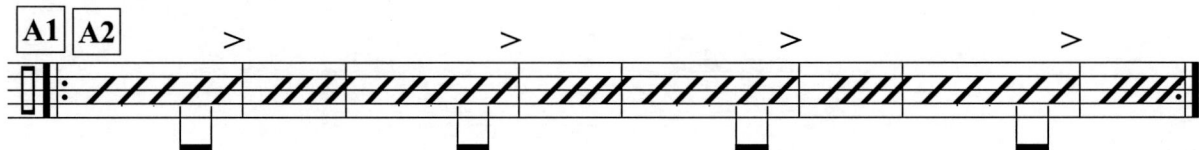

64

playthrough video - jazzdrumming.info/charts

groove video - jazzdrumming.info/more

*Simplified Jazz Mambo type grooves:

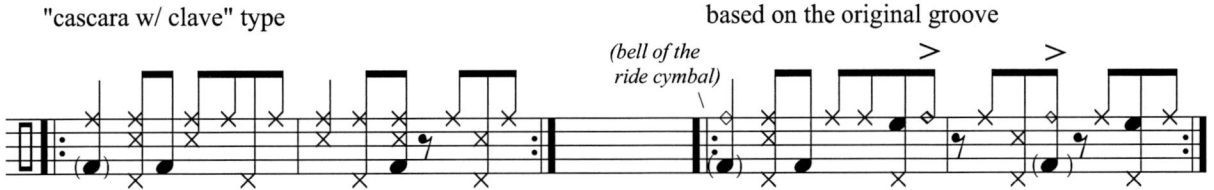

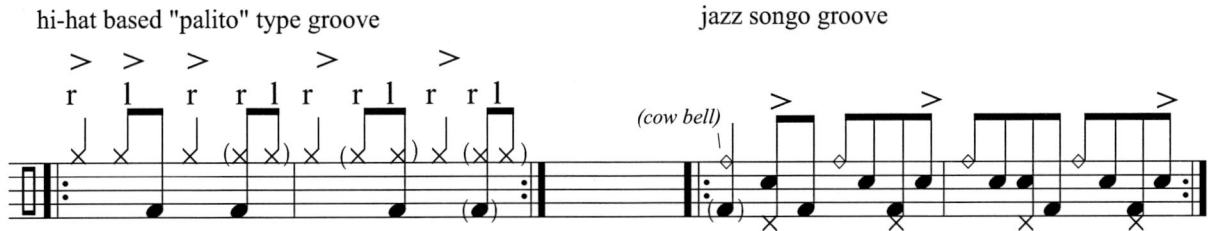

Suggestion: Memorize at least 2 of the above simplified Jazz Mambo type grooves and switch between them for different section of the tune.

Drum Set Legend:

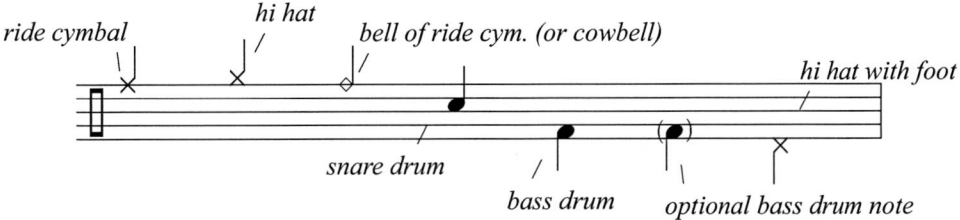

Notation Note:

Play groove, but also catch this accent.

65

SECTION 2 — DRUM CHART SUPPLEMENT

Suggested basic drumset part

Sir John

comp. by Blue Mitchell
drum arr. by A. Hall

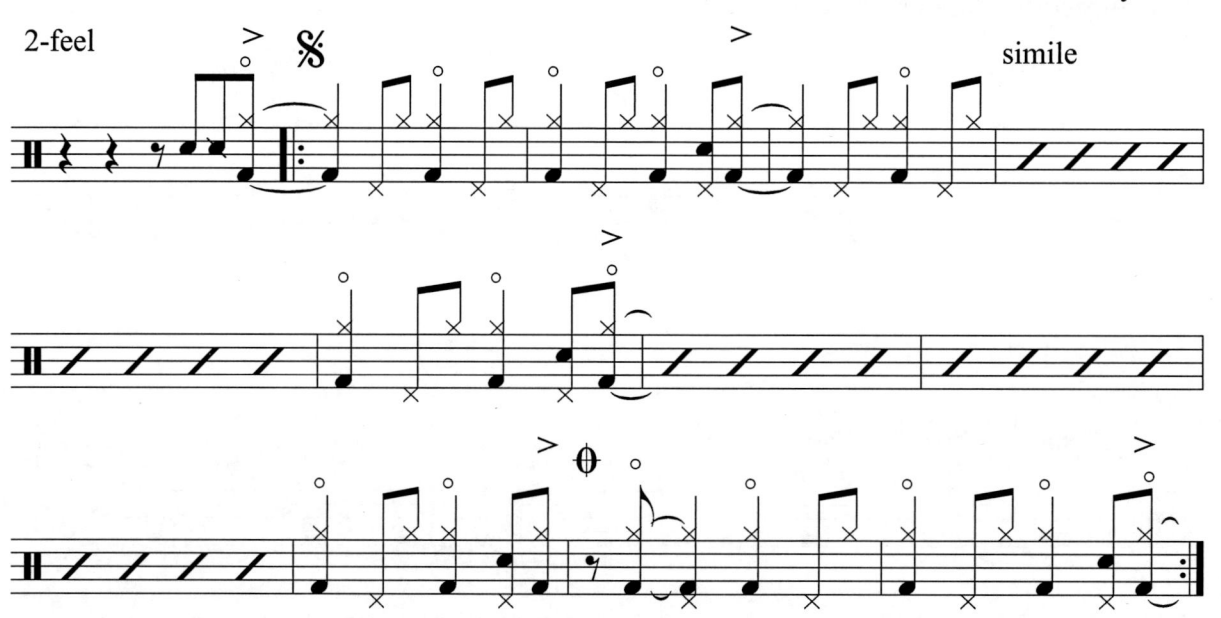

FOR SOLOS:
Play jazz time freely in 12 bar phrases, listen, interact, hold the pulse.
Watch for the cue to "background for solos" and "shout chorus".

On Cue: Background for solos

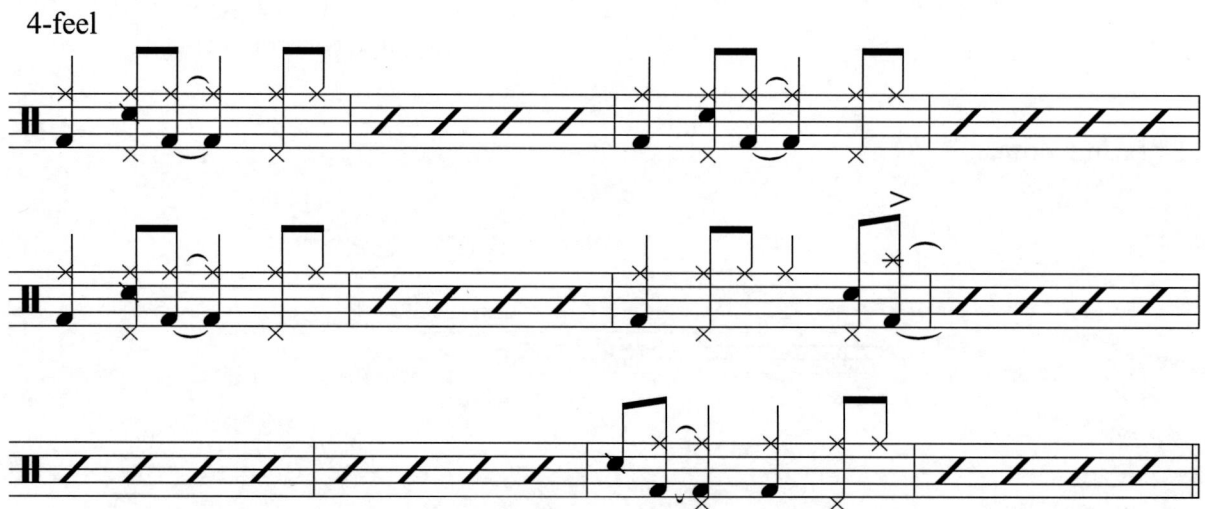

Drum Chart Supplement

playthrough video - jazzdrumming.info/charts

Shout chorus. Play after solos (optional)

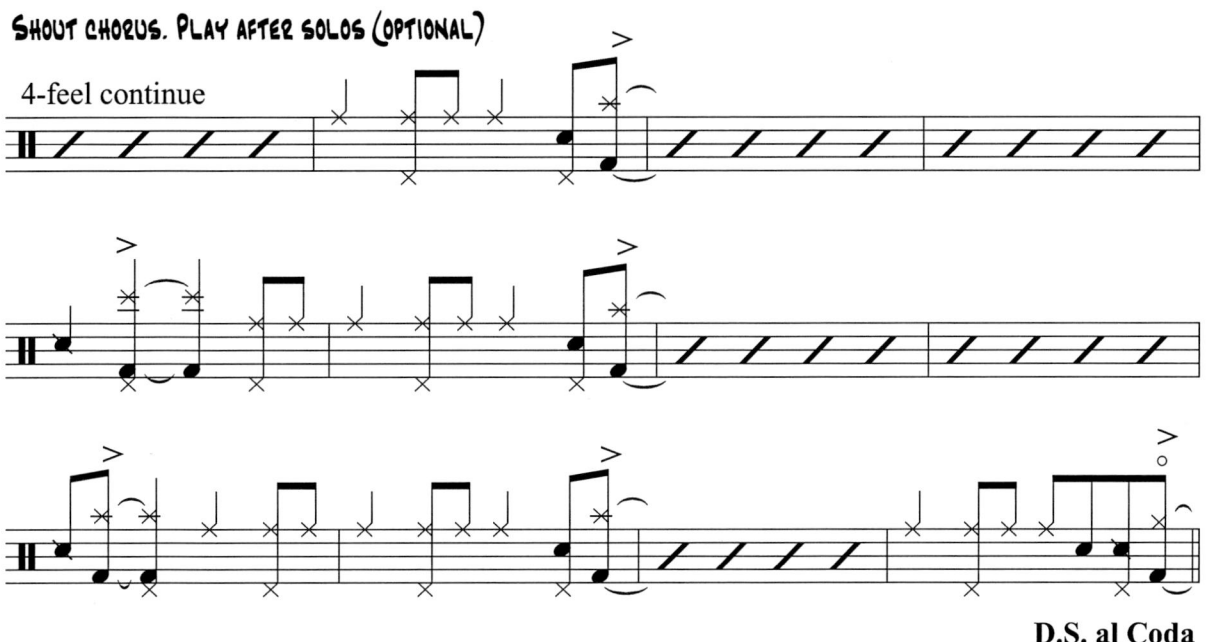

D.S. al Coda

Drum Set Legend:

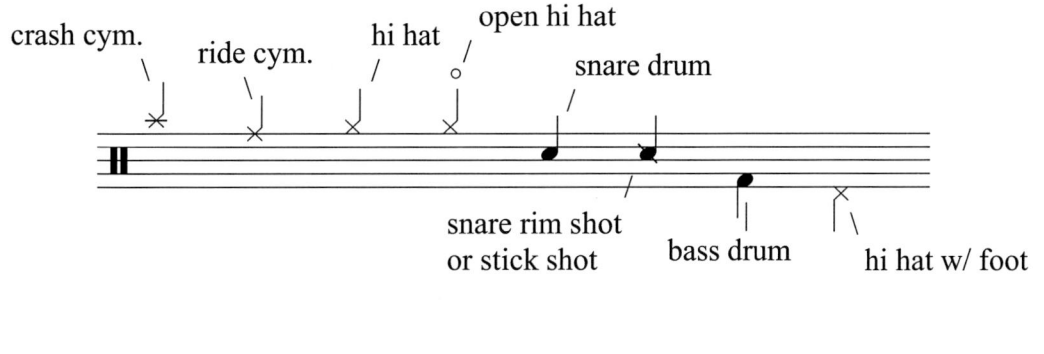

Notation notes:

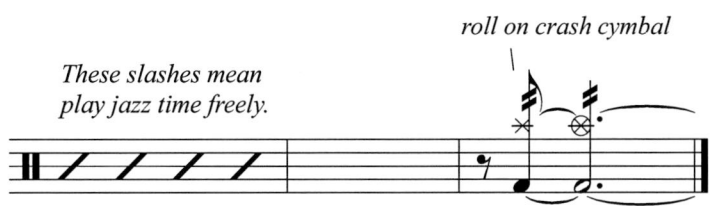

Sister Sadie

Suggested basic drumset part

"stop time"* into jazz shuffle

comp. by Horace Silver
drum arr. by A. Hall

FOR SOLOS:
PLAY JAZZ OR SHUFFLE TIME FREELY, INTERACT AND HOLD THE PULSE OVER A 32 BAR-AABA FORM.
WATCH FOR THE CUE TO "BACKGROUND FOR SOLOS"

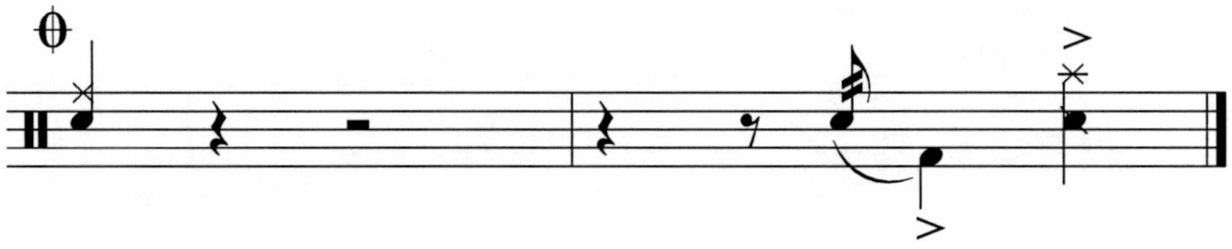

* "Stop Time" refers to an arrangement in which the rhythm section is playing short unison hits and rests, while the melody is played by the rest of the band.

playthrough video - jazzdrumming.info/charts

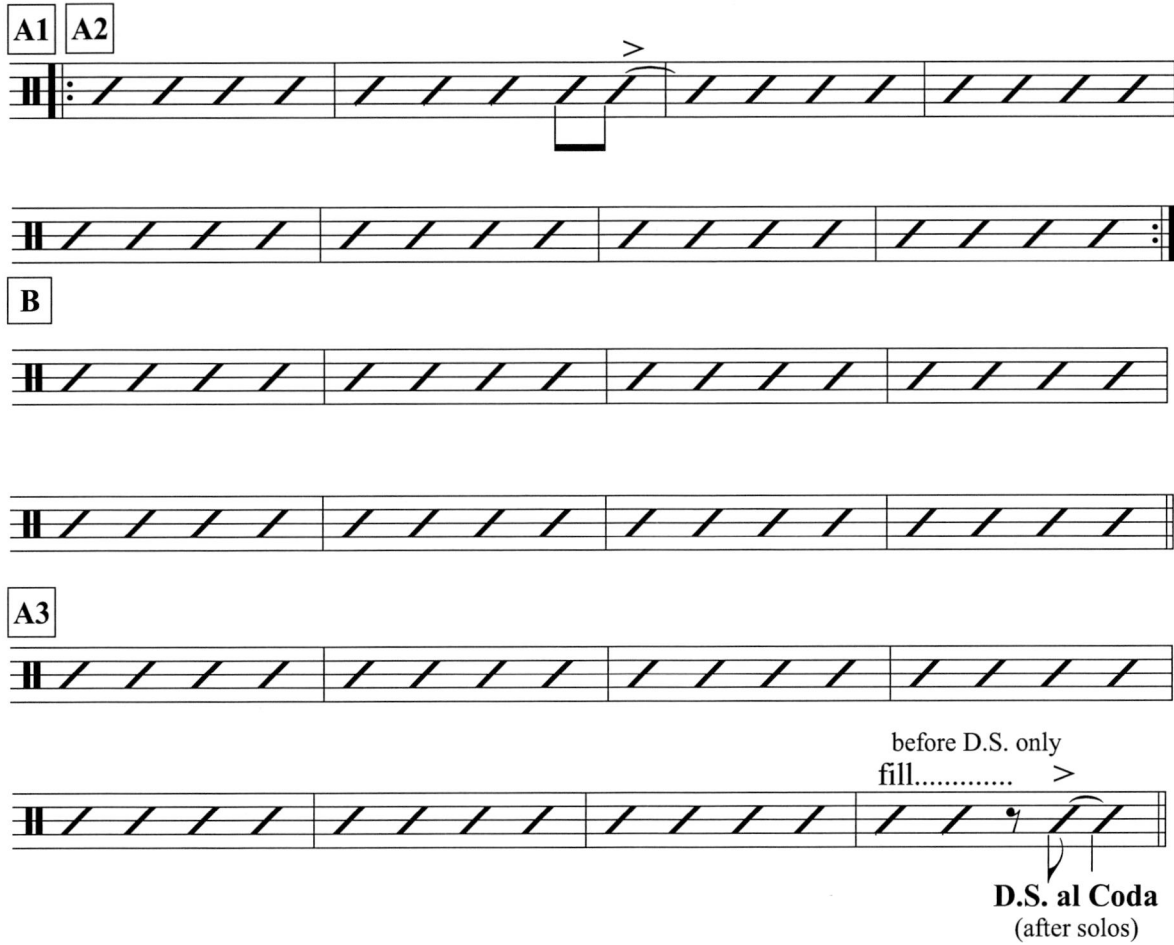

Drum Set Legend:

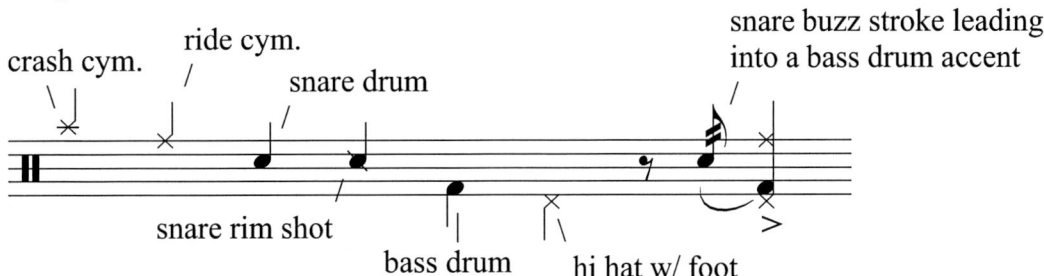

Notation Note:

So Danço Samba

Suggested basic drumset part

samba groove
• see simplified samba grooves

comp. by Antonio Carlos Jobim
drum arr. by A. Hall

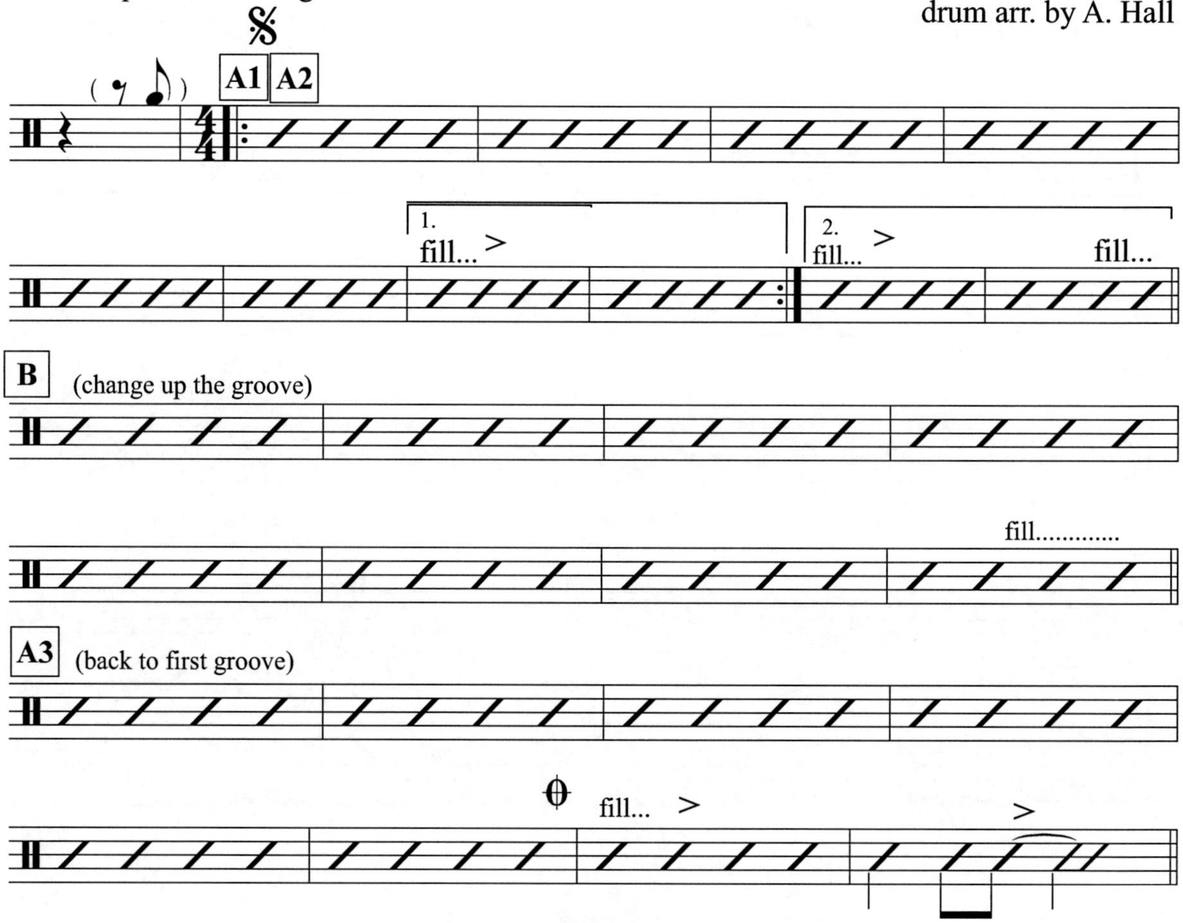

FOR SOLOS:
Play samba freely and hold the pulse over a 32 bar- AABA form.
Watch for the cue to "Background for Solos"

On cue: Background for Solos.

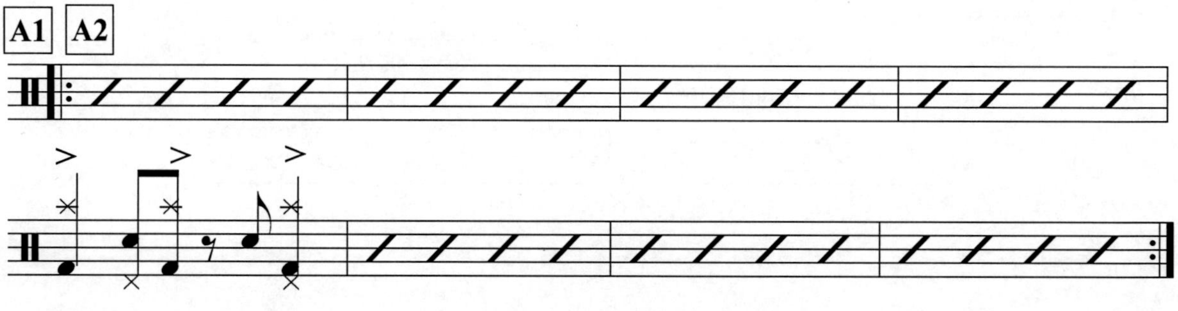

Drum Chart Supplement

SECTION 2

playthrough video - jazzdrumming.info/charts   groove video - jazzdrumming.info/more

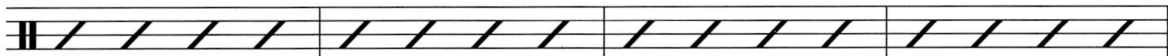

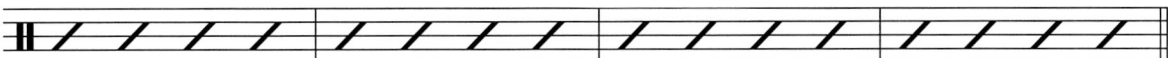

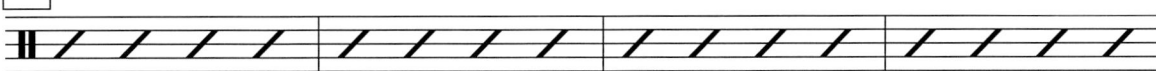

(after solos)
D.S. al Coda

- **Simplified samba type grooves:**

(Suggestion-memorize each, and switch out for different sections of the tune)

w/ brushes * on snare (or sticks on hi hat)
(w/ right hand lead sticking)

w/ sticks: #

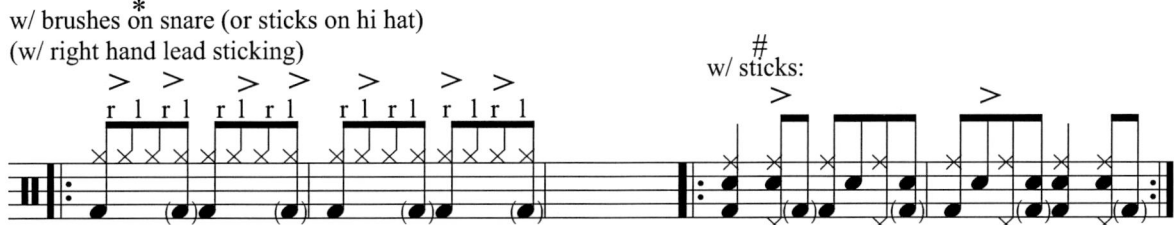

* *If playing all bd notes is too difficult, then just play bd on beat 1 and 3 until you're ready to play all.*

\# *These snare notes can also be played cross stick style, and the rhythms can be more varied.*

Drum Set Legend:

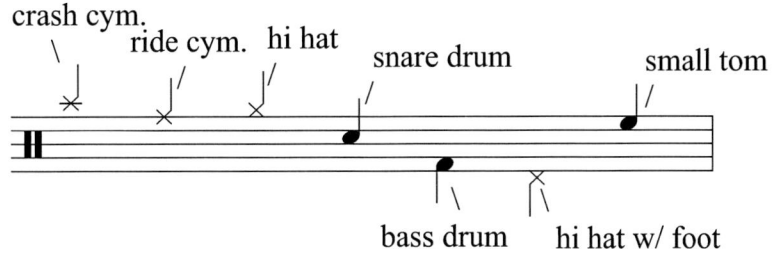

Notation Note:

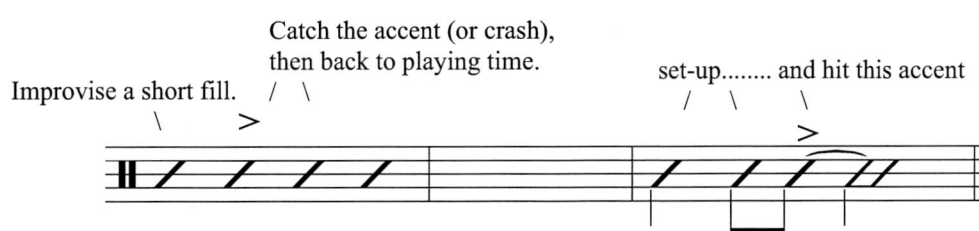

SECTION 2 — DRUM CHART SUPPLEMENT

Suggested basic drumset part

Song for My Father

comp. by Horace Silver
drum arr. by Alan Hall

Jazz Bossa Nova
(straight 8th feel)

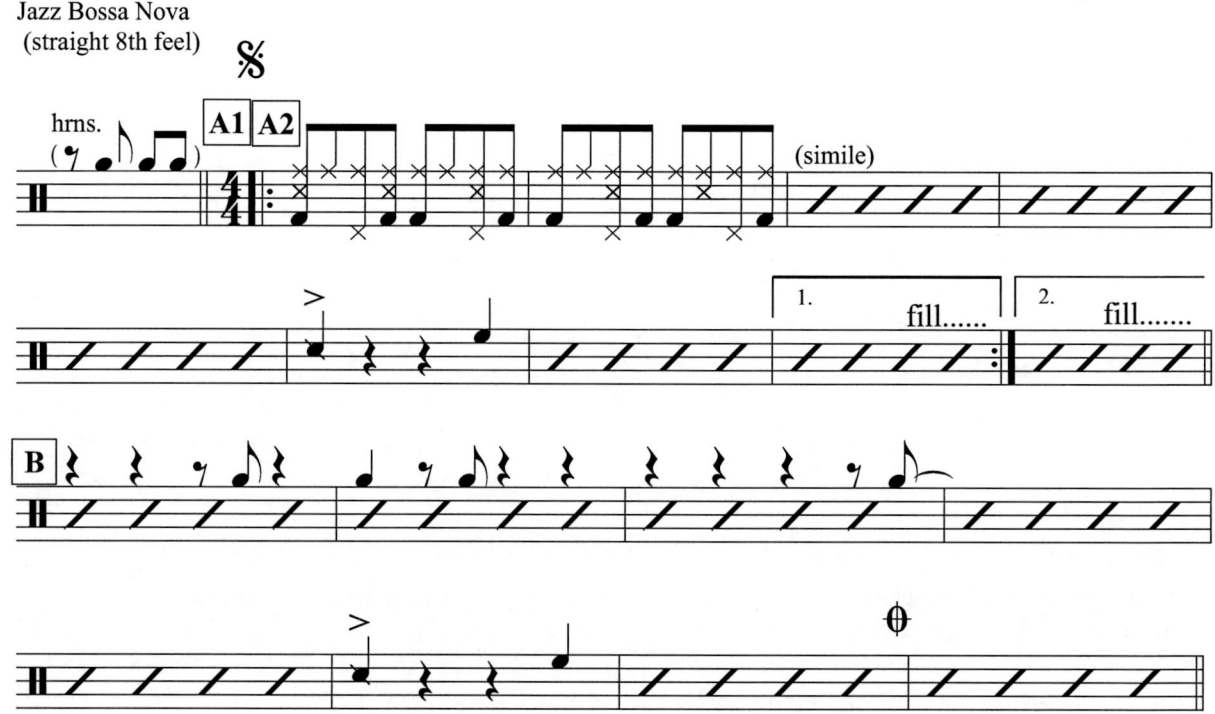

FOR SOLOS:
Play a varied jazz bossa nova, listen, interact, hold the pulse, keep the form (A A B)
Watch for the cue to "shout chorus"

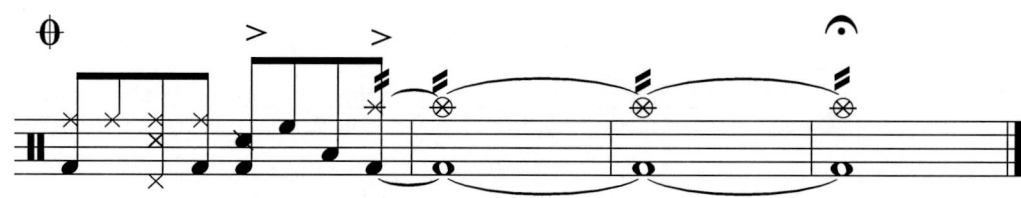

Drum Chart Supplement

SECTION 2

playthrough video at : jazzdrumming.info/charts

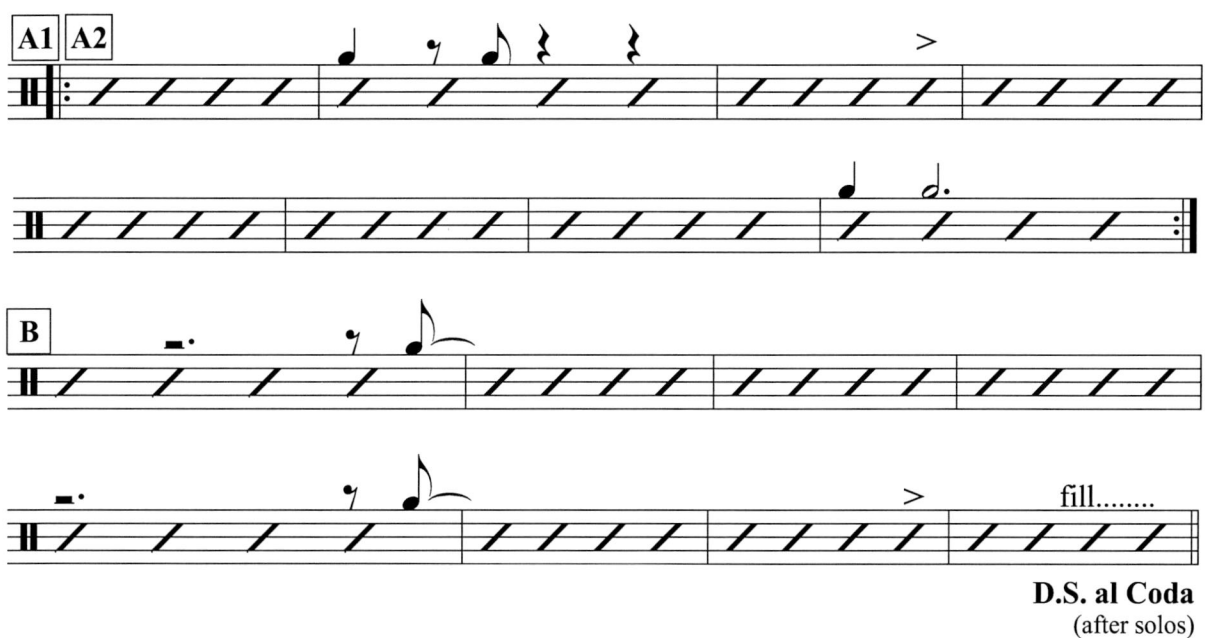

D.S. al Coda
(after solos)

Drum Set Legend:

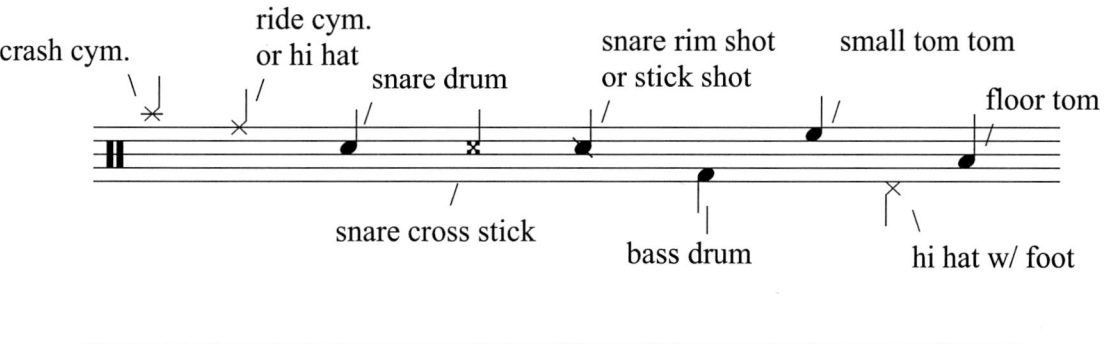

Notation Notes:

SECTION 2 — DRUM CHART SUPPLEMENT

Suggested basic drumset part

Sonnymoon for Two

comp. by S. Rollins,
drum arr. by A. Hall

Jazz Time

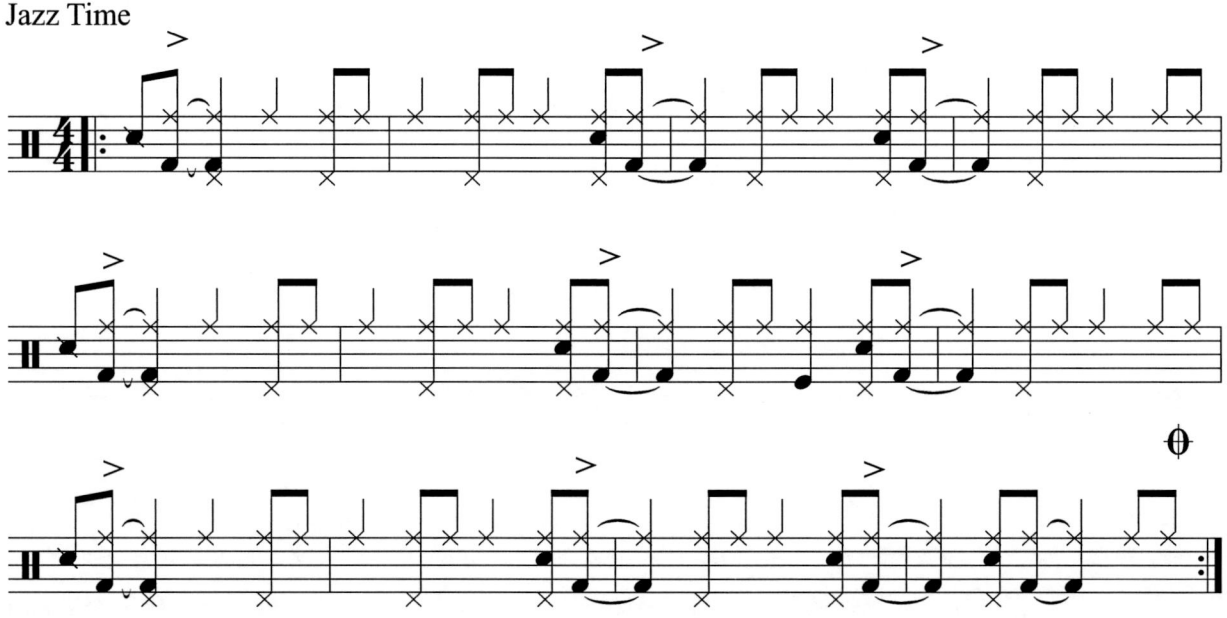

FOR SOLOS:
Play time freely in 12 bar phrases, listen, interact, hold the pulse.
Watch for the cue to "background for solos" and "shout chorus".

On Cue: Background for solos

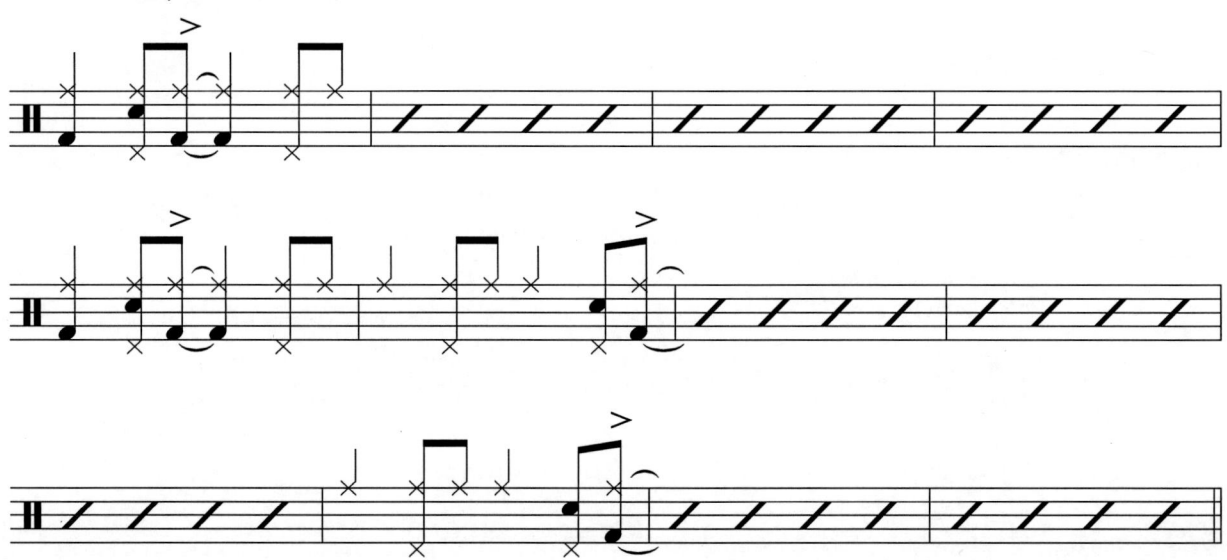

Drum Chart Supplement — Section 2

playthrough video - jazzdrumming.info/charts

Shout chorus. Play after solos (optional)

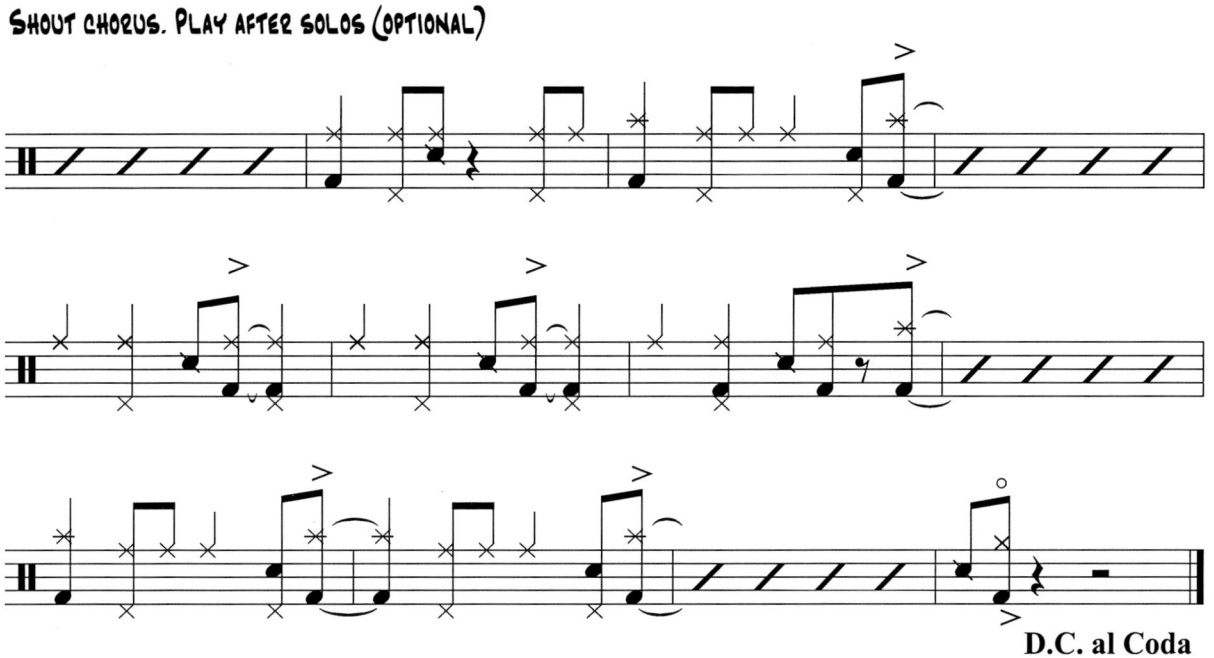

D.C. al Coda

Drum Set Legend:

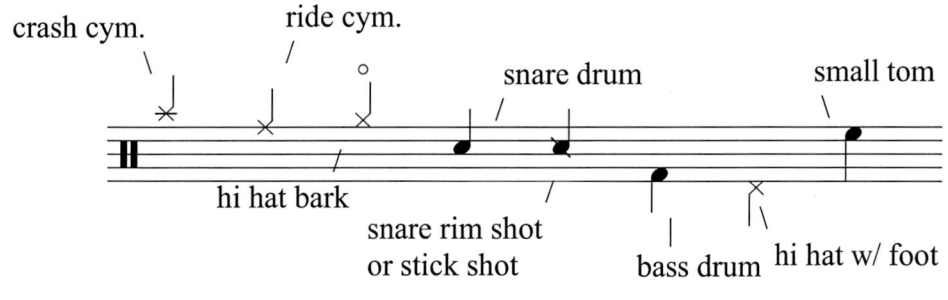

Notation notes:

SECTION 2 — DRUM CHART SUPPLEMENT

Suggested basic drumset part

St. James Infirmary

slow jazz 12/8 feel

comp. by Joe Primrose
drum arr. by A. Hall

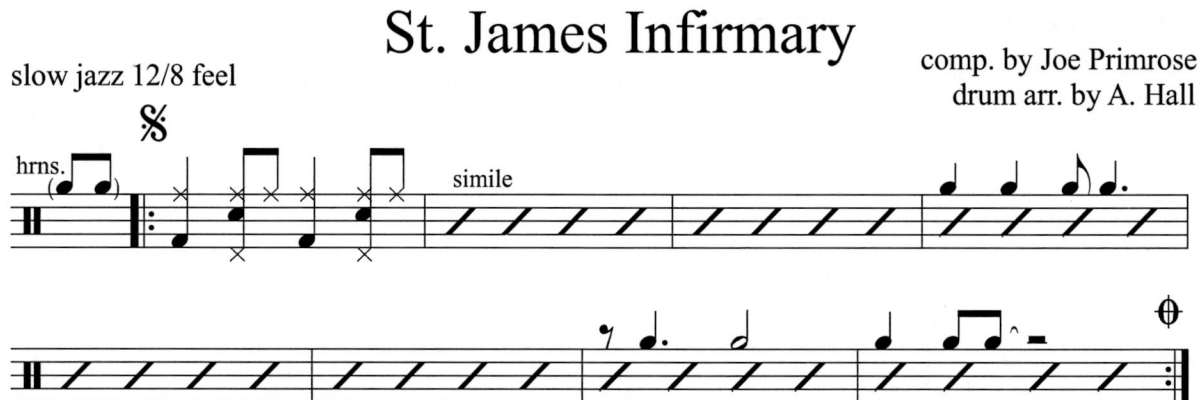

FOR SOLOS:
Play slow jazz time freely in 8 bar phrases, listen, interact, hold the pulse.
Watch for the cue to "background for solos" and "shout chorus".

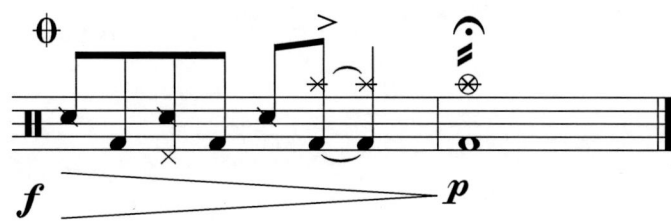

On Cue: Background for solos

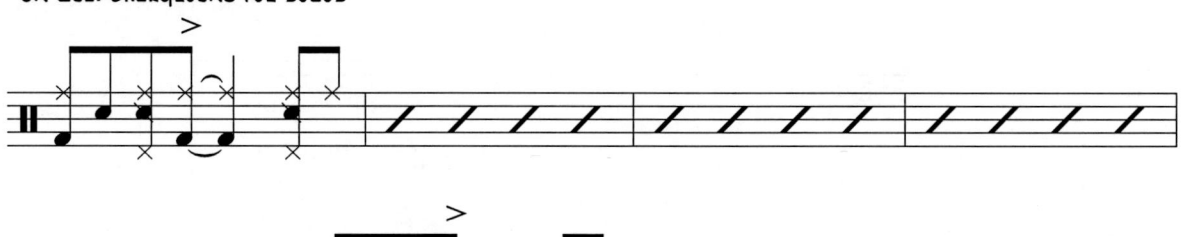

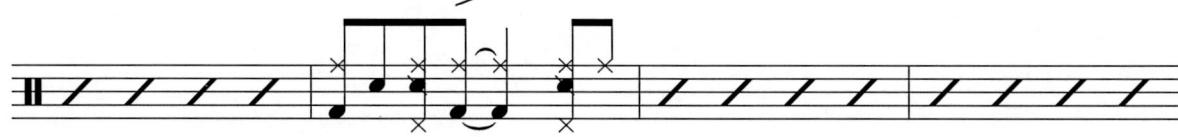

Shout chorus. Play after solos (optional)

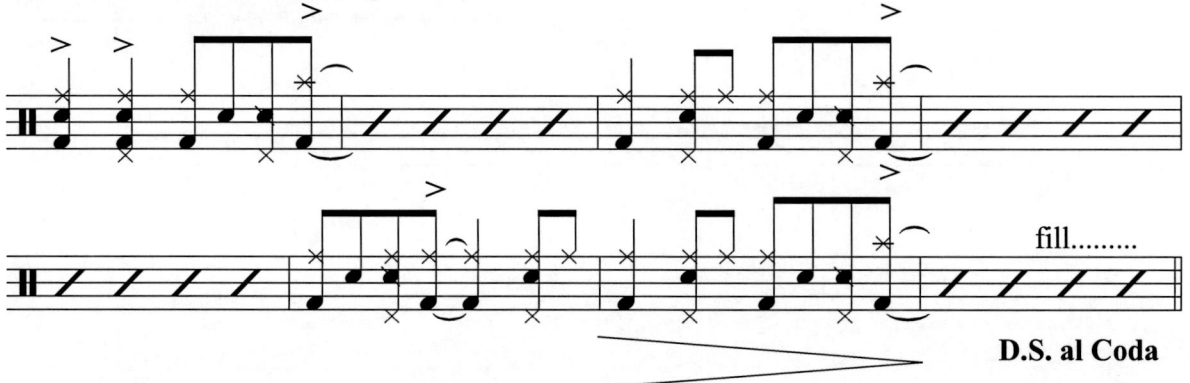

D.S. al Coda

Drum Set Legend:

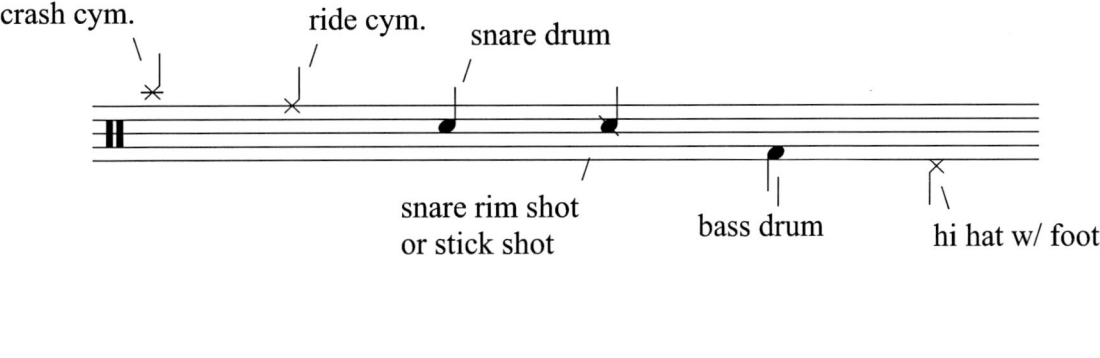

Notation notes:

SECTION 2 — DRUM CHART SUPPLEMENT

St. Thomas

Suggested basic drum set part

Soca Groove

comp. by Sonny Rollins
drum arr. by Alan Hall

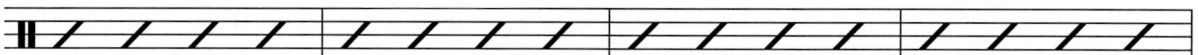

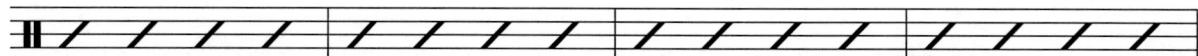

* you can substitute cross-stick for snaredrum hit for variety

FOR SOLOS:
Play a "soca" groove in 16 bar phrases, listen, interact, hold the pulse.
Watch for the cue to "background for solos" and also to the optional "shout chorus"

On Cue: Backgroud for solos.

continue "soca" groove

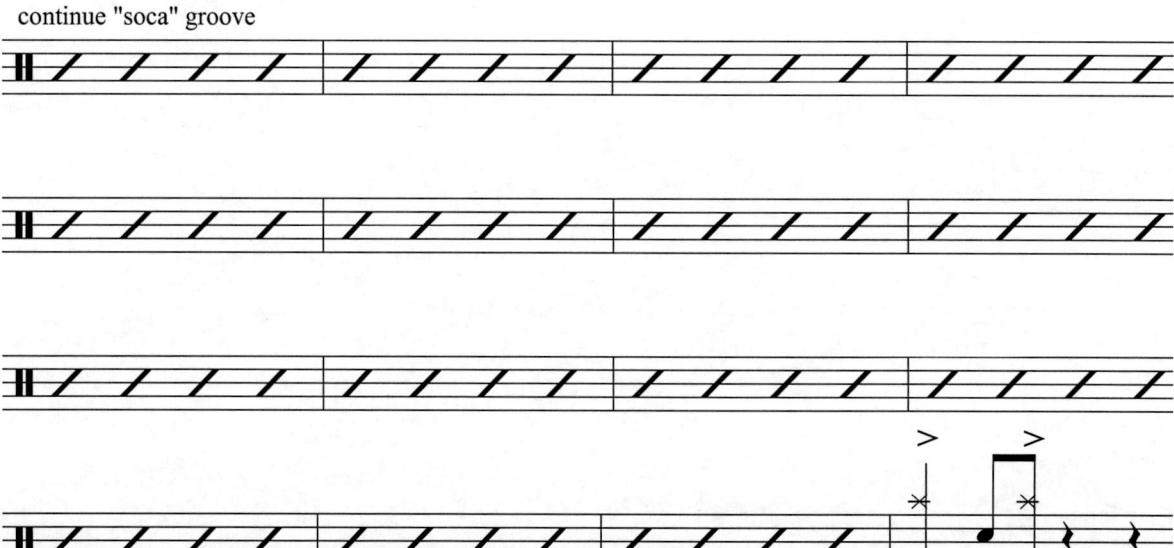

Drum Chart Supplement

playthrough video – jazzdrumming.info/charts   playthrough video – jazzdrumming.info/more

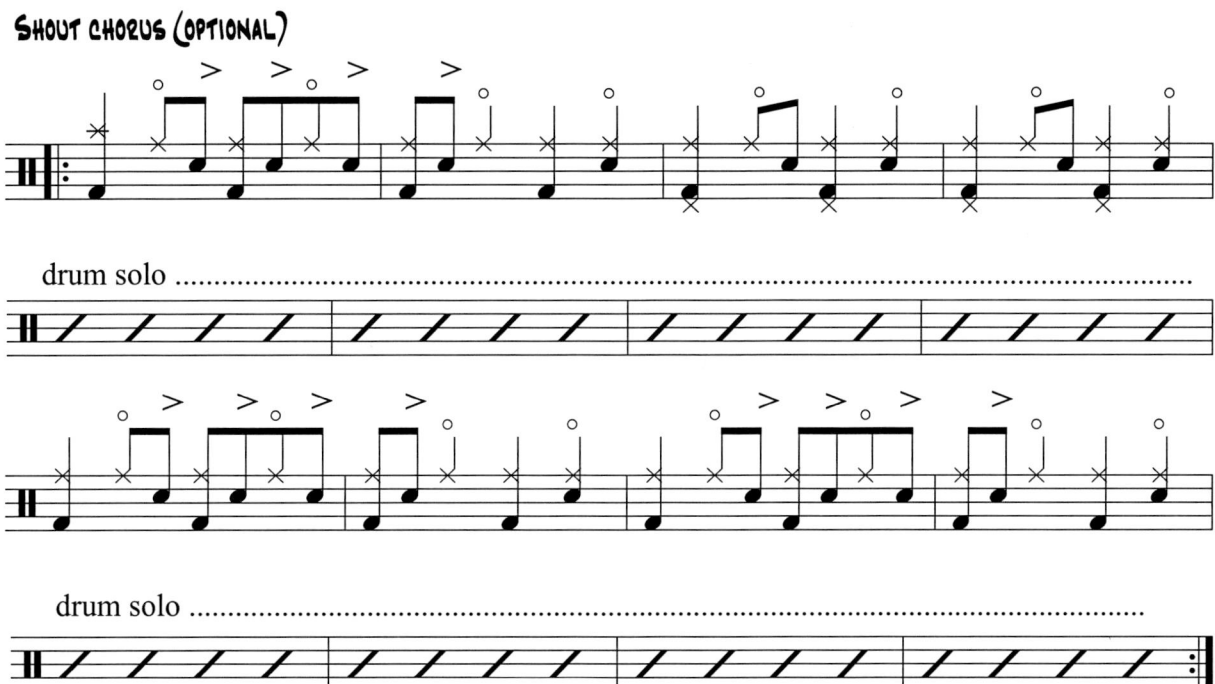

Drum Set Legend:

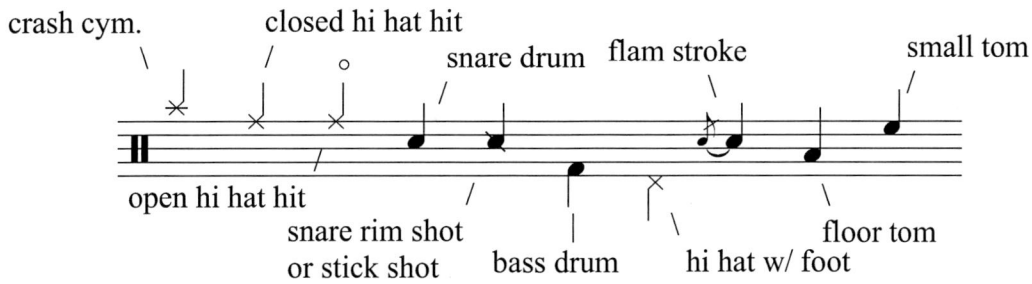

Notation Notes:

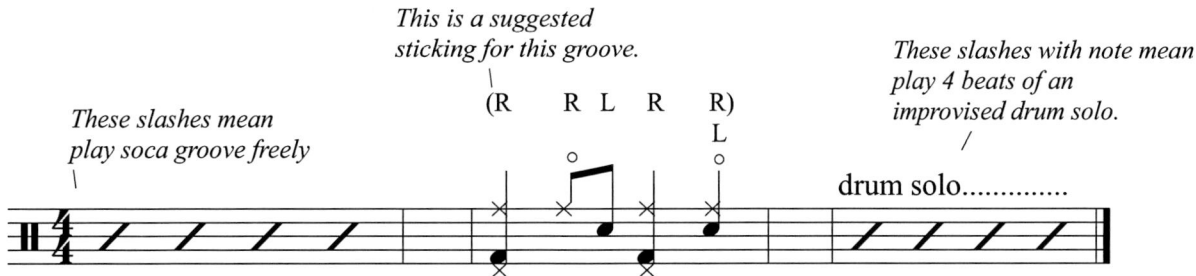

SECTION 2 — DRUM CHART SUPPLEMENT

Suggested basic drumset part

Straight Life

comp. by Freddie Hubbard
drum arr. by Alan Hall

Funk Rock
(with either a straight or swing 8th feel)
1/2 x feel

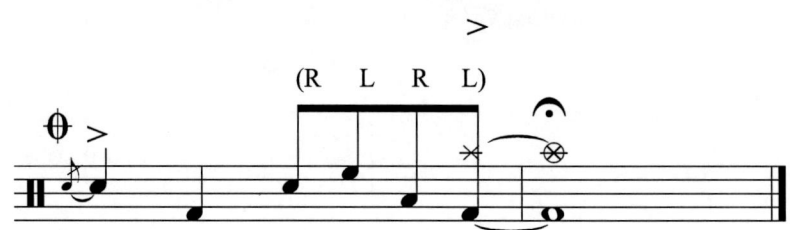

FOR SOLOS:
Play a loose, funk type groove, listen, interact, hold the pulse.
Watch for the cue to "background for solos"

Drum Chart Supplement

SECTION 2

playthrough video - jazzdrumming.info/charts

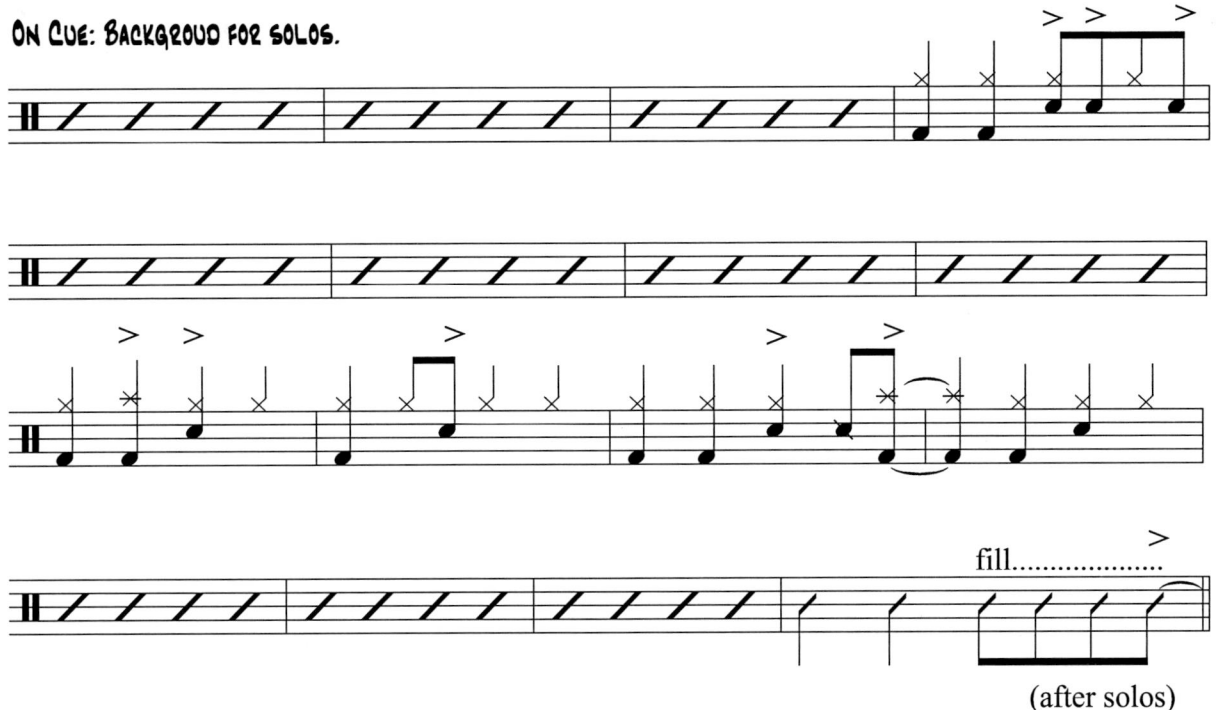

(after solos)

Drum Set Legend:

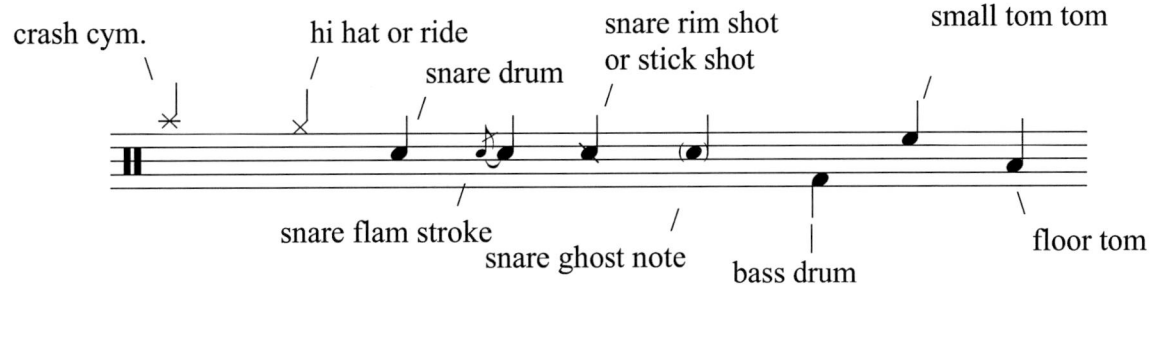

Notation Notes:

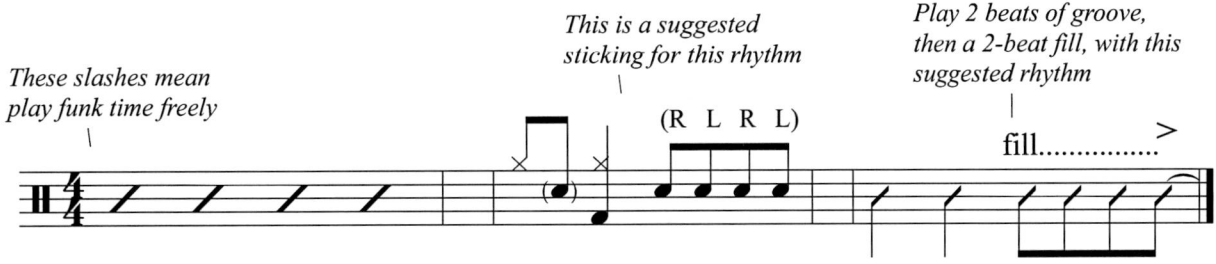

81

SECTION 2 — DRUM CHART SUPPLEMENT

Suggested basic drum set part

Tenor Madness

comp. by Sonny Rollins
drum arr. by A. Hall

jazz time

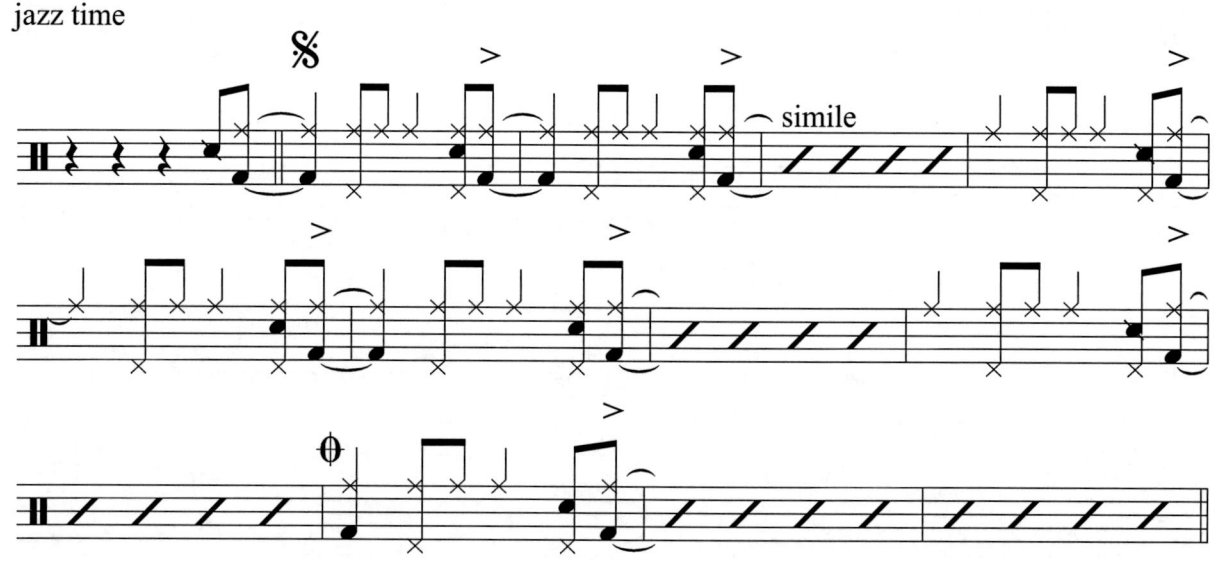

FOR SOLOS:
Play jazz time freely in 12 bar phrases, listen, interact, hold the pulse.
Watch for the cue to "background for solos" and "shout chorus".

On Cue: Background for solos

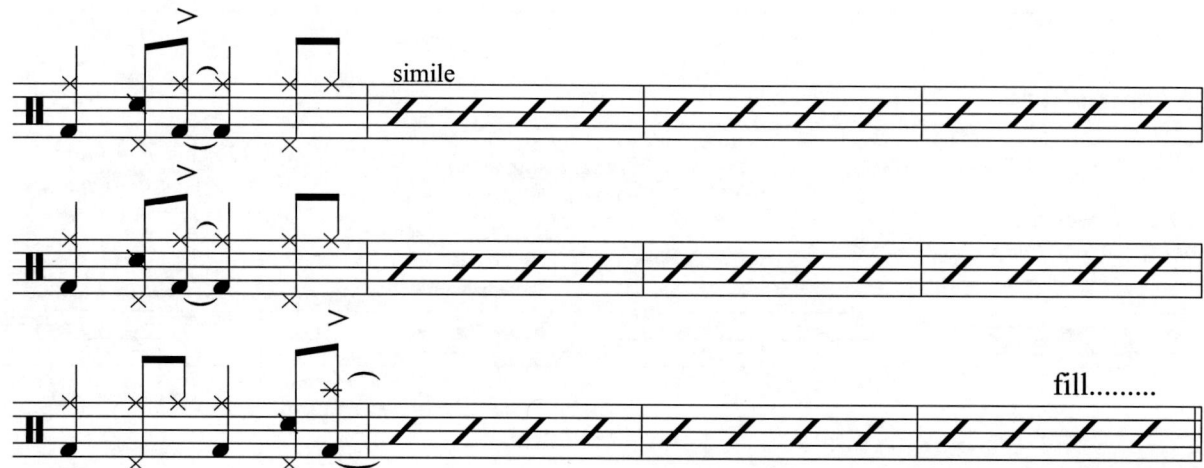

82

Drum Chart Supplement — Section 2

playthrough video – jazzdrumming.info/more

Shout chorus. Play after solos (optional)

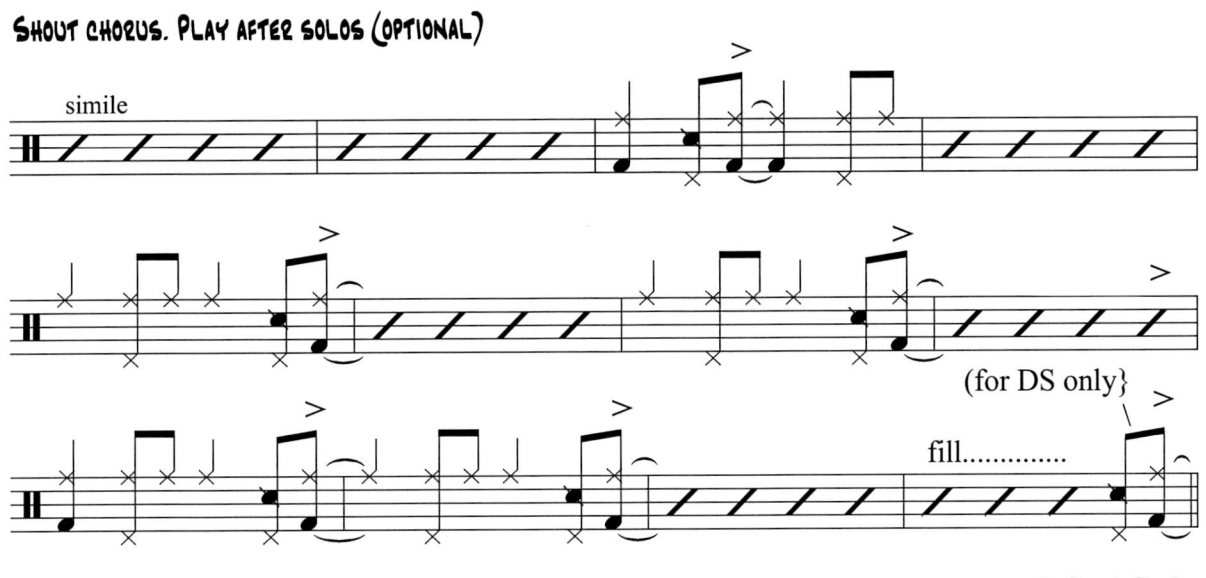

D.S. al Coda

Drum Set Legend:

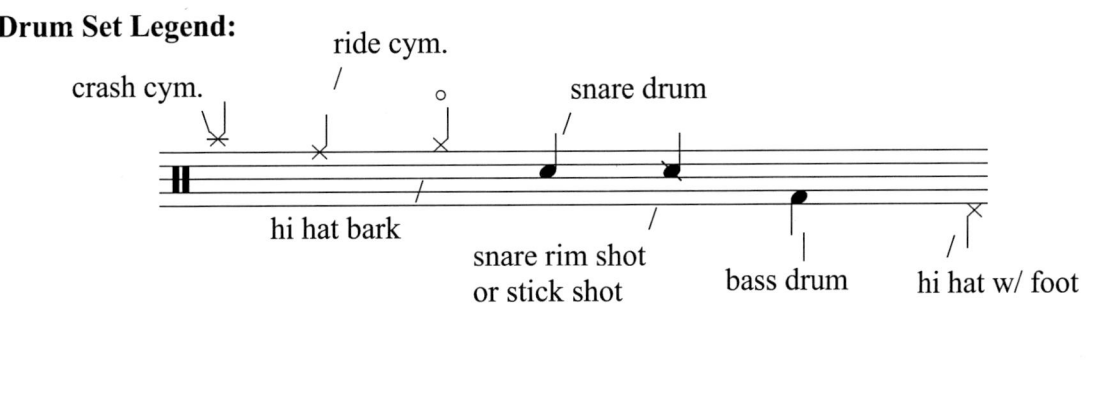

Notation notes:

These slashes (with simile) mean play jazz time freely.

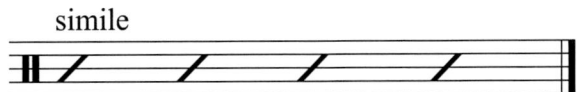

83

SECTION 2 — DRUM CHART SUPPLEMENT

Trail Dust

Suggested basic drum set part

comp. by Jim Rotondi
drum arr. by Alan Hall

Jazz Time

FOR SOLOS:
Play jazz time freely in 16 bar phrases, listen, interact, hold the pulse.
Watch for the cue to "background for solos" and "Shout Chorus"

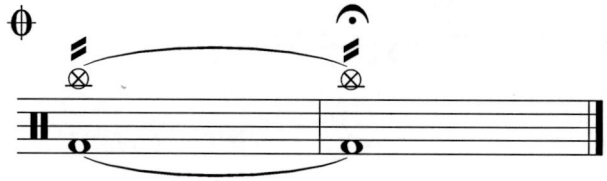

On Cue: Basckground for solos

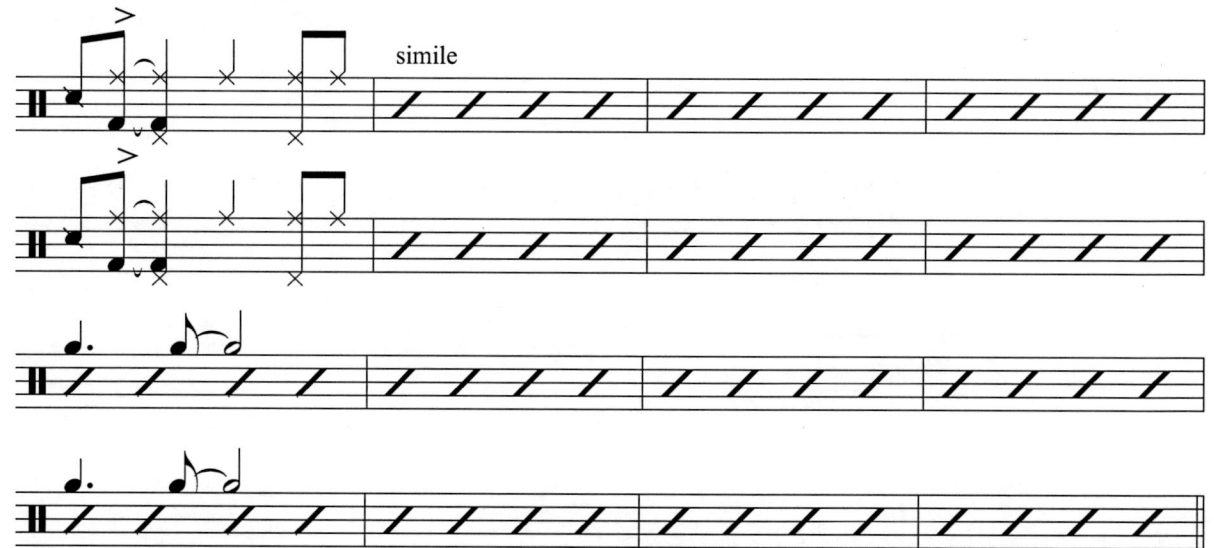

ON CUE: SHOUT CHORUS (OPTIONAL)

playthrough video - jazzdrumming.info/charts

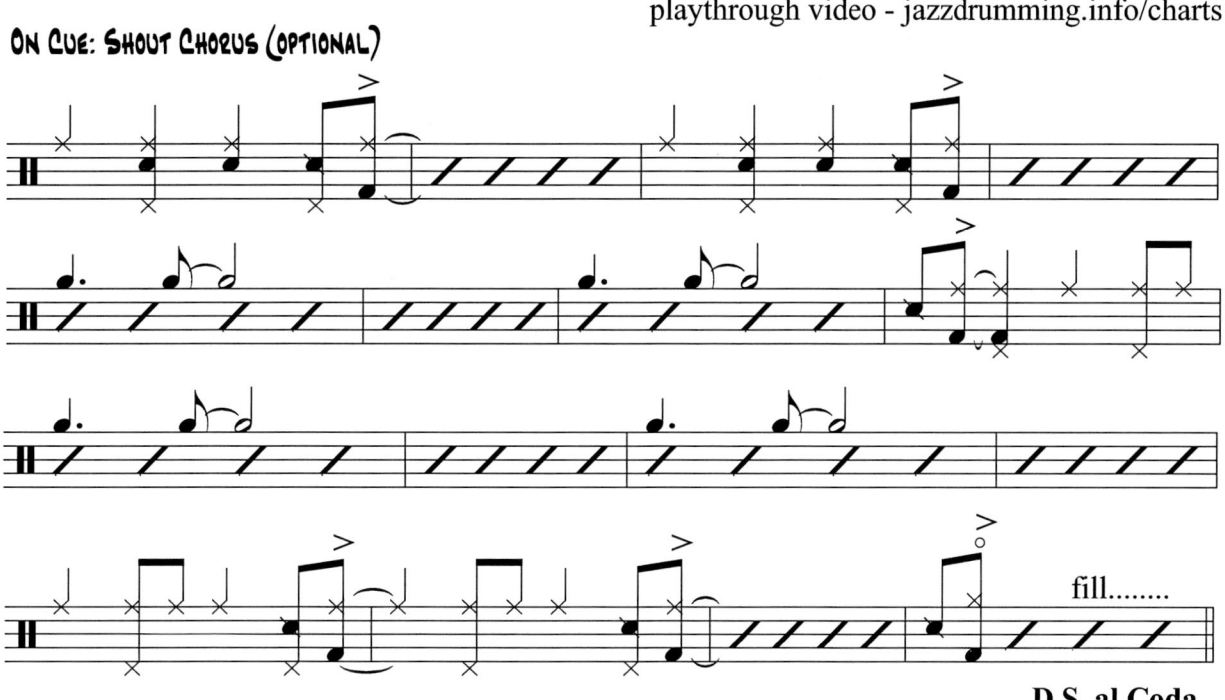

D.S. al Coda

Drum Set Legend:

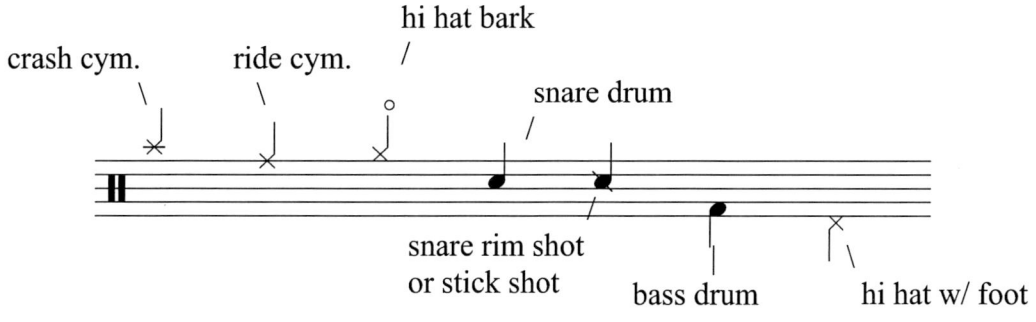

- -

Notation Notes:

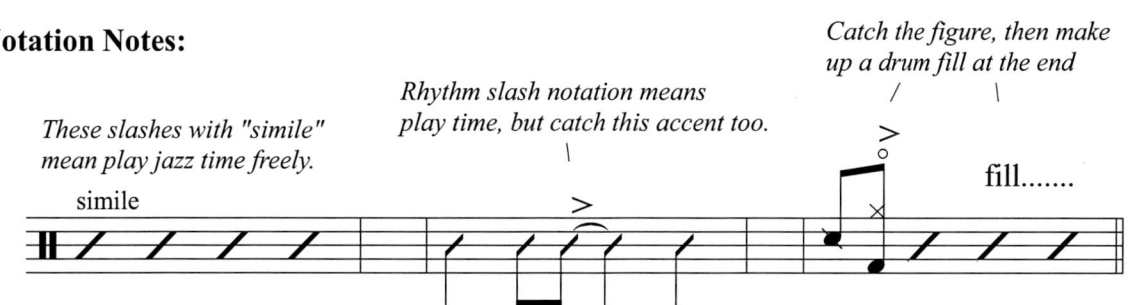

Section 2 — Drum Chart Supplement

Suggested basic drum set part

When the Saints Go Marching In

Traditional
drum arr. by Alan Hall

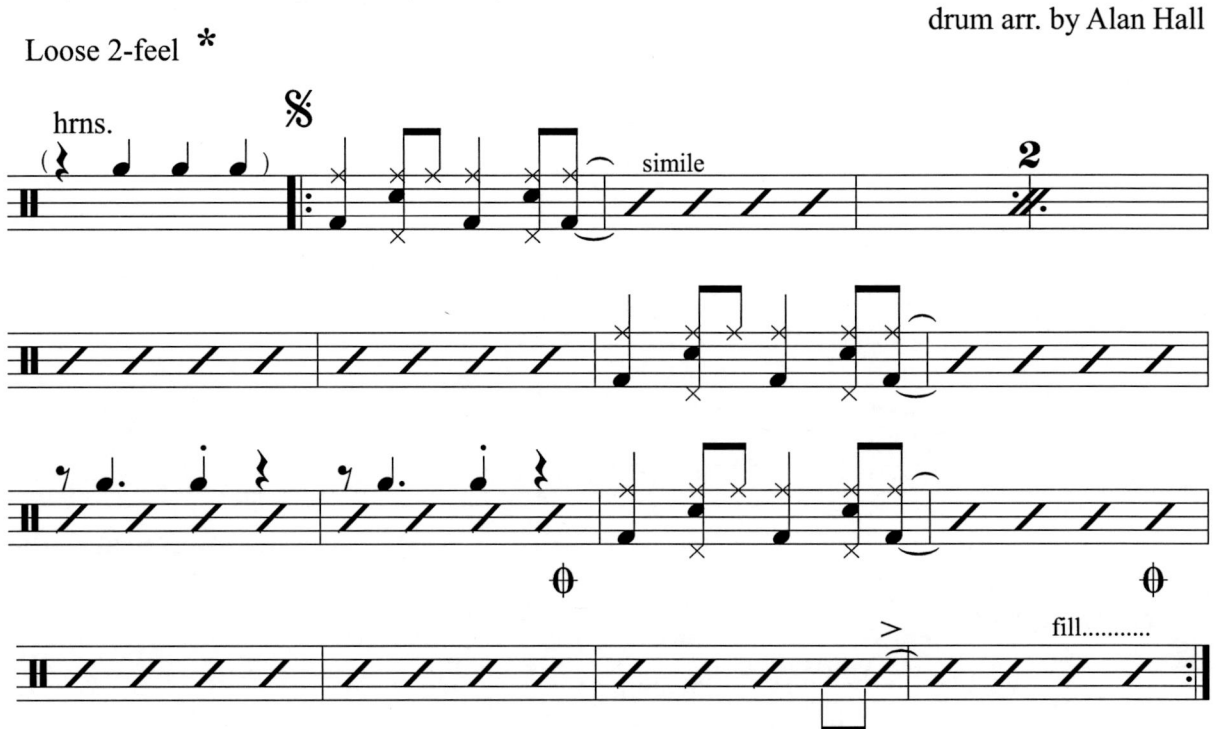

For solos:
Play time freely in 16 bar phrases, listen, interact, hold the pulse.
Watch for the cue to "background for solos"

On Cue: Background for solos.

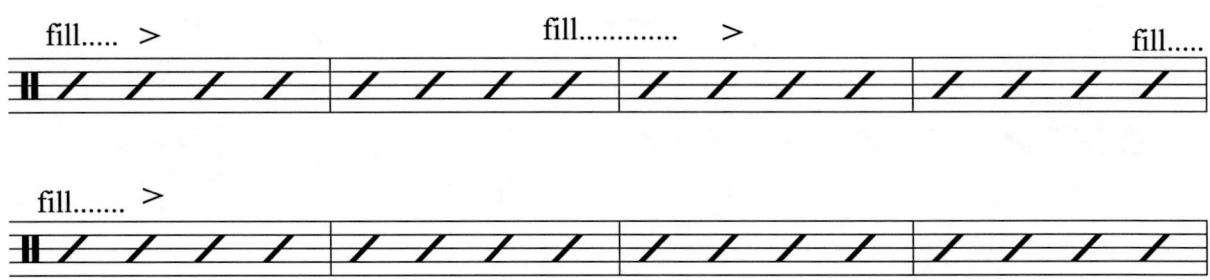

playthrough video - jazzdrumming.info/charts

fill............

D.S. al Coda
(after solos)

* Optional New Orleans "Second Line" flavored groove:

Drum Set Legend:

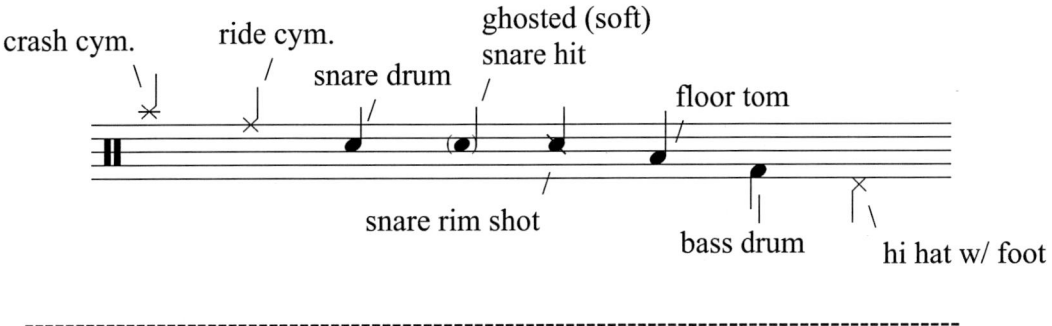

Notation Notes:

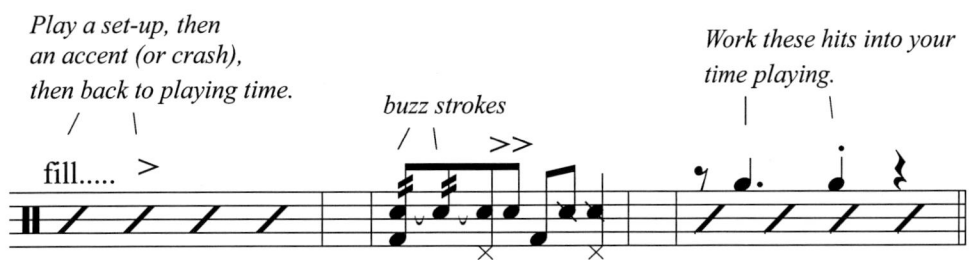

SECTION 2 — DRUM CHART SUPPLEMENT

Suggested basic drumset part

Work Song

Stop-time
Jazz Shuffle

comp. by Nat Adderly
drum arr. by Alan Hall

FOR SOLOS:
Play jazz shuffle time freely in 16 bar phrases, listen, interact, hold the pulse.
Watch for the cue to "background for solos"

playthrough video – jazzdrumming.info/more

ON CUE: BACKGROUND FOR SOLOS.

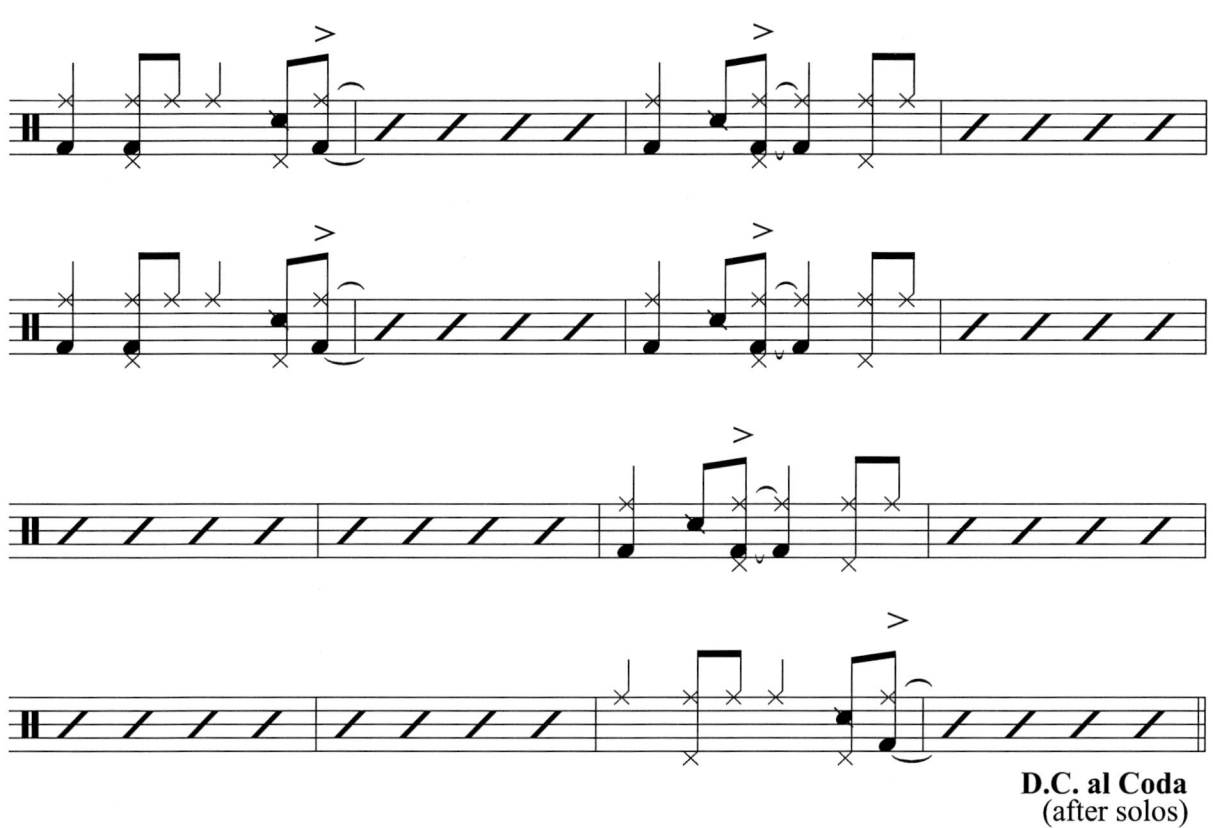

D.C. al Coda
(after solos)

Drum Set Legend:

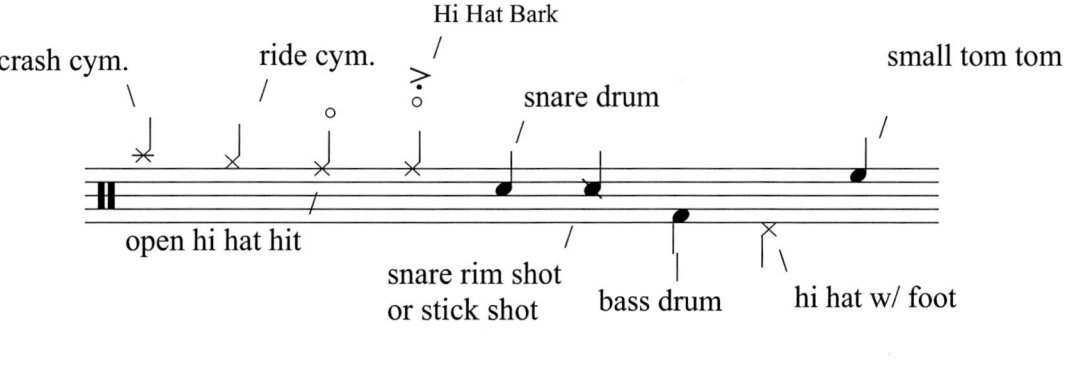

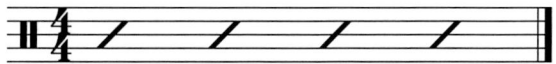

Notation Notes:

*These slashes mean
play jazz shuffle time freely.*

SECTION 2 — DRUM CHART SUPPLEMENT

Suggested basic drumset part

Yardbird Suite

comp. by Charlie Parker
drum arr. by A. Hall

bebop jazz feel

FOR SOLOS:
PLAY BE BOP JAZZ TIME FREELY, LISTEN, INTERACT, AND HOLD THE PULSE.
KEEP THE 32-BAR AABA FORM.
WATCH FOR THE CUE TO "BACKGROUND FOR SOLOS"

Drum Chart Supplement — Section 2

playthrough video - jazzdrumming.info/charts

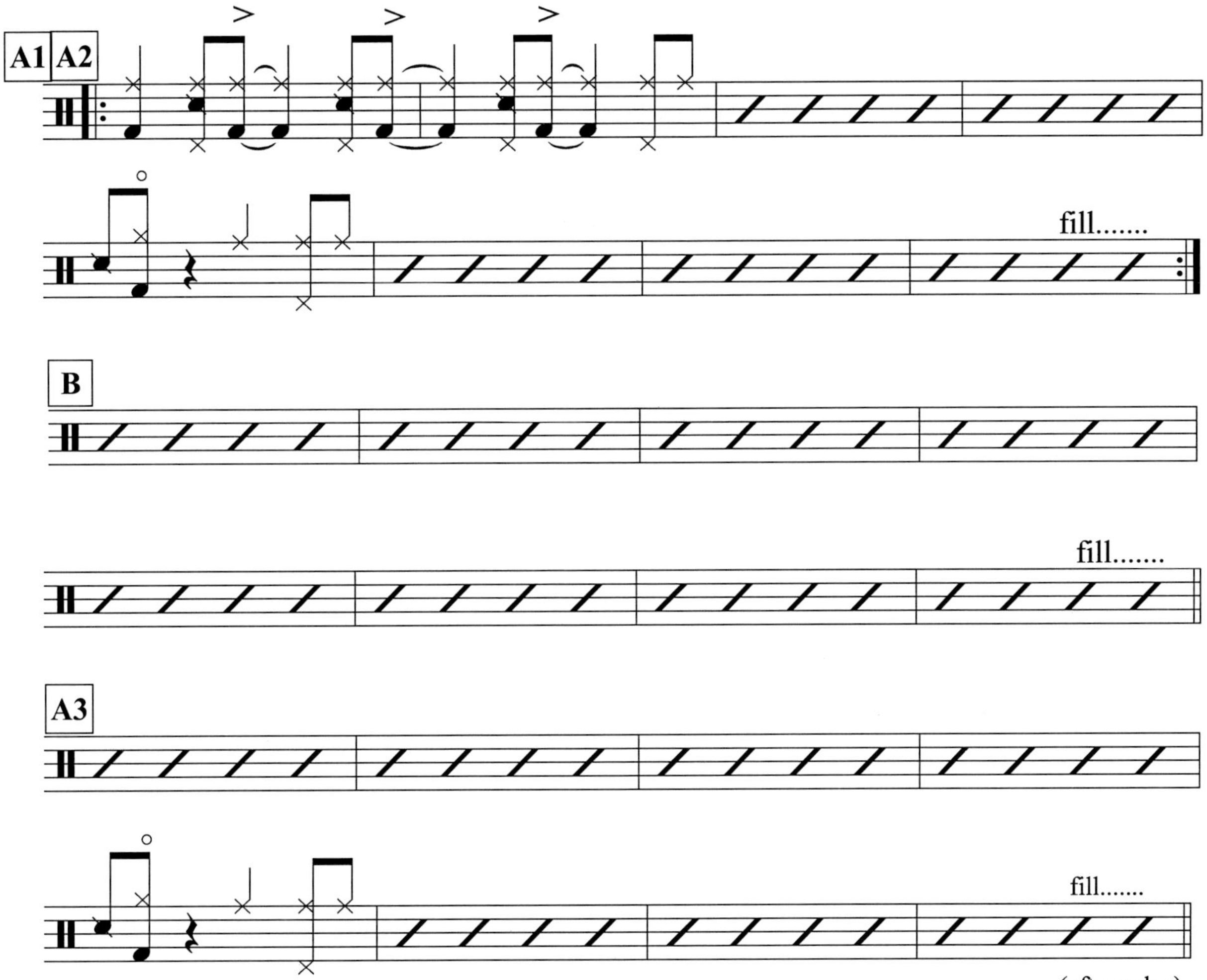

Drum Set Legend:

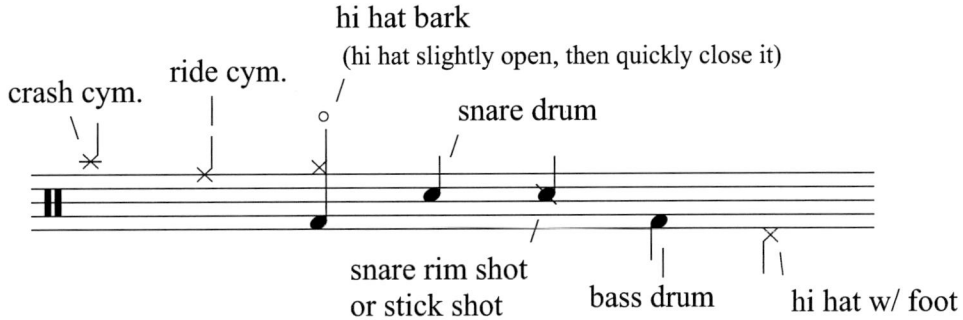

Notation Note:

Section 2 — Drum Chart Supplement

Suggested basic drumset part

Z's Blues

comp. by Eric Alexander
drum arr. by A. Hall

jazz feel

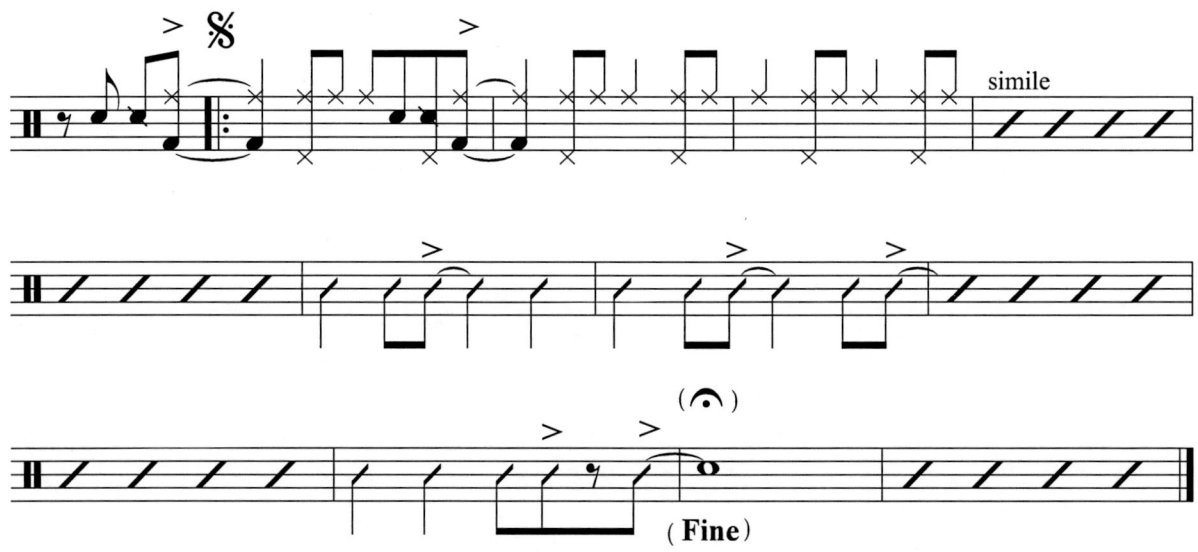

(Fine)

FOR SOLOS:
Play time freely in 12 bar phrases, listen, interact, hold the pulse.
Watch for the cue to "background for solos" and "shout chorus".

On Cue: Background for solos

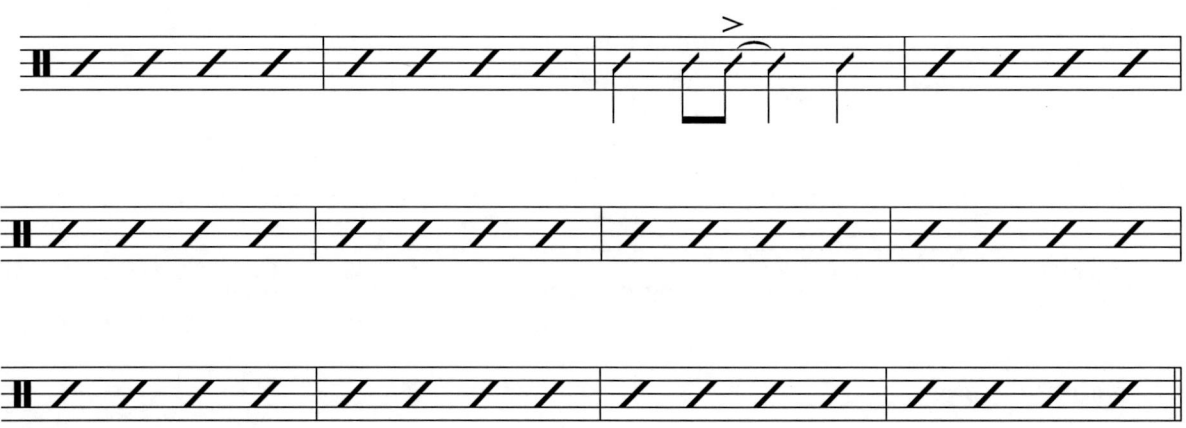

92

Drum Chart Supplement — Section 2

playthrough video - jazzdrumming.info/charts

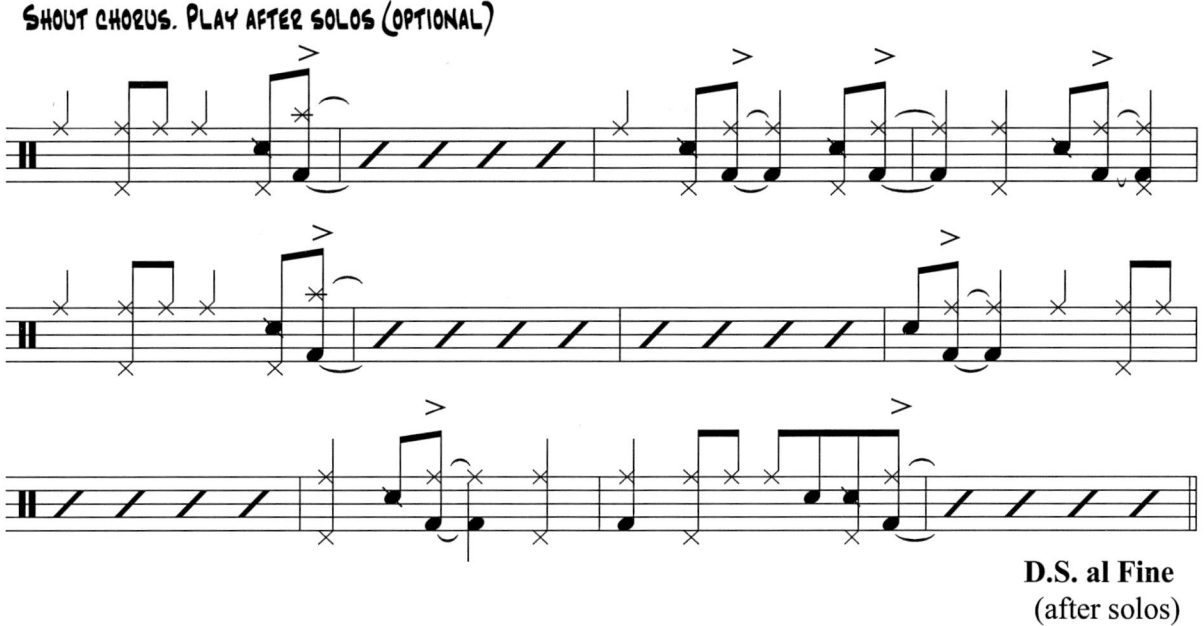

D.S. al Fine
(after solos)

Drum Set Legend:

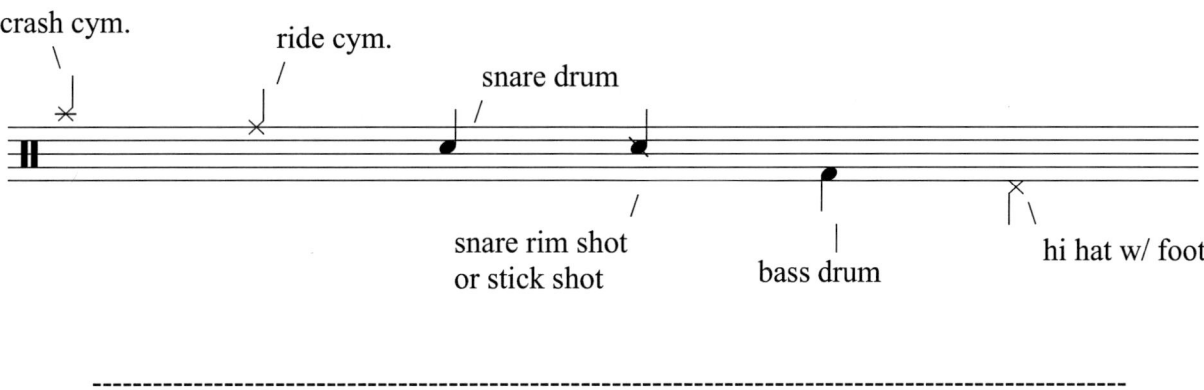

Notation notes:

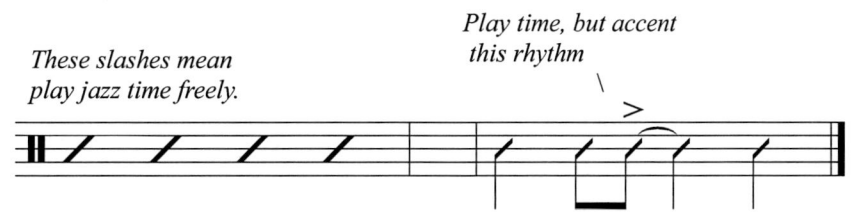

93

video at: **jazzdrumming.info/more**

Stop-Time / "Work Song" analysis

Stop-Time is an arranging technique which breaks the band into 2 voices basically: melody and rhythm section. It creates a *call and response* effect.

When you compare top stave (melody) with bottom stave (drumset part) in each system you can see that when the melody is busy, the drums are not: and vice-a-versa.

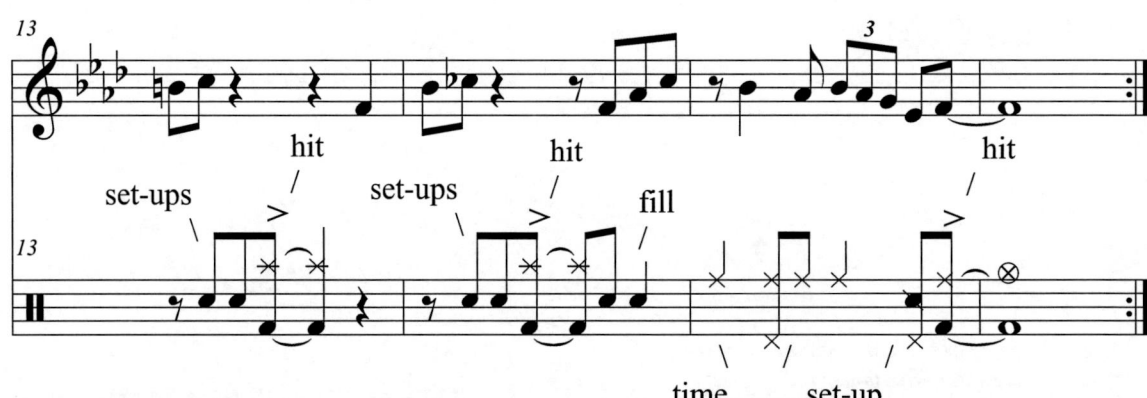

In the first 12 bars, the drummer plays the stops with the rhythm section. In bars 13-16 the drumset is setting up AND catching rhythm section hits as well as a final melody hit.

To Summarize:
When faced with a stop-time chart, be prepared to catch hits, wait in silence, and go to time-keeping. This can happen in different sections, and your approach might need to vary within any given tune.

video at: jazzdrumming.info/more

"Elvin" Style
This term refers to the rolling triplet innovations of the great drummer, Elvin Jones.

Jazz drumming is primarily based on an 8th note triplet "grid", which underlays the feel. Elvin Jones was one of the first drummers who fully integrated this grid into his comping and soloing

Prior to his innovations, the snare and bass drum "jabs" played against the ride pattern were mostly placed on the "lets" of various 8th note triplets. In order to explore this more fully, let's count out the 8th note triplet grid as follows:
"1-trip-let, 2-trip-let, 3-trip-let 4-trip-let"

Here is an example of a 2-bar comping pattern played before Elvin Jones' innovations. I will transcribe this in its full triplet form to better illustrate the differences.

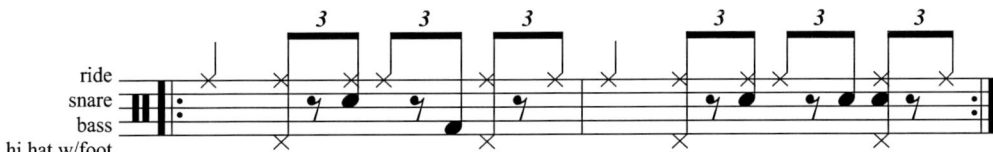

Notice the constant ride pattern, the steady hi hat on 2 and 4, and the absence of any middle triplet partials (the "trip")

In contrast, is an example of a 2-bar comping pattern as it might be played by Elvin:

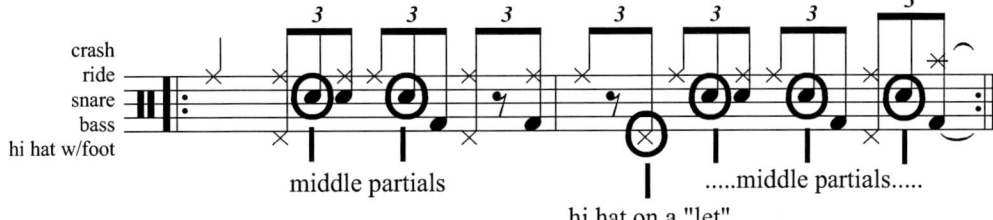

Notice all the places where the middle "trip" partial is played. Also notice the hi hat note sometimes played on a "let" instead of the standard "2 and 4".

To Summarize:
Comping in an "Elvin" style means to state the 8th note triplet partials often, among various limbs. This will add a driving, modern, "rolling triplet" feel to the groove. Remember though, the pulse and the "groove" must remain constant throughout. Use taste and musical judgement, always!

video at: jazzdrumming.info/more

The Jazz Shuffle
(swing all 8ths)

Basic Jazz Shuffle

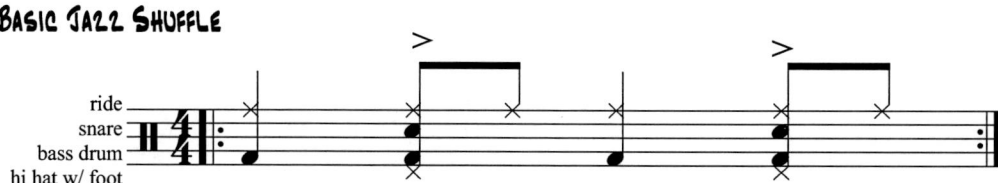

The main difference between a jazz shuffle and a blues shuffle is the ride cymbal pattern.

Here is a typical Blues Shuffle pattern:

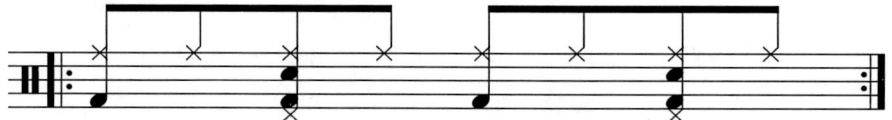

The main similarities between a blues shuffle and a jazz shuffle are the swing feel and the steady and consistent back beat (2 and 4) on the snare drum.

Jazz Shuffle Variations

variation 1)

variation 2)

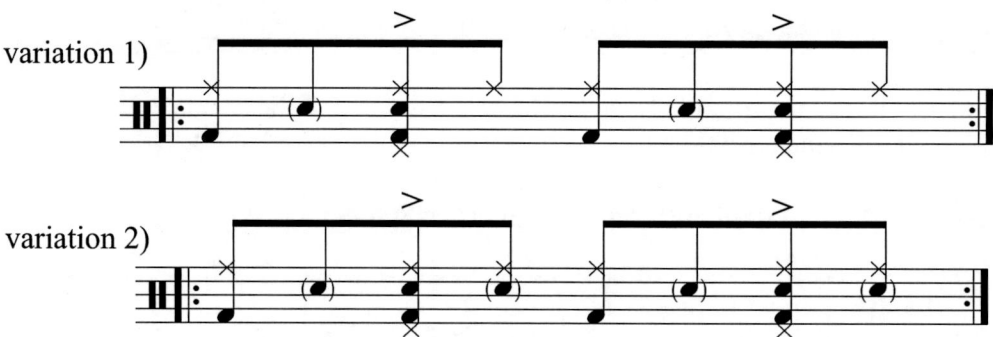

Below, the bass drum is reflecting a syncopated rhythm often played by the bass:

variation 3)

Below is an Art Blakey jazz shuffle with the hi hat on every quarter note and a syncopated bass drum:

variation 4)

Mix and Match:
Two bar jazz comping ideas in 3/4

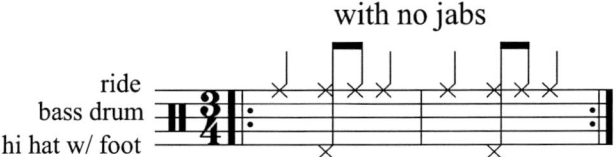

with no jabs

with snare "jabs"

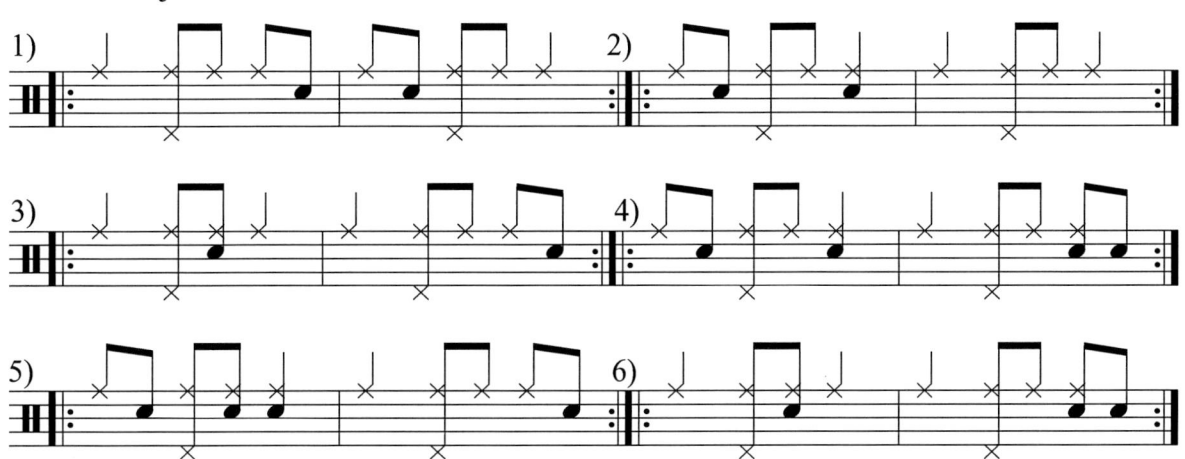

* throughout these examples, the ride cymbal and hi hat patterns remain unchanged.

with snare and bass drum "jabs"

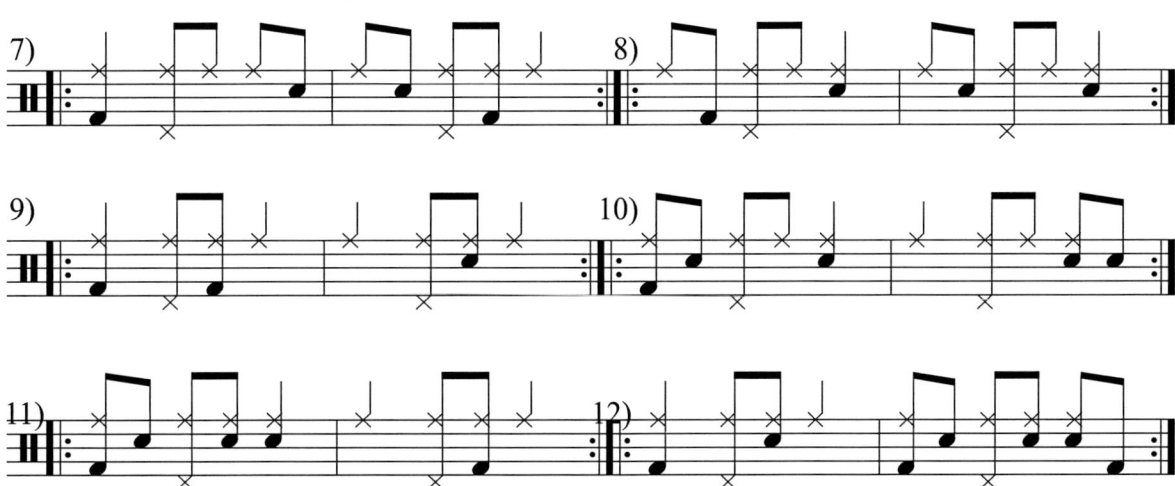

A solid approach to jazz waltz comping is to mix and match the *basic jazz waltz ostinato* with snare and bass drum jabs like above, freely. These are sample ideas that would be good to get "under your belt".

A 12/8 groove Example

Above is an example of a typical 12/8 groove, where all twelve 8th notes are explicitly played on the cym (or hi hat).

One can achieve the same feel in a slow 4/4, if it's written like this:

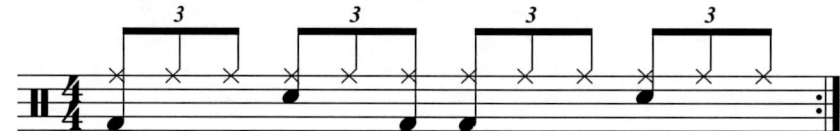

Playing with a 12/8 **"feel"** means to hint at, or suggest, or reference this groove, without actually explicitly playing it. These types of grooves are typically played at slower tempos.

Ballads played with brushes can also have this subtle 12/8 feel, without actually playing all 12 of the ride notes.

In this volume of *The Real Easy Book*, "St James Infirmary" should be played with a 12/8 feel.

video at: jazzdrumming.info/more

Advanced Latin Jazz Drumset Grooves

I've primarily notated *simplified* versions of the Latin drum set grooves in this edition of "The Real Easy Book". Here are more advanced versions of these grooves for those drummers who want to master them. This is NOT a complete guide; but these are versions that are used by many professional drummers playing in these styles.

Afro Cuban Styles

Mambo (2/3 Clave)

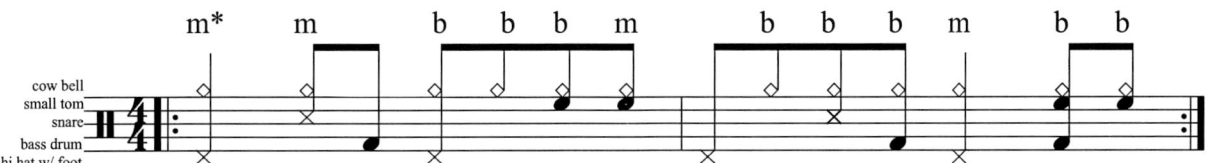

(These snare notes are notated to be played in "cross stick" style)

Mambo (3/2 Clave)

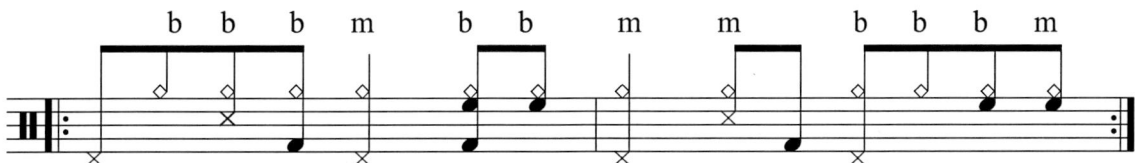

* m = mouth of the cowbell, b = back of the cowbell.
Optional: m = bell of cymbal w/ shoulder of stick, b = bell of cymbal with tip of stick

Cascara w/ Rumba Clave (2/3 clave)

*Play these snare drum notes cross-stick style, play the floor tom notes on the shell (or rim)

Cascara w/ Rumba Clave (3/2 clave)

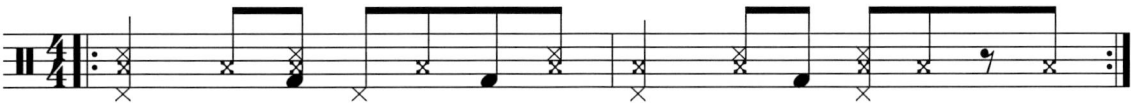

video at: **jazzdrumming.info/more**

Cascara w/ Son Clave (2/3 clave)

Cascara w/ Son Clave (3/2 clave)

Cha Cha (2/3 clave)

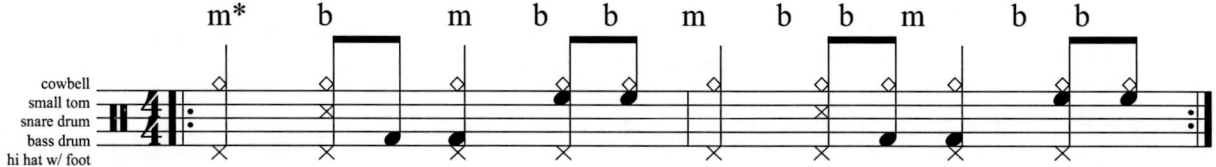

Cha Cha (3/2 clave)

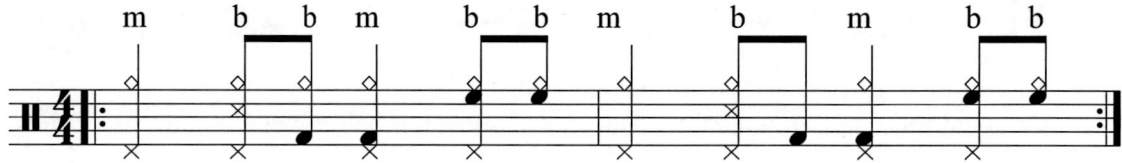

Songo (2/3 clave, full bell pattern)

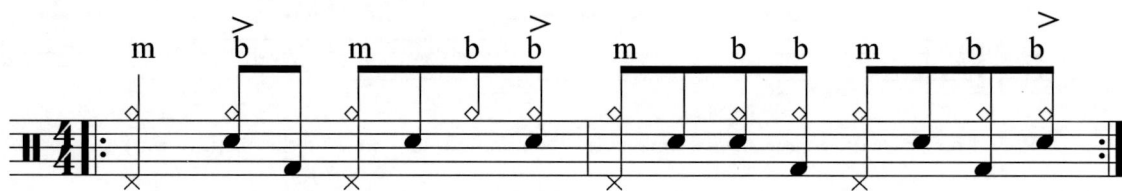

Songo (3/2 clave, full bell pattern)

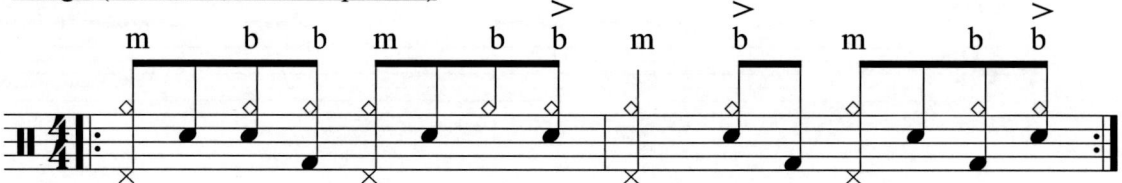

The accents (>) here refer to snare drum.

video at: jazzdrumming.info/more

Brazilian Styles

Bossa Nova (with one possible cross-stick pattern)

Jazz Samba abbreviated ride patterns

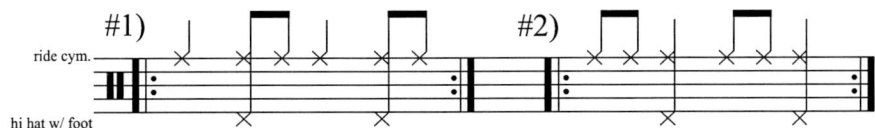

Jazz Samba Variation #1 (w/ abbreviated ride cym. pattern #1)[+]

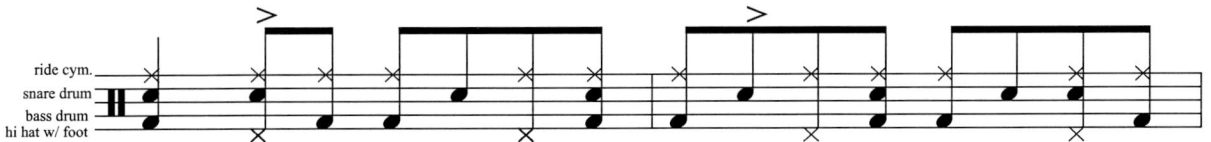

Jazz Samba Variation #2 (w/ abbreviated ride cym. pattern #2)

+ In both of these jazz sambas the snare drum notes can also be played cross-stick style.

The Brazilian ride and snare drum patterns here represent a fraction of the many possible variations typically used. If you're curious about other variations, I encourage you to check out the books about Brazilian drumming found in the references list at the back of this book.

TIP: In order to be able to concentrate on playing the music, and catching the figures, I encourage you to memorize all of the above Afro-Cuban and Brazilian grooves so you can move between them freely within each applicable chart.

References

Jazz Drumming

Progressive Steps to Syncopation - by Ted Reed (Ted Reed Publications)

The Art of Bop Drumming - by John Riley (Manhattan Music Publications)

The Drummer's Complete Vocabulary as Taught by Alan Dawson - by Alan Dawson and John Ramsey (Alfred Publishing)

Internalization (a non-reading intensive approach toward mastery of the jazz drumming language) - by Alan Hall (www.jazzdrumming.com)

Chart Reading

Big Band and Studio Drumming - by Steve Houghton (Steve Weiss Music)

Chart Reading Workbook for Drummers - by Bobby Gabriele (Hal Leonard)

Latin Jazz Grooves

Afro-Cuban Rhythms for the Drumset - by Frank Malabe and Bob Weiner (Manhattan Music Publications, Alfred Publishing)

New Ways of Brazilian Drumming - by Sergio Gomes (Advance Music)

Brazilian Rhythms for the Drumset - by Duduka Da Fonseca, Bob Weiner (Manhattan Music Publications, Alfred Publishing)

Practical Applications Afro-Carribean Rhythms for the Drum Set - by Chuck Silverman (Alfred Publishing)

SHER MUSIC CO.
The World's Premier Jazz & Latin Publisher!

BEST-SELLING BOOKS BY MARK LEVINE
- The Jazz Theory Book
- The Jazz Piano Book
- Jazz Piano Masterclass: The Drop 2 Book
- How to Voice Standards at the Piano

THE WORLD'S BEST FAKE BOOKS
- The New Real Book - Vol. 1 - C, Bb and Eb
- The New Real Book - Vol. 2 - C, Bb and Eb
- The New Real Book - Vol. 3 - C, Bb and Eb
- The Real Easy Book - Vol. 1 - C, Bb, Eb and Bass Clef (Three-Horn Edition)
- The Real Easy Book - Vol. 2 - C, Bb, Eb and Bass Clef
- The Real Easy Book - Vol. 3 - C, Bb, Eb and Bass Clef
- The Latin Real Easy Book - C, Bb, Eb and Bass Clef
- The Standards Real Book - C, Bb and Eb
- The Latin Real Book - C, Bb and Eb
- The Real Cool Book - West Coast 'Cool' Jazz Octet Charts
- The All-Jazz Real Book - C, Bb and Eb
- The European Real Book - C, Bb and Eb
- The Best of Sher Music Real Books - C, Bb and Eb
- The World's Greatest Fake Book - C version only
- The Yellowjackets Songbook - (all parts)

DIGITAL FAKE BOOKS (at shermusic.com only)
- The New Real Book - Vol.1 - C, Bb and Eb
- The Digital Standards Songbook
- The Digital Real Book
- The Jazz Songbook Series

LATIN MUSIC BOOKS
- **Decoding Afro-Cuban Jazz: The Music of Chucho Valdés and Irakere** - by Chucho Valdés and Rebeca Mauleón
- The Salsa Guidebook - by Rebeca Mauleón
- The Latin Real Easy Book - C, Bb, Eb and Bass Clef
- The Latin Bass Book - by Oscar Stagnaro and Chuck Sher
- The True Cuban Bass - by Carlos del Puerto and Silvio Vergara
- The Brazilian Guitar Book - by Nelson Faria
- Inside the Brazilian Rhythm Section - by Nelon Faria/Cliff Korman
- The Conga Drummer's Guidebook - by Michael Spiro
- Language of the Masters - by Michael Spiro
- Introduction to the Conga Drum, DVD - by Michael Spiro
- Afro-Caribbean Grooves for Drumset - by Jean-Philippe Fanfant
- Afro-Peruvian Percussion Ensemble - by Hector Morales
- Flamenco Improvisation, Vol. 1-3 - by Enrique Vargas

Bilingual or Libros en Español
- The Latin Real Book - C, Bb and Eb
- 101 Montunos - by Rebeca Mauleón
- Muy Caliente! - Afro-Cuban Book Play-Along CD
- El Libro del Jazz Piano - by Mark Levine
- Teoria del Jazz - by Mark Levine (digital only)

ALL METHOD BOOKS ALSO AVAILABLE IN DIGITAL FORM ONLINE

JAZZ METHOD BOOKS
BASS
- The Improvisor's Bass Method - by Chuck Sher
- Concepts for Bass Soloing - by Marc Johnson & Chuck Sher
- Walking Bassics - by Ed Fuqua
- Foundation Exercises for Bass - by Chuck Sher

GUITAR
- Jazz Guitar Voicings: The Drop 2 Book - by Randy Vincent
- Three-Note Voicings and Beyond - by Randy Vincent
- Line Games - by Randy Vincent
- Jazz Guitar Soloing: The Cellular Approach - by Randy Vincent
- The Guitarist's Introduction to Jazz - by Randy Vincent

PIANO
- Playing for Singers - by Mike Greensill
- An Approach to Comping: The Essentials - by Jeb Patton
- An Approach to Comping, Vol.2: Advanced - by Jeb Patton
- Wisdom of the Hand - by Marius Nordal
- Intro to Jazz Piano, A Deep Dive - by Jeb Patton

OTHER INSTRUMENTS
- Inner Drumming - by George Marsh
- Method for Chromatic Harmonica - by Max de Aloe
- Modern Etudes for Solo Trumpet - by Cameron Pearce
- New Orleans Trumpet - by Jim Thornton

FOR ALL INSTRUMENTS
- The Jazz Harmony Book - by David Berkman
- Jazz Musician's Guide to Creative Practicing - by D. Berkman
- The Jazz Singers Guide Book - by David Berkman
- Metaphors for the Musician - by Randy Halberstadt
- Forward Motion - by Hal Galper
- The Serious Jazz Practice Book - by Barry Finnerty
- The Serious Jazz Book II - by Barry Finnerty
- Building Solo Lines From Cells - by Randy Vincent
- The Real Easy Ear Training Book - by Roberta Radley
- Reading, Writing and Rhythmetic - by Roberta Radley
- Minor is Major - by Dan Greenblatt
- Jazz Scores and Analysis - Vol. 1 - by Rick Lawn
- Essential Grooves - by Moretti, Nicholl and Stagnaro
- The Jazz Solos of Chick Corea - transcribed by Peter Sprague

FOR STUDENT MUSICIANS
- The Blues Scales - by Dan Greenblatt - C, Bb and Eb
- **Rhythm First! - by Tom Kamp** - C, Bb, Eb and Bass Clef
- The Guitarist's Introduction to Jazz - Randy Vincent
- Jazz Songs for Student Violinists - by Keefe and Mitchell

CDs
- Poetry+Jazz: A Magical Marriage
- The New Real Book Play-Along CDs (for Vol.1) - #1, 2 and 3
- The Latin Real Book Sampler CD
- The Music of Charles Stevens

For more info, see SherMusic.com